D0886972

The Prevention of Crime

To Anne and Cathy

CONTENTS

Preface   1

PART I THE PROBLEM

The Criminal Society   7
1. Overview   7
2. The Lack of Prevention   9
3. The Criminal Society   10
4. Defining Crime   12

2. Homicide   15
   1. The Meaning of Homicide   15
   2. Geographical Variations   16
   3. The Homicidal Situation   19
   4. Prestige, Race, Age, and Sex of
      Offenders   21
   5. Other Characteristics of Offenders   25

3. Assault, Rape, and Robbery   29
   1. Aggravated Assault   29
   2. Forcible Rape   31
   3. Robbery   35

4. Burglary and Larceny   39
   1. Burglary   39
   2. Larceny and Auto Theft   43

5. Fraud   47
   1. "Black-Collar" Fraud   47
   2. "White-Collar" Fraud   50

6. Victimless Crime and Mass Disorder   55
   1. Victimless Crime: Drug Abuse   55
   2. The Nature of Rioting   58

7. Theory: Frustration and
Subcultural Learning   63
   1. Denial of Goals and Alienation   63
   2. Subcultures of Crime   68

8. Theory: Latent Functions
and Labeling   73
   1. The Functional Uses of Crime   73
   2. The Labeling Process   77
   3. Notes on Drug Addiction and Mass
      Disorder   79

9. The Control Process: I   85
   1. Self-fulfilling Prophecy   85
   2. The Conflicted Police Role   87
   3. The Overburdened Courts   93

10. The Control Process: II   97
   1. Prison and Beyond   97
   2. Notes on the Control
      of Drug Abuse   100
   3. Riot Control   104
   4. Punishing the Unconvicted   106

PART II PREVENTION

11. Basic Strategies: I   111
   1. The Discussion Ahead   111
   2. Needs and Latent Functions   114
   3. Reducing Frustration   118
   4. The Cooperation of Agents
      of Control   120

12.	Basic Strategies: II	125
	1. Organizational Mechanisms for Change	125
	2. Citizen Involvement in Action Programs	128
	3. Catalysts	131
	4. Research in relation to Action	134
13.	Public Education	139
	1. Concerning the Young	139
	2. Making School Meaningful	141
	3. Teaching Behavioral Science in the Public Schools	144
	4. Education Through the Mass Media	149
14.	The Neighborhood Service Center	153
	1. The Need for Service Centers	153
	2. Organization of the Center	156
	3. The Service Center and the Child	160
15.	Changing the Police	165
	1. The Police and The Community	165
	2. Professionalization	168
	3. Specific Offenses and the Police	171
	4. Riot Control	175
	5. A Promising Program	178
16.	Change in the Judicial System	181
	1. The Law	181
	2. Reorganizing the Courts	183
	3. Training of Judges and Other Personnel	189
	4. Note on Gun Control	191

17. Corrections: Training Programs 195
    1. Personnel 195
    2. Types of Training Programs 200
    3. The One-Year Professional Degree 206

18. Corrections: Treatment Programs 211
    1. Rehabilitation 211
    2. Treating Violent Adults 213
    3. Treating Children Who Steal 217

19. The Correctional Learning
    Center: I 221
    1. General Characteristics 221
    2. Professional Staff 225

20. The Correctional Learning
    Center: II 229
    1. Operation 229
    2. Leaving the Center 234
    3. Special Types of Offenders 237

21. A Concluding Word 245
    1. Recapitulation 245
    2. The Future 247

Appendix: Note on Evaluation
           of Preventive Programs 253
Footnotes 257
Index 269

PREFACE

The time for an extended discussion of the nature of crime and delinquency in the United States and of how we might more effectively control them is at hand. Few will hold that we have achieved a significant degree of success in preventing criminal and delinquent behavior. Alternately, many will argue vehemently that we know practically nothing about what gives rise to these forms of deviance. Those who so argue are misguided. We know from a scientific standpoint a great deal about the root causes of crime and delinquency. There is always much room for gaining greater knowledge. The fact remains that we are hardly ignorant about the forces that generate crime and delinquency. The layman may be ignorant about those forces; yet knowledge is available. The problem lies largely in a widespread lack of motivation to disseminate that knowledge and to take the steps necessary to deal effectively with crime and delinquency. There are numerous reasons why this reluctance permeates the society; they are one of the major concerns of this book.

This book is directed toward both concerned laymen and practicing profesionals. Included among the latter are judges, probation and parole officers, wardens and other personnel in correctional institutions, social workers who specialize in problems of crime and delinquency, police officers, and relevant officials at various levels of government. Sociologists and psychologists who specialize in the analysis of crime and delinquency should find the book of interest and, presumably, of value. But this book is largely directed to those who work

1

actively from day to day with the crime problem and to citizens in all walks of life who desire to take part in preventing crime and delinquency. In the long run, it will very likely be these citizens who most affect the course of events, who will most significantly determine whether violence, theft, and other crimes escalate or diminish.

The plan of the chapters ahead is this: Characteristics of various forms of crime are delineated. So too are social and psychological characteristics of offenders. Those sociological and social psychological forces that give rise to crime—and those that do not—are discussed at length. Present forms of social control in the United States, that is, ways of attempting to cope with the crime problem, are summarized. All of this provides a foundation for the major thrust of the book: considerations of a variety of programs that might be undertaken to prevent crime and delinquency.

Some of these projected programs are very broad, such as widespread public education in the lower schools concerning crime and other social problems and what effectively can be done about them. Other programs are relatively specific, for example, plans for improving the training of probation and parole officers. Various of the programs under consideration involve mundane yet necessary matters; increasing the physical equipment facilities and the communication systems of police forces across the country are illustrative. Others will be less ordinary and in some instances controversial. One that will be considered such by some is a program for detecting young children who have decided tendencies toward violence and for taking remedial action. A second is a proposal to conduct ongoing discussion sessions that involve small groups of prison inmates and parolees together with citizens in everyday life.

The crime and delinquency problem in the United States is vast and increasing. Frustration is one driving force behind violation of the criminal law. A major form of frustration is one-sided, uneven economic competition where the individual wants to win and yet is doomed to lose. A shortage, especially in the lower socio-economic strata, of persons who can serve as noncriminal role models is another primary source of crime.

The crime control process accomplishes ends quite diametrically opposed to those ostensibly sought by the society's members. Much of the control apparatus, much of the action in police departments, courts, prisons, and so on, serves to increase frustration and limit adequate role models. In this way, crime is facilitated.

When a society is overly competitive, when competition is rigged as well, when individuals are frustrated in countless other ways, sadistic and masochistic needs run high. The creation of criminals serves the need of those who create them to hurt still others. It serves also to make the creators targets of crime and so to fulfill whatever needs they possess to be hurt. The creation of criminals serves the needs of the offenders themselves to be hurt, punished, by the larger society. And it provides the offender with opportunity to fulfill his need to strike actually or symbolically at other persons. It provides still others—"average   citizens"—with   opportunities   for vicarious involvement in crime and punishment.

We become dependent on crime. It becomes part of our way of life. It becomes an integral component of *social organization*. Crime in the United States provides activity and rewards not only for violators and for the average citizen. It provides as well a livelihood for several millions who are directly employed in the abortive attempt to control it.

We abhor the deaths and injuries that result from crime, the grief, the loss of property. We need crime and yet we detest it. This is our ambivalence regarding crime and the criminal. That ambivalence is at the root of our failure to carry on a rational and reasonably effective national program of crime control.

The amount of discussion of the crime and delinquency problem is very large. The propensity to assign blame is great. But how much attention is actually given in practice to prevention and rehabilitation? Almost none.

We might well be called, in regard to crime and delinquency, the unpreventive society. Little wonder. We are reluctant to wipe out that which is a part of us. We are reluctant to go to the source of a problem we have come to need.

Part I
The Problem

1. THE
CRIMINAL SOCIETY

1. OVERVIEW

Crime and delinquency in the United States are exceedingly widespread and pervasive. It will be clear that this condition is not the result of chance. A complex variety of social forces combine to perpetuate in great numbers the several forms of violence and theft and such other crimes as drug abuse, prostitution, homosexuality, and abortion. Homicide, assault, rape, robbery, burglary, and larceny abound at the lower end of the social class scale. Embezzlement, price-rigging, and various other types of fraud are extremely prevalent, if seldom prosecuted, at the upper end of the scale.[1]

The social system gives rise to severe psychological frustrations, especially deprivations in relation to the success goals of the society. These in turn have as consequences criminal violations on a large scale. Defective practices for training children in the customs and values of the general culture play their part as well. Moreover, when crime has been and is so much a part of so many aspects of everyday life, then a society's members come, however unwittingly, to depend upon it. The mechanisms of social control that are manifestly designed to reduce crime and delinquency take on a latent function of serving unerringly to perpetuate and even to propagate crime and delinquency.[2]

It is to these matters and to how, in the light of them, crime might to some significant degree be effectively prevented that this book is addressed. The concern is with youth crime, that is, delinquency, as well as with adult crime. Characteristics of crimes and of offenders in the United States, and to some extent of victims as well, are first assessed. There is virtue, sometimes easily forgotten, in seeing a problem clearly before moving on to proposed remedies. The social conditions that generate crime as those conditions are reflected in theories of crime are assayed. As a nation we are impatient with theory, especially social theory. This is another way of saying that we are driven to avoid resolution of our myriad social problems. It is only on the basis of theory that any preventive or remedial action can be taken. That action will be as effective as the theory is valid.

The social control process in regard to crime as it now operates is considered at some length. If that process is to be changed, to be made effective, it too must be understood. Only then can those parts of the process that serve to induce crime be neutralized or removed such that effective controls replace abortive ones. Finally, processes of social control that may serve to actually reduce crime are set forth in some detail. Several of these are broadscale measures to be instituted in the society at large. Others are pinpoint measures to be selectively introduced only at certain junctures in the social system.

It is usual to distinguish three broad areas of social response to the crime problem: prevention *per se*, which occurs before the fact; control, in the sense of apprehension of violators by police, judicial processes, punishment, and other action which follows the commission of criminally deviant acts; and rehabilitation, which also follows the violation and has to do with avoiding further crime by the individual.

All three of these can rightly be seen as aspects of prevention broadly construed, however, and are so seen here. Certain types of response by police, courts, and prisons will serve to impede crime while others will actually further it. And rehabilitation is, after all, prevention of further crime by the given person. Each of these then is treated as a form of prevention.

2. THE LACK
OF PREVENTION

We are not a preventive society. We tend to take action after a problem has attained large-scale proportions. In medicine, the emphasis has traditionally been on treating the ill individual rather than on broad preventive measures.[3] It is the surgeon at the operating table who receives the plaudits, not the behind-the-scenes specialist in preventive medicine. Regarding the mental health field, there is much emphasis on psychiatric intervention into the lives of emotionally disturbed persons. There is little concern with preventing mental illness at the outset.[4] In problems of the physical environment, air and water pollution and related matters, the emphasis has been on remedial action rather than on prevention at the source.

So it is with crime. Very, very little attention is given to preventing the development of individuals who will be criminal. Much concern and vast resources are expended in the apprehension of violators, in court proceedings, and in punishment.[5] It would be difficult consciously to design a system of social control that was so inefficient as our crime control apparatus. Devoid of early preventive measures, that system emphasizes detection, fines, and incarceration. It is a remarkable commentary on our system of control that two-thirds of those who are currently prison inmates were imprisoned at an earlier time, and a majority of those who are now imprisoned will after release return to prison.

3. THE CRIMINAL SOCIETY

By any reasonable standard we are an exceedingly criminal society. With something over two hundred million population, a conservative statement is that eight million distinctly serious crimes, felonies, are committed annually.[6] Many millions more that are less serious, misdemeanors, occur each year. For 1970, the Federal Bureau of Investigation reports 5,568,200 felonies.[7] This is an estimate of crimes *known to the police* across the country. And included are the following types only: murder and manslaughter, forcible rape, aggravated assault, robbery, burglary, and grand larceny, including auto theft. The figure would be much higher of course if other forms of crime and if crimes not now known to the police were also included. But taking the known figure of 5,568,200 only, one can calculate that in 1970 a serious crime occurred for every 37 persons in the population. On the average during that year one of these serious crimes was committed every six seconds.

During 1970, 4,836,800 major property crimes were known to have occurred in the United States: 2,169,300 of those were burglaries; 1,746,100 grand larcenies; and 921,400 auto thefts.[8] Violent crime is of course also great in this society. The Federal Bureau of Investigation reports that during 1970 there were committed 15,810 murders; 37,270 forcible rapes; 329,940 aggravated assaults; and 348,380 robberies. These total almost three-quarters of a million crimes of violence.[9] If violent crimes unknown to the local police and the F.B.I. were included, obviously the figure would be much higher. As the figure stands, the violent crime rate for the United States for the year 1970 was 360 per 100,000 population.[10] This means that during the year, 360 of the above types of violent crimes were committed for every 100,000 persons.

(Crime rates are usually computed on a base of 100,000 population.) Put differently, it means one violent crime for every 276 persons. On the average one murder was committed every 33 minutes; one forcible rape every 14 minutes; one aggravated assault every minute and a half; and one robbery every minute and a half. Taking those crimes together, a violent crime occurred every 43 seconds on the average.

As Table 1 indicates, known crimes of violence rose markedly over the 1960's. The rate of 360.0 (per 100,000) in 1970 was well over double that of 156.4 in 1961. As noted, these are known rates. The increase is in part due to greater efficiency by police in recording and reporting crime. A significant portion of the increase, however, reflects an actual rise in violence. Murder is a useful index of violent crime in general. For years it has been unlikely that it would go undetected and it has been well re-

TABLE 1
Changes in Rates of
Violent and Property Crimes
(per 100,000 Population)
in the United States,
1961-1970*

Year	Violent Crime	Property Crime	Total
1961	156.4	981.8	1,138.2
1962	160.5	1,030.8	1,191.2
1963	166.2	1,125.8	1,292.0
1964	188.2	1,251.7	1,439.9
1965	197.6	1,314.2	1,511.9
1966	217.2	1,449.4	1,666.6
1967	250.0	1,671.7	1,921.7
1968	294.6	1,940.2	2,234.8
1969	324.4	2,152.5	2,476.9
1970	360.0	2,380.5	2,740.5

*Source: Federal Bureau of Investigation, *Uniform Crime Reports*—Washington, D.C.: U.S. Government Printing Office, 1971, p. 65.

ported.[11] Murder rates in the United States were rather stable during the early years of the 1960's and then rose rapidly. The rate for 1970 was 7.8; this was over sixty-five percent greater than the 1961 rate of 4.7.[12]

Property crimes (burglary, grand larceny, and auto theft) more than doubled in rate from 1961 to 1970. Table 1 shows that the known rate in 1961 was 981.9 (per 100,000). In 1970 the rate was 2,380.5. The combined rate for violent and property crimes rose from 1,138.2 to 2,740.5 over the ten-year period. Both the present very high rate and the enormous increase in recent times are indicative of a highly criminal society.

One significant footnote: At any given time in the United States over 1,300,000 persons are in the custody of the over-all criminal corrections system.[13] That is, about one-and-a-third million people are either in prisons, jails, or juvenile reformatories or are on probation or parole. This obviously is a considerable segment of the population. Moreover, most of those incarcerated or on probation remain inmates or probationers for less than a year. Hence the volume of persons moving through the correctional process is enormous.

4. DEFINING CRIME

Most violations of law are torts rather than crimes. Torts are violations of civil law. They are violations against particular individuals rather than against the state, the society. The question of intent is not at issue in civil cases. And in the legal sense violators are not punished. Frequently, however, they are required to make reparations to the injured party.

Crimes, on the other hand, are considered essentially to be acts against the state although particular individuals may suffer the direct consequences. There must be intent, premeditation, if there is to be a crime. Crimes are punishable by the state and often the victim is not indemnified. Crimes are violations of social morés, of those customs that society's members consider critical for survival. Torts, in contrast, are violations of certain folkways rather than morés. The society's members do not view such violations as endangering the fabric of the society.

To illustrate: in many jurisdictions it is a civil offense to let ice accumulate on the sidewalk in front of one's home. The local government owns the sidewalk but the homeowner has the responsibility of keeping it free of ice and snow. Assume that a pedestrian approaches a homeowner's portion of sidewalk, slips, and breaks his leg. The pedestrian is free to sue the homeowner in civil court. The question of intent on the part of the homeowner does not arise. He is expected to keep the sidewalk clear, intent aside. If the pedestrian wins the case, the homeowner can be ordered by the court to pay his medical costs, income lost from work, and so on. Keeping the sidewalk clear of ice is seen as a personal responsibility. Failure to meet that responsibility is not viewed, however, as a threat to the over-all social organization.

In contrast, assume a homeowner sees a man coming down the street, rushes out, and strikes him. The pedestrian falls and breaks his leg. A crime has been committed. There is intent. The action is punishable. It is considered a threat to the society as a whole. If everyone went around striking everyone else the society would soon be in chaos.

One main way of classifying crimes is in regard to the seriousness of the offense. Felonies are significantly more serious offenses than misdemeanors. Felonies include murder, manslaughter, assault with intent to kill, forcible rape, robbery, burglary, and grand larceny. Examples of misdemeanors are petty larceny, public drunkenness, and vagrancy. Felonies are usually punishable by more than a year's incarceration in a state or federal prison or by death. Punishment for misdemeanors tends to involve confinement of a year or less in a local jail.[14]

A second important form of classification has to do with the content of criminal acts. Major forms are crimes of violence, crimes against property, and crimes without victims. Any of these may include both felonies and misdemeanors. Violent crimes, sometimes termed "crimes against the person," are in the main murder, manslaughter, assault, and forcible rape. Burglary and larceny are the most prevalent types of property crimes. "White-collar crimes" of embezzlement and the like are essentially property crimes. Robbery is the taking of goods or money from a person by force or threat of force. As such it is both a violent and a property crime. Victimless crimes are those considered by the society's members to be threats to the social organization although no one, except possibly the violator himself, is in the usual sense a victim. The use of addictive drugs, prostitution, homosexuality, abortion, and some forms of gambling are examples.

In the chapters immediately ahead, characteristics of various types of crimes and offenders are considered. Attention is first given to the violent crimes: criminal homicide, assault, forcible rape, and robbery as well. Following that, several property crimes are reviewed: the "black-collar" violations of burglary, larceny, and auto theft; confidence games and forgery; and the "white-collar" violations of embezzlement and price-rigging. Finally, the several victimless crimes and, separately, mass rioting, are the focus of concern.

2. HOMICIDE

1. THE MEANING OF HOMICIDE

Homicide is a broad category that includes many forms of killing of one person by another. Justifiable homicide is killing performed in a socially approved line of duty. The killing of an escaping arrestee by a police officer is an example. Criminal homicide is the killing of another which is intentional, that is, not accidental, and not in the line of socially sanctioned duty. In practice it is often exceedingly difficult to determine whether the act was intentional, that is, premeditated. Was it clearly planned sometime before the killing occurred? Was it unconsciously "planned"? Was it planned, forgotten, and then carried out? One of the burdens of the courts is, of course, to make this determination.

There are four major forms of criminal homicide; two fall within the category of murder and two within that of manslaughter. First-degree murder is the most serious form. It is characterized by an especially "high degree of premeditation" and, in legal terms, "maliciousness." Second-degree murder involves somewhat lesser degrees of premeditation and maliciousness. Nonnegligent manslaughter is a slightly less serious crime although significant degrees of premeditation and maliciousness must be present. Negligent manslaughter is still less serious. Nevertheless in relation to all crimes it is a highly serious transgression. While some intent must exist, the act of negligent manslaughter is, as the name implies, considered to be one of negligence rather than of malice. Fatal automobile accidents where the driver has been drinking are likely to lead to convictions for negligent manslaughter. In many sociological studies, first- and second-degree murder and nonnegligent manslaughter are grouped together as major forms of criminal homicide. Negligent manslaughter is often treated separately because of the greater emphasis on sheer negligence.[1]

2.   GEOGRAPHICAL VARIATIONS

A summary of homicide rates for 61 modern, literate societies, circa 1960, shows the median rate to be 1.8. Our rate of 5.0 for that year was almost three times the median rate.[2] Among those 61 countries we ranked fifteenth from the top. Societies with higher rates than ours tend to be technologically underdeveloped countries, especially those of Latin America: Columbia, Mexico, and Nicaragua headed the list. Countries with particularly low rates are in the main highly stable and technologically well developed, such as The Netherlands, Norway, and Denmark. The Netherlands' rate of 0.3 was but one-seventeenth of ours.

Iceland is an excellent illustration of a technologically developed society with an exceedingly low homicide rate. Icelanders are individualistic and yet they must cooperate against a difficult physical environment. They socialize their children well in regard to matters of overriding importance and otherwise give them a free hand. While they are neither strongly competitive nor uncompetitive, Icelanders have a wide range of aggression outlets: they argue, they fight; the small children have a game in which they choose sides and throw rocks at each other until one side gives way. Yet it is very rare in these activities that anyone is seriously hurt.[3]

Columbia, in contrast, is a society in the throes of technological transition. It has an exceedingly high rate of homicide, 36.0 in 1960. The extremely competitive major political parties in Colombia have been involved in a running state of undeclared war. Feuding and killing have spread to many nonpolitical groups as well. The *violencia,* as this condition of violence is known, has accounted for well over 200,000 murders (in a population of 14,000,000) during the past several decades.[4]

It is instructive to look briefly at nonliterate, so-called "primitive" societies around the world. In general, homicide is lower among them than among their literate counterparts. A study by the author of some 40 nonliterate groups shows their median rate to be decidedly below that of literate societies. And there do not appear to be nonliterate societies where rates reach the heights that they do among literate groups.[5] While this study is concerned with but a sample, and not necessarily a representative sample, of nonliterate societies, it is clear from other sources as well that "primitives" are less violent than "moderns."[6]

The Hopi of our southwest provide a good example of a traditionally nonliterate society that has little homicide and little outward physical violence of any kind. (They do, however, have a rather high suicide rate.) The Hopi are a highly cooperative, self-effacing people. They are group-oriented rather than individualistic. What competition there is in Hopi life tends to be of an inverted kind: The aim in their highly popular footraces is to avoid winning; coming in second or third is more prestigious than taking first place.[7]

In striking contrast are the traditional Maori, a particularly violent people. Their everyday life was characterized by lengthy periods, perhaps of a year or more, of excessive competition. These alternated with periods of a similar length in which cooperation predominated. Homi-

cidal and assaultive behavior were especially prevalent
during the latter parts of, and directly after, the periods
of competition. Suicide, interestingly, was high toward
the end of, and immediately following, the cooperative
periods.[8]

Turning now to some characteristics of criminal homi-
cide in the United States: Rates are especially low in New
England and are particularly high in the South. As
Table 2 shows, in 1970 the New England rate was 3.1

TABLE 2
Criminal Homicides, Aggravated Assaults,
Forcible Rapes, and Robberies,
per 100,000 Population,
for Regions of the
United States, 1970

Region:	Criminal Homicide*	Aggravated Assault	Forcible Rape	Robbery
Northeast	5.8	134.0	12.7	232.8
New England	3.1	83.6	9.7	74.2
Middle Atlantic	6.7	150.0	13.7	283.4
North Central	6.5	127.0	17.0	172.7
East North Central	7.2	139.6	18.0	202.3
West North Central	4.9	95.8	14.7	99.7
South	11.2	202.7	18.0	130.2
South Atlantic	11.8	227.0	18.0	168.5
East South Central	10.6	165.1	14.7	60.2
West South Central	10.7	188.8	20.3	116.0
West	6.4	187.3	28.9	157.5
Mountain	6.7	155.5	23.0	90.6
Pacific	6.3	197.2	30.8	178.4
Total United States	7.8	162.4	18.3	171.5

*Includes first- and second-degree murder and nonnegligent man-
slaughter.

From Federal Bureau of Investigation, *Uniform Crime Reports,*
1970, Washington, D.C.: U.S. Government Printing Office, 1971, pp.
66-71.

while the rate for the South Atlantic states was almost four times that, 11.8. (Both black and white rates were low in New England and high in the South.) The Puritan ethic still holds sway to some degree in New England, apparently causing inhabitants to suppress violent tendencies. The severe frustrations of everyday life among lower-class blacks and whites in the South generate strong aggressive tendencies. The socialization, the training, of children in those groups is often quite minimal and so controls regarding outward violence are weak.[9]

Homicide is most prevalent in large cities, those with populations of over 250,000. In 1967 in the United States, these cities had a rate of 11.9. (See Table 3. For ease of calculation, the year 1967 was used. Present rates are similar.) The rate for rural areas was 5.0 and for suburban areas, 3.3. It is in considerable part the frustrating strains of black ghetto life that account for the high rates in large urban areas.

3. THE HOMICIDAL SITUATION

Homicide occurs most frequently late at night and in the early morning hours and especially on weekends. Peak rates are often in the early hours of Sunday at the tail-end of Saturday night carousing and arguing. One study, of homicide in Philadelphia, found that the rates for Fridays, Saturdays, and Sundays were several times higher than rates for other days of the week. While the over-all rate for Philadelphia was 6.1, the rate on Saturday was five times that, 31.8. Regarding hours, *half* of the homicides occurred in the six-hour period between 8:00 p.m. and 2:00 a.m.[10]

The usual site for homicide is a home or other nonpublic place. Bedrooms and kitchens are common scenes of homicidal attacks.[11] A majority of homicides in the Unit-

TABLE 3
Rates of Criminal Homicides, Aggravated Assaults, Forcible Rapes, and Robberies by Size of City and by Suburban and Rural Place, United States, 1967

Place:	Criminal Homicide*	Aggravated Assault	Forcible Rape	Robbery
over 250,000	11.9	257.0	27.3	330.2
100,000 to 250,000	7.4	158.8	13.8	107.8
50,000 to 100,000	4.0	101.4	10.3	69.0
25,000 to 50,000	3.5	85.3	7.8	44.5
10,000 to 25,000	2.9	79.2	7.0	26.2
under 10,000	2.5	76.0	5.1	14.8
Total for cities	6.8	156.3	15.5	152.8
Suburban	3.3	78.9	10.9	38.4
Rural	5.0	67.2	9.2	11.5
Over-all Total	6.1	131.9	14.4	113.8

*Includes first- and second-degree murder and nonnegligent manslaughter.

From Federal Bureau of Investigation, *Uniform Crime Reports, 1967,* Washington, D.C.: U.S. Government Printing Office, 1968, pp. 100-101.

ed States are committed by firearms; knives and clubs are also much used.[12] Efforts to reduce violence by a restricting the sale of firearms should take into account a variety of complex factors. To what extent would individuals be motivated to obtain guns simply because it was illegal to do so? How many homicides now committed by firearms would be committed by other means if firearms were not at hand. On balance, the staggering number of firearms in this country appears to be more a symptom of violent tendencies in the society than a cause of those tendencies.[13] We shall return to this matter in a later chapter.

The role of the victim in the homicidal act is much

greater than is commonly realized. Criminal homicide is very often the end result of a spiraling escalation of antagonism between two persons. They argue, they scuffle, one strikes a lethal blow at the other. In a study of almost 600 homicides, Wolfgang found that 26 percent were precipitated by the victim.[14] That is, the victim was the first to use physical force in the interchange between him and the subsequent offender. If strong psychological provocation had been included within the definition of victim-precipitation, then the 26 percent figure would of course have been considerably greater.

Offenders and victims usually live near each other, and tend to be of the same race and social class.[15] As a rule, homicidal victims are the relatives, friends, or acquaintances of offenders; seldom are victims and offenders strangers to each other.[16] One typical study found that in 25 percent of the cases, victim and offender were relatives; in 28 percent close friends; in 13 percent acquaintances; in 10 percent paramours; and only in 12 percent were they strangers.[17] The remaining percentage included homosexual partners, and so on. During 1966 for the United States as a whole, 29 percent of all criminal homicides involved victims and offenders of the same family. In slightly over half of those cases, one spouse killed the other; in one-seventh of the cases, parents killed their children.[18] Homicide, then, is an intensely personal crime, carried out between people who know each other at least moderately well.

4. PRESTIGE, RACE, AGE, AND SEX OF OFFENDERS

Criminal homicide varies decidedly by social class. The lower the class standing of individuals, the higher the homicide rate.[19] Numerous studies show that recorded homicide rates in the United States are from 10 to 15 times higher for blacks than whites.[20] In the black ghettoes the rates are especially high. The society's denial to blacks of access to educational and economic opportunity channels is well known and requires little documentation. In 1968, only six percent of those enrolled in institutions of higher education in the United States were black although the percentage of blacks in the country's total population was approximately double that.[21] For 1967, nonwhites were one-third as likely as whites to hold prestigious occupations as professionals, managers, or technical workers. They were three times as likely as whites to be in unprestigious nonfarm laboring jobs.[22] In 1971, the median annual family income for whites was $10,670; for blacks the figure was $6,440.[23]

This institutionalized blockage of blacks to success in American terms is a major source of the frustration that drives homicidal behavior. At the same time it is true, as previously indicated, that blacks generally kill blacks. Since homicide is as a rule the result of an escalating altercation among individuals who know each other fairly well or better, there is actually little opportunity for blacks to murder whites. They seldom have white friends with whom to quarrel. Blacks *could* go out into the community and kill whites at random. But homicide seldom occurs in that way although such killing is increasing—particularly where white police officers are the victims. In general practice blacks become substitutes for whites as the objects of black rage.

To be sure, blacks are sometimes arrested and charged with homicide when whites would not be. And they are sometimes convicted when whites would be found innocent. On the other hand, in the northern ghettoes and in parts of the south, officials occasionally look the other way when blacks kill blacks; these homicides then go unrecorded.

In the United States and around the world as well,

homicidal offenders quite definitely tend to be males. Rates in this society have been found in different studies to be from three to nine times as great for males as for females.[24] The Federal Bureau of Investigation reports that in 1970 five males were arrested for homicide for every one female.[25]

Homicide rates vary greatly by age of offender also. Here and in other societies homicide is low in childhood, rises in late adolescence to a peak in early adulthood and then gradually declines with age. Rates are often about five times as great for those in their twenties as for those over 50 years of age.[26] In the United States the rates are of the order of 14.0 for the former and 2.0 to 3.0 for the latter.[27] The general pattern is roughly the same for both sexes. For those in their twenties, male rates tend to be somewhat between 20.0 and 30.0 and female rates about 5.0. For those over 50 years old, male rates are approximately 5.0 and female rates approximately 1.0.[28]

In early adolescence the individual still has hope of achieving to some degree his aspirations. If the gates to economic success and to prestige and power are to slam shut, then it is in very late adolescence or early adulthood that this is likely to become obvious to the individual. For many, of course, those gates will remain open. For others, the resentment of social deprivation will grow rapidly and can erupt in explosive violence.

This will be so with greater intensity for males than for females. Certainly females suffer many deprivations in our society. Yet it is upon males much more than females that the onus is placed in regard to success or failure in gaining income, prestige, and power. Frustration regarding these goals grows unbearably severe for males much more often than for females.

When one considers age, sex, and race in conjunction with each other these themes stand out all the more strikingly. Table 4 shows homicide rates by age, sex, and race of offender as reported in Wolfgang's Philadelphia study, a study reasonably typical of the urban United States. In all age categories, rates for black males exceed those for white males and for white and black females. The highest rate is for black males in the 20 to 24 year age range; the rate is 92.5. This is over 300 times greater than the rate for white females, age 40 to 44, who have the lowest reported rate, 0.3.

At all ages, except 15 to 19 years, rates for black females are greater than for white males. In the 25 to 29 year category, the rate for black females is 22.3. These are likely to be women with several children, whose father is permanently absent or at home only occasionally. The women must support themselves and their children in a hostile economy. The only jobs available, if any, are low-paying and physically and psychologically demanding. These are frustrated, bitter, angry women.

TABLE 4
Criminal Homicide Rates by
Age, Race, and Sex of Offender,
Philadelphia, 1948—1952

Age:	Black			White		
	Total	Male	Female	Total	Male	Female
Under 15	.2	.4	.4	.2	.3	—
15-19	38.0	79.2	2.9	2.5	4.6	.4
20-24	46.6	92.5	12.4	4.6	8.2	1.2
25-29	47.4	77.8	22.3	2.5	4.6	.6
30-34	44.3	75.1	19.3	2.8	5.2	.6
35-39	35.4	65.5	9.8	3.3	6.0	.9
40-44	30.0	47.1	14.6	2.4	4.7	.3
45-49	30.8	44.0	18.2	2.5	4.4	.7
50-54	15.9	29.4	1.9	.5	1.1	—
55-59	19.7	30.6	8.5	.8	1.7	—
60-64	5.9	7.9	4.0	1.5	2.6	.5
65 and over	6.0	10.5	2.2	.8	1.8	—
All ages	24.6	41.7	9.3	1.8	3.4	.4

From Marvin E. Wolfgang, *Patterns in Criminal Homicide, Philadelphia: University of Pennsylvania Press, 1958, p. 66.*

5. OTHER CHARACTERISTICS
OF OFFENDERS

Regardless of race, age, and sex, homicidal offenders have experienced much frustration in childhood, both physical and psychological.[29] A study by the author found that severe birth traumas, serious surgical operations, serious illnesses, and accidents and beatings were considerably more common in the early lives of male offenders than of a sample of nonoffenders.[30] The nonoffenders were the offenders' nearest-age brothers. There was a pattern in the offenders' childhoods of increasing antagonism between mother and son. Beginning with a difficult birth, with feeding problems of the infant and illness of the mother, there developed a see-sawing pattern of interpersonal difficulties between mother and child. The child irritated the mother; the mother, crying, confined herself to a bedroom, leaving the child unattended for hours. The child later retaliated; the mother in turn retaliated, and so on.

In the study noted above, offenders tended in childhood to have used socially unacceptable forms of releasing aggression, symbolic and otherwise. Compared with their nearest-age brothers, offenders showed strong tendencies to kill animals, attack other children, steal, swear, and lie. Brothers were more likely to use such socially acceptable releases as arguing, sports, and the like.

What should be made clear is the depth of both frustration and aggression in the early lives of homicidal offenders.[31] Often offenders have been, throughout their early years, sick, battered children, targets for the aggressive behavior of those around them. Frequently they have been quiet children, given to sporadic outbursts of a distinctly sadistic nature.

It is characteristic of male offenders to have had dominant mothers and fathers who were either exceedingly passive men or who were absent from the home most of the time.[32] In either case the boy lacked an adequate sex role model. Other role models were also lacking. The white boy in the slum and the black boy in the ghetto have few even moderately successful individuals to emulate. Their role models come in considerable part from the mass media, one-dimensional gross distortions of living persons that are impossible to attain.

It will be understandable then that the homicidal offender's conception of himself, his identity, is weak and ill-formed. He is extremely insecure about his maleness and about his ability to compete as a person. His lack of identity makes him especially vulnerable to status threats. At the same time it drives him to take aggressive action against an overpowering and uncertain social environment. And the homicidal act provides the offender with an instant identity as a "murderer" who has the strength to control events.

Individuals subjected to the pressures of severe frustration and of high insecurity tend to become delusional.[33] Those who have frustrated them severely have also, in most instances, rewarded them much of the time. It is unusual and difficult for interaction to proceed without reward. Thus if a mother has on many occasions deprived a boy emotionally and perhaps beaten him as well she very likely has also rewarded him on other occasions. Since the mother's varying behaviors will tend to be responses to her needs rather than to what the boy does, he comes to have a picture of others as undependable people who reward one minute and disappoint through frustration the next. He becomes highly suspicious. If he has been frustrated in the extreme he becomes delusional and paranoidal.

Generally speaking, homicidal offenders are not psychotic.[34] But of those who are psychotic, many have strong paranoid tendencies. They believe that others seek to destroy them and so they take violent action in what they construe to be self-defense. However irrational such a belief may be, it is likely to have a certain basis in past truth. That is, there once were grounds for the belief; the offender has misplaced them to the present.

There is no conclusive evidence that alcoholics as such commit a disproportionately great amount of homicide. However, alcohol is involved in a majority of cases. In about one half the cases offenders have been drinking at the time of the crime. Victims have been drinking also in three-quarters of those cases. In an additional 10 percent of cases, victims have been drinking and offenders have not.[35] While alcohol is sometimes a distinctly precipitating factor in criminal homicide, there is little reason to think that if alcohol were prohibited homicide would decrease. As with firearms, the widespread use of alcohol appears to be a symptom of underlying social tensions more than a basic cause of extreme violence.

3. ASSAULT, RAPE, AND ROBBERY

1. AGGRAVATED ASSAULT

In the United States the legal definition of assault refers to the threat to do bodily harm to another rather than to the harmful act itself. Battery means the actual injury of one person by another. However, the term aggravated assault is in practice frequently used to denote serious battery; intent to kill is often involved.

The known aggravated assault rate in the United States for 1970 was 162.4 (per 100,000 population). An estimated 253,000 such assaults occurred.[1] Referring back to Table 2 (Chapter 2) the South Atlantic states have the highest assault rate, 227.0, of any region in the United States. This is almost three times greater than the rate of 83.6 for the New England states, the region with the lowest rate. It can readily be seen in that table that assault and homicide rates vary together. The higher the assault rate in a region, the higher the homicide rate tends to be. As Table 3 (Chapter 2) shows, assault as well as homicide decreases steadily as city size grows smaller. Suburban rates for both are slightly higher than for the smaller cities. On the other hand, the rural assault rate of 67.2 is lower than for cities of any size or for the suburbs, while the rural homicide rate, 5.0, is higher than for all but the larger cities.

Sex, age, race, and social class patterns for aggravated assault are similar to those for criminal homicide both in

29

this society and around the world. For 1970, arrests of males outnumbered arrests of females by seven to one.[2] By age, assault rates are highest in late adolescence and early adulthood and then gradually decline as age increases.[3] Blacks commit assault much more frequently than whites. About half of the arrests for assault in the United States are of blacks who comprise slightly over 11 percent of the population.[4] Race aside, assault tends decidedly to increase as the socio-economic standing of offenders decreases.[5]

There is a pattern of seasonal variation, aggravated assault rates being highest in the summer months and lowest during the winter.[6] Regarding weapons, the Federal Bureau of Investigation reports that for the United States as a whole in 1970, knives or other cutting instruments were the most frequently used, 28 percent of the time. Personal weapons—hands, fists, feet—were employed in 23 percent of the cases; blunt objects and firearms were each used about one-quarter of the time.[7]

Few detailed, quantitative studies of aggravated assault are available.[8] One of the best is by Pittman and Handy.[9] Those authors analyzed 241 cases of aggravated assault known to the police in St. Louis during 1961. They found that assaults predominated between 10:00 p.m. and 11:00 p.m. Almost half occurred on Fridays and Saturdays. The most usual weapons were knives; firearms were the second most usual. In about two-fifths of the cases, assault took place in a residence; in the remainder, outside of a residence. Three-quarters of the offenders were males; over four-fifths were black. Generally, offenders and victims were of the same sex and race. Both tended to be in the 20 to 34 year age range. The vast majority of offenders, and of victims as well, were blue-collar workers. Most offenders had previous arrest records. The authors add: "Females assault males with whom they have had a previous close relationship (such as dating, sexual intimacy, or common law marriage); but this is not the case with males assaulting females."

Pittman and Handy go on to compare their findings with Wolfgang's results regarding homicide. Both crimes tend to occur on weekends and late at night. While knives were most common in assault, firearms were the most usual weapon in homicide. Verbal arguments preceded both types of crimes, but alcohol was involved more often in homicidal than in assaultive cases. Victim and offender were typically of the same age, sex, and race in both homicide and assault. Young, male, lower-class blacks were disproportionately highly involved in both crimes.[10]

2. FORCIBLE RAPE

Forcible rape is the carrying out by a male of sexual intercourse with a female "forcibly and against her will."[11] Varying degrees of violence may be involved, from the threat of force to severe beating and choking. *The Uniform Crime Reports* list 37,300 forcible rapes in the United States during 1970.[12] This means a rate of 18.3 (per 100,000 population). As is understandable, forcible rapes are greatly underreported to the police. Victims often seek to avoid publicity. In any case, referring to Table 2 (Chapter 2), known rates for rape are decidedly highest in the western states, where the rate is 28.9, and next highest in the south, the rate there being 18.0. In contrast, homicide and aggravated assault are highest in the south. Rates for all three forms of violence—homicide, assault, and rape—are low in the northeast and especially so in New England.

As for the relation between population concentration and rape, Table 3 (Chapter 2) shows that rates for rape are greatest in large cities and decrease as city size de-

creases. Cities of over 250,000 population have a rate of
27.3 while cities under 10,000 population have a rate of
5.1. Rates for suburban areas and rural places exceed
those of the small cities but are well below the over-all
rate for the United States.

By age, arrests for forcible rape are concentrated in
the 17-19 year group, and almost two-thirds of arrests
during 1970 were of persons under the age of 25.[13] Regarding race, of those arrested during that year, 48 percent were black, 50 percent white, and two percent other
races.

Gebhard *et al.* found that those offenders who raped
adults tended to be psychologically normal while offenders who raped children were likely to be emotionally disturbed and from socially disorganized backgrounds.[14] A
second study indicates that of 1605 offenders, about half
were *legally* considered to be "not deviated" psychologically.[15] Most reports show little evidence of prior criminality.[16] And there is not a pattern of repeated rape by
the same individual. Sagarin and MacNamara report
that of a group of about 1,000 rape offenders, 15 percent
had previously been arrested for rape.

Of the few quantitative studies of forcible rape, that by
Amir is of special merit.[17] Amir analyzed rape in Philadelphia during 1958 and 1960. There were 646 cases of
rape—646 victims and 1292 offenders. While 370 cases
were single rapes, a considerable minority, 276, were multiple rapes, meaning that in a given incident one victim
and more than one offender were involved. Basing rates
on "potential population," those whose age and sex were
such that they could be offenders or victims, Amir found
that black rates for both offenders and victims were four
times higher than white rates. When he employed the
usual basis for computing rates, a 100,000 base of all persons in the population, Amir found that offender and victim rates were each about 12 times higher for blacks than

for whites. Most of the 646 cases involved offenders and victims of the same race.

The highest rates for both offenders and victims were found in the 15 to 25 year age bracket. Victims tended more than offenders to be minors. As a general rule, the older was the offender, the younger was the victim. Both offenders and victims were likely to be unmarried. The occupational prestige of offenders was low. Ninety percent held either skilled worker jobs or ones of lower prestige. Highest rates for offenders were found, then, among young, lower-class black males.

In about one-third of the rape cases in the Amir study, alcohol was present in one or more participants. In almost two-thirds of those cases, alcohol was present in both offender and victim. Alcohol and the use of extreme violence in the course of rape were positively associated with each other. Alcohol was more likely to be involved in cases that occurred on weekends than on weekdays. Unlike most other studies of rape, Amir found that a relatively high proportion of offenders, about half, had previous arrest records. Of those, only one-fifth were in connection with crimes against the person and only about one-tenth were for forcible rape. A fifth of the victims had records of arrest for some type of criminal violation.

Slightly over half, 53 percent, of the 646 cases occurred on weekends. And almost half took place between 8:00 p.m. and 2:00 a.m. While there was a tendency for rape to predominate during the summer months, that tendency was not a strong one.[18] Rape tended to occur in those areas of Philadelphia where homicide and aggravated assault rates were also high.

In about half of the cases offender and victim knew each other at least fairly well, had carried on, according to Amir, "primary relationships." Offender and victim lived in the same neighborhood in slightly over four-fifths of the cases. One-third of the time the offender met the victim at the latter's residence and the offense was committed there. If severe violence was involved, it usually took place in the home of the victim or offender. Automobiles were the scene of rape in but one-seventh of the cases. Most of the rapes, almost three-fourths, were clearly planned, and were not explosive actions "on the spur of the moment."

Fifteen percent of the time no force was actually used although threats of force may have been made. "Roughness," meaning very mild force, was employed in 29 percent of the cases; "nonbrutal" beatings in 25 percent; "brutal" beatings in 20 percent; and choking in 12 percent. The latter two forms of extreme violence were positively associated with blacks raping blacks and with cases where the offender was black and the victim white.

All in all, Amir reports extreme resistance by the victim was unusual. Victims were "submissive" slightly over half of the time, "resisted" about one-quarter of the time, and put up "a strong fight" in just under one-fifth of the cases. These figures were about the same for both black and white victims. The younger the victim, the less likely she was to resist. Of special interest is the finding that victims resisted most strongly when they were most intimidated in the initial stages of the encounter or when force was most used against them.

Of the 1292 offenders, 71 percent were involved in multiple rape cases (one victim and more than one offender). Multiple rapes tended to be intraracial. The younger the offender the more likely he was to take part in multiple rape. A high proportion of multiple rape offenders had previous records of crimes against the person or of sexual offenses. To a greater extent than single rapes, multiple rapes occurred in neighborhoods where both offenders and victims lived. However, multiple rapes took place among strangers more often than did single rapes. There was an especially strong tendency for multiple rapes to be planned rather than unplanned.

Amir distinguished between two types of multiple rapes: pair rapes, where two males raped one female; and group rapes, in which three or more males and one female were involved. Characteristics of pair rapes were decidedly more similar to single rapes than they were to group rapes. The author notes especially: "The futility of resistance and fight by the group rape victim is revealed by the fact that in group rape situations the victim was more submissive or resisted the offender but was less inclined to put up a strong fight."[19]

Amir defined victim-precipitated cases as either those where the victim agreed to intercourse and then changed her mind or where she voluntarily entered a highly sexually charged situation. About one-fifth of the 646 cases were classified as victim-precipitated. Such cases were especially prevalent when the victims were white and also when both offender and victim in the given incident were white.

3. ROBBERY

Robbery is the taking of goods or money from another individual by force or by threat of force. As such it is a crime of violence as well as of theft. Armed robbery involves the use of weapons such as firearms or knives. In strong-arm robbery the offender uses fists, arms, and so on. A majority of robberies are of the armed type, 60 percent in 1970, with the remainder, 40 percent, being strong-arm cases. Of the known armed robberies in that year, 63 percent were committed with a firearm, 24 percent with a knife, and 13 percent with a blunt instrument such as a club.[20]

Robbery in the United States is reported by the Federal Bureau of Investigation to be somewhat more prevalent than aggravated assault. In 1970, 348,400 robberies were recorded as compared to the 330,000 assaults. The rate per 100,000 population was 171.5 for robbery (and 162.4 for assault).[21] *The Uniform Crime Reports* indicate that robbery is the most rapidly increasing serious crime. The year 1970 showed a 16.4 percent increase over 1969 for the robbery rate as contrasted with 10.6 percent for the various major felonies. For the period 1960 to 1970 there was a rise of 224 percent in the number of robberies. During that time, the rate for robbery rose 186.3 percent. (Use of a rate means in effect that population is held constant.) The volume of bank robberies increased especially rapidly, by 29 percent from 1969 to 1970 and by 409 percent from 1960 to 1970.[22]

Unlike the other forms of violent crime, robbery rates are highest in the northeast (excluding New England) and lowest in the south. In 1970, the figure for the northeast was 232.8; for the south it was 130.2 (See Table 2, Chapter 2). More than homicide, assault, and rape, robbery is a big city crime. During 1967, the robbery rate for cities with populations of over 250,000 was 330.2 (Table 3, Chapter 2). There were 56 such cities and they accounted for 71 percent of the known robberies.[23] In striking contrast, the rural rate was 11.5. That is, the rate for the large cities was 29 times the rate for the rural areas.

Robbery offenders tend to be young. Seventy-seven percent of arrestees for this crime in 1970 were under 25 years of age; 57 percent were less than 21; and 33 percent were under 18.[24] Only six percent were females. Blacks made up 65 percent of the arrestees, whites 33 percent, and other races two percent.[25] Evidence indicates that robbery offenders are even more likely than those who commit other types of violent offenses to be of low prestige. A Philadelphia study reports that the prestige of 92 to 97 percent of robbery offenders was equal to that of skilled laborers or less.[26]

Roebuck and Cadwallader analyzed various social and psychological characteristics of 32 black males incarcerated in Washington, D.C. for armed robbery. They were compared with 368 black males incarcerated for other offenses. The authors summarize their findings: "The armed robbers were a group of hardened, anti-social recidivists, the products of disorganized homes and slum neighborhoods where they came in contact with criminal norms and activities at an early age. Rejected and ill-supervised, in homes charged with emotional conflict, they entered street corner society early—between the ages of six and nine." Case histories of the offenders indicated a pattern of maladjustment at school, at home, and in the wider community. Most had been leaders of gangs and were prone to violence and to destroying property. Offenders were physically large and strong and had excess energy. Most, 20 out of the 32, had been amateur boxers. In maturity, "they sought out criminal companions of a similar type, that is, other robbers. They took real pride in their criminal style—the taking of property by force or threat of force."[27]

While homicide, assault, and rape offenders and victims tend to be acquaintances and of the same race, this is not so for robbery. The Eisenhower Commission (National Commission on the Causes and Prevention of Violence) conducted a survey of 17 cities and found the following: 45 percent of robberies involved black offenders and white victims; in 38 percent of the cases both offenders and victims were black. There was a decided tendency for the victim to be older than the offender. The robberies analyzed were not "crimes of passions" as are homicide, assault, and rape. Rather, there was a degree of impersonal calculation.[28]

All in all, it is clear that in the United States violence is committed largely by individuals who are male and young. Blacks are greatly overrepresented among offenders. Victims tend to have social backgrounds similar to those of offenders. With the exception of robbery, violent crime is personal crime. It occurs among neighbors who are likely to know each other or among relatives. As with homicidal offenders, those who commit assault, rape, and robbery, tend to have led lives of great frustration. They have been weakened by continual psychological and physical hurts and their tolerance of frustration is low. They lash out against their frustrators or substitute figures. To some this may not seem applicable to armed robbers, who are supposedly "hardened and tough" offenders. However, apparent hardening and toughening can very well be an outer defense against an inner insecurity born of deprivation.

4. BURGLARY
AND LARCENY

1. BURGLARY

Two major types of property crime are burglary and larceny. Burglary refers to unlawful entry into a residence or place of business in order to commit theft. Larceny is theft without force or fraud. Larceny includes shoplifting, pocket-picking, purse-snatching, theft of vehicles, and so on. Robbery, previously discussed, is both a violent and a property crime: force or the threat of force is used against an individual in order to steal from him.

Burglary is the most prevalent serious crime (felony) in the United States. In the year 1970, 2,169,000 burglaries were recorded. These accounted for 39 percent of the crimes listed in the Federal Bureau of Investigation's Crime Index. As noted earlier, the Index includes murder and first-degree manslaughter, forcible rape, aggravated assault, robbery, grand larceny, and auto theft. And burglaries accounted for almost half—45 percent—of the property crimes included in the Index.[1]

The over-all rate for burglary in the Unied States in 1970 was 1067.7 per 100,000 population. Burglaries predominated in the Western states. As Table 5 indicates, the rate there was 1541.8. The North Central states had the lowest rate, 896.6. The rate for the Northeast was 1065.5. Rates for grand larceny and auto theft were also very high in the West. While there is no simple explanation for this, the fact is that a greater proportion of the

TABLE 5
Rates per 100,000 Population
for Burglary, Grand Larceny,
and Auto Theft
by Geographical Region,
United States, 1970

Region:	Burglary	Grand Larceny	Auto Theft
Northeast	1065.5	823.2	571.9
North Central	896.6	759.7	419.3
South	960.7	750.2	327.1
West	1541.8	1269.3	570.2
Total U.S.	1067.7	859.4	453.5

Source: Federal Bureau of Investigation, *Uniform Crime Reports—1970*, Washington, D.C.: U.S. Government Printing Office, 1970, pp. 66-71.

population in the western states is composed of migrants than in the other states. Rootlessness and impersonality in relationships tend to give rise to property crimes as well as to crimes of violence.

Table 6 shows that burglary, like robbery, is a big city crime. The same is true for grand larceny and auto theft. Rates for these crimes are distinctly lowest in rural areas and they are in the middle range in the suburbs. The burglary rate is two-and-a-half times greater in the large cities than in rural places; the grand larceny rate is over four times greater in the large cities; and the rate for auto theft is more than 11 times greater. Crimes of violence are also prevalent in the large cities although the difference in rates between those cities and rural areas is not as great as it is for property crimes. Again, impersonality of life in the large city is one significant force behind the commission of property crime and of violent crime also. And relative deprivation strikes the impoverished much more glaringly in urban areas than in rural settings. Differences in wealth and power are vastly greater and are highly visible.

Eighty-three percent of those arrested for burglary are under 25 years of age. Slightly over half are younger than 18. This is also the case for the other major property crimes of grand larceny and auto theft. Fifty-one percent of those arrested on grand larceny charges and 56 percent of arrestees for auto theft are under 18.[2]

The enormous emphasis in our society on material goods as signs of prestige and power impels the young who are without those signs to gain them illegally. There is of course in the symbolic sense an element of aggression in these forms of theft. The material possessions of those of some affluence are confiscated by those who are deprived. The deprived thereby vent some of the aggression that is a consequence of their myriad frustrations.

Only five percent of those arrested for burglary in 1970 were females.[3] Like robbery, burglary does not fit into the female role as that role is defined in this society. The idea of a second-story woman or of a strong-arm female simply has very great connotations of a lack of feminin-

TABLE 6
Rates per 100,000 Population
for Burglary, Grand Larceny,
and Auto Theft in Cities,
Suburbs, and Rural Areas,
United States, 1967

Place:	Burglary	Grand Larceny	Auto Theft
All Cities	998.3	668.8	463.4
Cities over 250,000	1473.8	912.7	776.0
Suburbs	678.8	459.8	205.4
Rural Areas	403.7	218.6	67.7
Total U.S.	868.7	565.3	360.5

Source: Federal Bureau of Investigation, *Uniform Crime Reports—1967*, Washington, D.C.: U.S. Government Printing Office, 1968, pp. 62-67.

ity; it connotes, in fact, masculinity. As we shall see, this is quite definitely less so for larceny.

There are eight times as many whites as blacks in the United States. Blacks constitute over 11 percent of the population and whites about 88 percent. The remainder is made up of other races. Yet approximately one-third of those arrested for burglary, grand larceny, and auto theft are black.[4] As with arrests for violent crime, there is always the likelihood that some blacks will be arrested simply because they are black and powerless. Yet such discriminatory practices cannot account for much of the three-fold overrepresentation of blacks in arrests for property crimes. As discussed earlier, blacks share but little in the success goods of the society. Relative deprivation is very great.

Both thieves and police officers categorize those who engage in burglary into two groups: regular and cat-burglars. Regulars attempt to burglarize when residents or workers are away. Cat-burglars enter dwellings while the residents are there. They tend to be viewed by regulars and by police as "odd." They are seen as persons who "get their kicks" out of performing by stealth.

Burglars, and larcenists as well, may be professionals or amateurs. Professionals make an occupation of theft and are skilled in a wide avariety of techniques for gaining goods and money illegally. They have established ongoing contacts with lawyers, fences, and often with the police as well. Burglars who make a living from theft are usually termed professional heavies.[5] They define themselves as criminals. They are above average in intelligence. They have had much contact with others who display criminal behavior patterns. They grew up in lower-class urban areas and were members of delinquent gangs. They were apprehended and arrested by police early in life and many times since. They have served sentences in reformatories, jails, or prisons. They dislike intensely those who are a part of the formal control system: police, court personnel, and correctional officers.[6]

2. LARCENY
AND AUTO THEFT

Larceny is the theft of money or goods where force or fraud are not involved. Grand larceny usually refers to thefts of items valued at 50 dollars or more and petit larceny to situations where lesser amounts are involved. The Federal Bureau of Investigation reports that 1,746,000 grand larcenies were known to occur in 1970. This means a rate of 859.4 per 100,000 population. There were an additional two-and-a-half million known petit larcenies. The largest category of stolen goods was auto accessories. These made up 20.6 percent of the total. Next were items left in autos, 19.0 percent; then items from buildings, 16.3 percent; then bicycles, 14.6 percent. Shoplifting accounted for 8.8 percent; purse-snatching for 2.6 percent; and pocket-picking for 1.2 percent.[7]

As was made clear in the preceding section, larceny in the United States occurs predominantly in large cities, in the western states, and among the young and the black. Females commit grand larceny to a greater extent than they do most other crimes. Twenty-eight percent of arrests for this crime in 1970 were of females. Only in the misdemeanor of drunkenness were women represented in greater proportions, relative to males.[8]

Shoplifting is especially a female form of larceny. Mary Owen Cameron conducted an extensive study of shoplifting in a large Chicago department store.[9] She distinguishes boosters and snitches. Boosters are professional shoplifters. They make their living by selling the goods they steal. Snitches or pilferers are amateurs. They steal goods they would like to have, often small luxury items such as costume jewelry or food delicacies. Many pilfer goods that they could otherwise obtain only by using part of the family budget, thereby drawing money away from important family needs.

Most shoplifting is habitual, Cameron finds. Shoplifters are not predominantly from the lower class. They range across the entire social class spectrum. They have had little contact with the adult criminal subculture. Some, however, have earlier been members of delinquent gangs. The professional booster sees himself or herself as a law violator. The amateur snitch, the pilferer, clearly does not.

When apprehended by store police, snitches rationalize their actions, attempt to pay for the item, and cannot believe they will be arrested and brought to trial. Cameron holds that those snitches who are apprehended by store detectives and then released without being turned over to the municipal police for arrest and trial seldom repeat their larceny. She says in effect that they recognize that the goods they steal are not worth the stigma that can come to them if they are arrested. If the case is prosecuted, then the offender begins to take on the self-image of thief and is more likely to commit larceny in the future. Those disgraced seek the support of self-professed thieves in or out of jail. That support in turn serves to increase the process of self-labeling as thief. To quote Cameron: "Crime prevention would seem best achieved by helping the law violators retain their self-image of respectability while making it clear to them that a second offense will really mean disgrace."[10]

Cameron does not believe that kleptomania plays a part in shoplifting. She contends that if amateur shoplifting were neurotic-compulsive behavior, then those apprehended by store detectives and shortly released would continue their larcenous behavior and they do not. There are a number of researchers who agree. For example, Gibbons cites research by Robin, whose findings substantiate Cameron's. "'Kleptomania' turns out," Gibbons writes, "to be nothing more than a social label hung on 'nice people' who steal and withheld from 'bad people' who are simply 'crooks'!"[11]

However, kleptomania need not be so strong a compulsion that it continues regardless of events. Compulsive behavior patterns do extinguish under suitable conditions. Probably shoplifting is for many shoplifters more a compulsion than Cameron, Gibbons, and Robin believe. Probably in most cases it is not a very strong compulsion, however. Perhaps apprehension by store detectives is a stronger deterrent, in the face of moderate compulsion, than those researchers give it credit for being. And, finally, it may be that far more amateur shoplifters who are apprehended but not arrested continue to shoplift than are known to do so.

Auto theft is in the broad sense a form of grand larceny. The Federal Bureau of Investigation treats it separately in part because there is so much of it. In 1970, 921,000 motor vehicles were known to have been stolen. This was one out of every 100 registered vehicles. The rate for 1970 was 453 per 100,000 population. The average value of the stolen vehicles was between 900 and 1000 dollars. Two-thirds of auto thefts take place at night. Over one-half occur in residential areas.[12]

While females commit a substantial amount of larceny, their rate for auto theft, as for burglary and robbery, is distinctly low. About four percent of those arrested for auto theft are females. It is a male crime, then, and as noted earlier, it is committed predominantly by the black and the young. *Of all major offenses, auto theft has the largest proportion of arrestees under age 18.* Fifty-six percent are less than 18 years old and 36 percent are black.[13]

The car remains the primary and most portable symbol of success, power, affluence, and prestige in the United States. It is a dominant feature of the American reality as well as the American dream. If the automobile is not a part of the reality of many poor Americans, then it can readily become so through theft.

This reasoning applies with somewhat lesser intensity to the other forms of larceny, to robbery, and to burglary. Goods or money are appropriated by the individual. Above all, they promise the prestige he so desperately needs. Seldom is prestige actually delivered in significant degree. The amounts of money stolen, the value of the goods taken, are often small. But the promise is there—there can always be a next time. Meanwhile, the individual, denied prestige and therefore frustrated, releases aggression in the defiant act of theft.

5. FRAUD

1. "BLACK-COLLAR" FRAUD

Confidence games, forgery, embezzlement, and price-rigging are forms of fraud. Generally, confidence games and forgery are viewed as "black-collar" crimes, as are all of the crimes previously discussed. Embezzlement, price-rigging and other types of crime in business settings are usually termed "white-collar" crime. First, to consider confidence games and forgery: Most if not all "con-men" are professionals. It takes time and effort to learn the subtle art of conning. Confidence games cannot readily be carried out on a highly limited time basis. However, it would be possible for a person with a more or less legitimate occupation to have a second occupation as con-man. Confidence games usually involve a get-rich-quick idea. The con-man gradually persuades the mark, the victim, that he can with a modest investment make a large profit. In the process the con-man acquires the mark's modest investment under the guise that the project has in some way failed.[1]

Professionals who are con-men have much prestige among thieves. They come from a wide variety of social class backgrounds. Few are from homes of poverty. Conning requires verbal fluency and intelligence, confidence of manner, a certain savoir-faire. One study indicates that while con-men come mainly from the middle class they have experienced exceedingly difficult early lives.[2] They

47

have learned to excel in deceit as a way of responding to adversity. They take pride in this skill and now use it for profit.[3]

Confidence swindling is exceedingly widespread although hard figures are impossible to obtain.[4] It is a low-risk crime. Probably no more than five percent of offenders are arrested.[5] American culture emphasizes quick success, willingness to take risks, to gamble, to play the game hard and to beat the other fellow. Confidence swindling has much in common with super-salesmanship in the United States. And it requires marks, victims, who are willing to participate in a "deal" that will supposedly swindle someone else. Such individuals, obviously, are not difficult to find. In the process they, the real victims, are swindled. Having gotten involved in illegal dealings they are reluctant to attempt to prosecute the con-man.

Check forgers tend to be either semiprofessionals or amateurs. Whichever the category, most are from middle class backgrounds. They are white, they are male, and they are older than most other types of offenders, often being in middle age or beyond. Many have experienced much marital strife.[6]

Edwin Lemert has conducted some of the best analyses of check forgery. Regarding "naive forgers" (his term for amateurs), Lemert suggests that relatively honest individuals turn to an occasional forgery when they are socially isolated and when other sources of funds are closed to them. For example an alcoholic who has not worked for some time and who has been temporarily rejected by his family and friends may pass a bad check or two in order to get money for alcohol.[7]

Professional check forgers are most properly viewed as semiprofessionals.[8] The skills required are neither many nor complex. Forgery consists essentially of being able to cash a check when funds are not available to back it up.

Seldom is forgery a full-time, week-in and week-out occupation. It is a cyclical activity. A series of bad checks are "spread" in a community and then the forger moves on. Further, in interviews forgers testify to having "a need" to pass bad checks at some times and not at other times. That is, occasionally they are motivated to experience "the thrill" of dissembling.

Check forgers are loners. They avoid others in part because of fear of being given away. But this avoidance is also due to the fact that many are middle class and do not wish to consort with other criminal offenders, the most likely candidates for friendship. Moreover, since they must keep on the move or soon be identified, their opportunities for friendship are considerably limited.

Forgers must give the appearance of being at least moderately affluent. There is, of course, much reluctance to cash checks of persons who appear "seedy." Affluence combined with travel is costly. Forgers must cash more and more checks to pay the costs. A vicious circle eventually sets in: The more checks they cash, the more they need to keep moving. The more movement, the more need to cash checks. The more checks, the greater the probability of being apprehended. Forgers perceive this and experience rapidly increasing strain. The business community and the police are especially incensed at their crimes and make special efforts to apprehend them. This too the forger knows.

At the same time, the forger's identity suffers. He plays but partial roles. For example, to the victim he may appear as a successful businessman on a trip. But he does not play that role all day every day. As noted, he sees few people in close relationships. An ongoing stable self-image is thus very difficult. As Lemert puts it, there is an "erosion of identity." The forger becomes more and more isolated. As greater and greater numbers of checks are passed and success temporarily increases, the noose of apprehension by legal authorities tightens. Paranoia often arises. Any small cue—a knock on the door, whatever—is taken as a sign of impending apprehension by the police.

The suspense becomes unbearable. There is in Lemert's phrasing a "final bankruptcy of motivation." The forger cannot go on because of fear and because of a rapidly diminishing identity. He makes an obvious mistake and is caught or gives himself up to the police. It is only at this point that there is public knowledge of his "ability" to pass bad checks. Now he gains identity as a forger and later as an inmate. The vast majority of such forgers are apprehended in this way.[9]

2. "WHITE-COLLAR" FRAUD

As noted earlier, fradulent violations committed by businessmen in the course of their occupations are termed white-collar crimes. These take two main forms: stealing, largely through embezzlement, for direct personal gain, and other criminal acts designed to enhance profits of the business organization.[10] Embezzlement takes many forms: "borrowing" bank and real estate deposits, directly stealing the assets of the organization, "juggling the books," and the like.

A great amount of embezzlement goes unreported. It is estimated that no more than one percent of crimes of embezzlement are prosecuted. Nevertheless it is clear from those data available that embezzlement accounts for more theft in dollar terms than all black-collar theft combined. One analysis estimated embezzlement at well over a billion dollars in 1960.[11] Known black-collar thefts through burglary, pocket-picking, robbery, and auto theft amounted to $570,000,000 in that year.[12]

Donald Cressey carried out a detailed analysis of embezzlement.[13] He confined his study to "criminal violations of financial trust." The employee must have accepted a position of financial trust offered him in good faith. And he must have then violated that trust by committing fradulent theft in the business setting. Cressey found that individuals become violators when the following conditions obtained: They saw themselves as having a financial problem that they could not share with others. They perceived that their problem could be resolved in secret by a violation of trust. That is, they saw that they had the opportunity to resolve the problem in that way. And they were able to rationalize their violation before committing it.

Trust violators are middle class, middle-aged, have had no significant contact with the criminal subculture, and possess no previous criminal record. Not many individuals have the opportunity to violate financial trust. They must be in a position of some financial responsibility. This generally excludes the lower class and the young. And if a person has a criminal record he is unlikely to be given financial trust in the first place.

Edwin Sutherland conducted a large-scale study of corporate crime, of violations by employees in order to benefit the company.[14] He analyzed the life histories of 70 firms. They were the largest manufacturing, mining, and mercantile corporations in this country. Sutherland collected data on such violations as misrepresentation in advertising, unfair labor practices, rebates, financial fraud, restraint of trade, and infringement of patents, copyrights, and trade-marks. He found a total of 980 violations, an average of 14 per corporation. While it is questionable that all of these violations would technically qualify as crimes, Sutherland firmly established his main point: The conduct of the corporation involves an enormous amount of law violation.

The most notable series of violations *for* the firm in recent years was the conspiracy of high-level employees in the electrical industry to fix prices in violation of the

Sherman Antitrust Act.[15] Criminal charges were brought against 29 corporations and 45 officials of those corporations by the United States government. Officials met more or less secretly in various parts of the country and conspired to rig bids on various electrical products and to fix prices across the industry in a number of other ways.

The biggest violator was the General Electric Company. Fines levied against that company totaled $437,500; 32 executives were known to have been involved. The Westinghouse Company was fined $372,500. In all, seven officials served jail sentences, most for 30 days. Twenty-four other officials received suspended jail sentences. Some officials were fired by their companies and others were retained in much the same capacities they had filled prior to conviction.

Competition was very great in the electrical field. In General Electric, top officials set sales quotas impossibly high. (Those officials had long issued directives pointing out that price-rigging was illegal. Yet some knew the practice existed. None of these officials was convicted.) The market was extremely uncertain and unstable. Demand fluctuated greatly and prices shifted rapidly unless stabilized through conspiracy. Some senior employees had the choice of either being fired or entering in collusion with representatives of other companies to fix prices. All violators knew they were breaking the law. Many viewed their behavior as technically illegal but not criminal and not unethical. They considered their actions to be usual in the industry, which they were. They felt they should be excused because they were acting under orders. And they believed that their actions were ethical and necessary because they stabilized the market. Few were able to see that that which is usual, which is done because someone else orders it, and which contributes to stability can also be unequivocally criminal.[16]

Employers are reluctant to face the adverse publicity that will come with trial for white-collar crime. And they fear also that public opinion may conclude that the company is persecuting an employee. Further, there is considerable sympathy in firms for the trusted long-term employee who "borrows" funds because of some personal problem that only money can cure. Especially is this so for the employee who has spent many years at modest salary. Moreover, no one individual loses when a company is embezzled; many lose. Harm to the individual is thus less clear. And this leads to decreased motivation to prosecute. Also, these crimes are difficult to discover and once discovered it is difficult to obtain sufficient evidence for successful prosecution. At the same time, the threat and fact of negative sanctions such as a jail term are far more effective deterrents in white-collar crime than in black-collar crime. The white-collar thief stands to lose his respectability. The black-collar thief has less respectability to lose. Finally, persons in a position to commit white-collar crime are in a loose sense at least part of the "establishment." Black-collar offenders are not.[17]

Both black- and white-collar perpetrators of fraud differ in several significant ways from those who commit crimes of violence and the theft crimes of burglary and larceny. Fraudulent offenders tend to be distinctly older. They are seldom black. They are of decidedly higher prestige. And they matured in family environments of greater prestige than the other offenders.

6. VICTIMLESS CRIME AND MASS DISORDER

1. VICTIMLESS CRIME: DRUG ABUSE

In this chapter two broad forms of criminal violation, not necessarily related, are discussed. The first is victimless crime and the second is mass disorders. Victimless crime involves willful exchange among adults of goods or services that are strongly demanded yet proscribed by criminal law. Persons directly taking part seldom complain to legal authorities. Essentially what is involved is the attempt to legislate morality for its own sake.[1] Examples are the sale of addictive drugs; homosexual relations; the exchange between prostitute and client; the expectant mother and physician who "collaborate" in an illegal abortion.

Organized crime often infiltrates the networks of exchange that develop. People want the goods and services. Given the criminal law, the distribution of those goods and services cannot be organized and facilitated on a legitimate basis. It is an apt situation for massive exploitation by professional criminals who are part of a large-scale organization. The sale of drugs and prostitution both involve exchanges particularly conducive to this type of exploitation.[2]

Here we shall focus on one form of victimless crime: drug addiction and abuse. The general nature of the problem will be briefly explicated. In later chapters theories of addiction, the present control process, and possibilities for more constructive and efficient control will be detailed. Few areas of human concern are so confounded by misconceptions and ambivalence as the use of drugs and their abuse.[3] Addiction has many meanings.[4] The effects of different drugs depend to varying degrees on personality and social setting. Estimates of the numbers of persons in the United States who use various types of drugs vary widely.

The opiates are the most common physiologically addictive drugs used in this country. They include opium, morphine, codeine, and various derivatives. These drugs are depressants; they have much medical value. In this country, heroin, a derivative of morphine, is the most commonly used opiate. Usually it is "shot" into the vein with a needle. Cocaine, a stimulant, is psychologically addictive. It is little used here.

Marihuana is quite a different type of drug. Usually marihuana is smoked. Depending on personality and social context, it may have stimulating or depressing effects. It is not addictive in the purely physiological sense. It does not appear to have serious, harmful effects. Marihuana is relatively inexpensive, compared to heroin and other forms of morphine.

The amphetamines are stimulants, often called "pep pills." They are used medically, frequently in cases of overweight or excessive fatigue. They are not physiologically addictive. Their "abuse" stems in large part from the "energy" and elation they seem to provide. The barbiturates are depressants. Called "goof balls," they induce sedative or anesthetic reactions. They relieve anxiety and are often prescribed as "sleeping pills." The barbiturates can be addictive physiologically. They are overused largely because of their anxiety-reducing function.

The hallucinogens produce unusual or bizarre states of

consciousness. Two major traditional forms are peyote and mescaline. LSD is a synthetic drug made of lysergic acid and other components. It is many times stronger than peyote or mescaline. Common practice is to place it in liquid form on a sugar cube and swallow it. It is also available in pill form. In some instances psychosis—which may or may not have been latent in the individual—is induced by hallucinogens. Apparently the hallucinogens are not physiologically addictive.

Broadly speaking all of these drugs possess either depressant or stimulant properties. Individuals often become psychologically dependent on them although some are not, as we have seen, physiologically addictive. They vary greatly in the harmfulness of their effects. These drugs tend to temporarily decrease feelings of frustration. Most temporarily reduce conflict among the user's roles. On the other hand, the withdrawal effects of the addictive drugs can cause great suffering. And certain of the psychotic symptoms that may be brought about by the hallucinogens are severely frustrating.

Heroin and other opiates are imported largely by organized crime groups. Marihuana comes in the main from Mexico although it can be grown here. Some marihuana is made available through organized crime channels. Much is imported in one way or another by individuals operating alone or in small groups. The barbiturates and amphetamines are readily available because physicians prescribe them in large numbers. And pharmacies fill forged prescriptions. LSD is manufactured and sold illicitly by small companies and by individuals from various walks of life.

It is practically impossible to estimate reliably the number of persons in the United States taking various of these drugs other than on legitimate prescription. Compared to other drugs heroin is not widely used.[5] Marihuana is in great demand and its use is increasing. This is true also of the amphetamines and barbiturates; after all, they are presently in millions of medicine cabinets. Use of the hallucinogens, definitely on the rise in recent years, particularly on college and university campuses, appears now to be waning.

2. THE NATURE OF RIOTING

Mass disorders of a riotous nature usually involve components of violence, property damage, and often theft in the form of looting. Riotous behavior can be defined as physical or psychological aggression toward others consciously carried out by relatively large numbers of individuals acting more or less in concert with each other.[6] Psychological aggression implies that frustration is inflicted upon others through verbal attack, destruction of other's property, and so on. Relatively large numbers of persons refers to something larger than a small, intimate group. Some coordination among individuals in space and time is necessary if a riot is to occur. Hence the phrase, "more or less in concert with each other." Aspects of riotous behavior may be or may not be patterned. That is, riot behavior may be "institutionalized" or it may not be.

Two major forms of rioting in the United States have revolved around racial conflicts and campus protest. The former have involved much more violence, damage, and theft than the latter.[7] There has been much resentment in various quarters of the society over the rebellious behavior *en masse* of considerable numbers of college students. This has been in part due to alienation between younger and older people. It has also been due to the resentment felt by many that college rebels seem to them to have taken for granted a right to abuse the privilege of attending college. In any event, few, albeit too many, have been killed or seriously wounded on the campuses.[8] And property damage has not been high compared to that growing out of racial conflict.[9]

The emphasis here will be on race riots in the United States in relatively recent times. Let it be noted at the outset that racial rioting in the United States is not at all a recent phenomenon. Race riots by Indians and blacks punctuated all centuries since the early 1500's.[10] During the first half of the twentieth century, there was much serious rioting. In the East St. Louis riot of 1917, 39 blacks and nine whites were killed and hundreds wounded. In the Chicago riot of 1919, 15 whites and 23 blacks were killed and many more wounded. There were race riots during World War II, the 1943 Detroit riot being the worst with nine whites and 25 blacks killed.[11]

The years 1967 and 1968 were periods of extreme racial turbulence. An analysis by the Lemberg Center for the Study of Violence showed the following: During 1967 there were 233 major disorders. A large number, 251, occurred during the *first four* months of 1968. Of those, 202 took place in April, directly after Martin Luther King's death. Beyond doubt, King's assassination had a widespread effect as a precipitant.[12]

During 1967 the 233 disorders occurred in 168 cities and 35 states. About 19,000 persons were arrested, 3,400 injured, and 82 killed. Property damage was estimated at $69,000,000. Considering April, 1968 alone: The 202 racial riots took place in 172 cities and 37 states. Twenty-seven thousand were arrested, 3,500 were injured, 43 were dead. The estimate of damage to property was $58,000,000.[13] As is well known, property damage is usually inflicted on stores owned by whites, and sometimes blacks, who are believed by local residents to be exploiting them. As one example, in the Newark riot of 1967, 1029 retail establishments were damaged. About 5,000 employees were directly affected. These establishments were largely of the exploitive type.[14]

Race riots in recent years have taken place to a significant degree in black areas of northern and midwestern cities more than elsewhere. About half of the local black inhabitants have been involved, some very tangentially, others closely. Ten to 15 percent of the inhabitants were active rioters. Twenty-five percent were by-standers. Ten to 15 percent acted as counter-rioters, trying to "cool" the situation.[15]

Rioters tend to be young black adult males. They are unmarried and lifelong residents of the riot area. Females, however, are not greatly underrepresented. One-third to two-fifths of the rioters are female, mainly young adults. Rioters are a cross-section of the lower socio-economic group of the community. Most are employed, and in skilled or semiskilled jobs. They are better educated than their neighbors. They are not especially prone to have criminal records. And they are acutely aware of what they consider to be racial prejudice and discrimination. Thus rioters do not conform to the "riff-raff" image of being unemployed, uneducated trouble-makers.[16]

Precipitating incidents in racial riots are many. They symbolize fundamental black grievances. Usually two related factors are involved: First, there is a physical or verbal attack or degradation directed against a black by a white. Second, authorities refuse to take appropriate action. Often there is a series of similar incidents in the given locale over the weeks or months preceding a riot. And frequently the police are involved. As an illustration, white police may hound young black men. Complaints are lodged; nothing is done. A final incident occurs and the black community erupts.

Major social forces that generate the broad conditions necessary for race riots have been analyzed at some length by the Kerner Commission and by other groups.[17] Police prejudice, discrimination, hostility, and brutality form one clear complex of factors. These police attitudes

and actions are more than precipitants. They are basic
elements of the social system as well. Numerous studies
confirm this.[18] White police prejudice toward blacks is extremely common. As but one brief example, many white
police officers talk glibly of "going out and getting me a
nigger tonight."[19]

Pervasive prejudice and discrimination toward blacks
in the society at large, that is, apart from the police, is of
course another major force behind racial rioting. So too
is the white exodus from the inner cities, the black migra-
tion there and the consequent coalescing of ghetto communities. Other central social forces behind racial riots
are these: The day-in and day-out frustration of black
powerlessness; a new black racial pride that catalyzes *action;* the terroristic behavior of some members of the
white power structure that provides a basis for blacks to
rationalize their own terroristic activities; the frustrated
hopes of blacks for large gains in the face of the small
gains they have actually made (blacks are now little better off economically relative to whites than they were in
1945).[20]

Further social factors conducive to black rioting are:
the encroachment on black areas of new white residential and business projects; a scarcity of black involvement in neighborhood businesses; an especially low percent of blacks on city police forces; a severe lack of communication between local government and average
voter, both white and black.

The day-in and day-out degradation of black by white
has brought about the following extraordinarily serious,
pervasive and dangerous personality characteristics:
Many blacks suffer from a lack of identity. They often
strongly disapprove of themselves. They are suspicious
of whites, sometimes to the point of paranoia—although
with good reason. The repressed rage of blacks is conse-
quently very great.

Reaction of the community to the *possibility* of a racial riot is of course of much importance in determining whether a riot actually occurs. What the police, public officials, and other community members actually do and do not do when racial tensions are high may impede or impel the development of riotous behavior. These matters are considered further at later points in this book.

7. THEORY: FRUSTRATION AND SUBCULTURAL LEARNING

1. DENIAL OF GOALS AND ALIENATION

It will hardly be possible in several score of pages to summarize adequately the extraordinarily complex array of forces that generate crime. As indicated at the outset, there is much need for further knowledge as to the sources of crime. At the same time much knowledge is at hand and ready to be used. Some indication of the nature of sociological and psychological variables behind crime has already been given in the preceding discussion.

The problem now is to proceed without undue oversimplification and without misleading the reader not closely versed in criminological theory. Hence we shall proceed with care. But we shall not allow the discussion to become stuck on dead center either because "we do not know enough" or because the pitfalls of oversimplification are supposedly insurmountable.

Theory is, after all, a simplified picture of what happens in some part or another of the universe. It is not necessarily ivory-towered. It is not necessarily impractical. Theory is a symbolic representation, more or less abstract, of what appears to lead to, or cause, something else. In criminology, there are presently three major and related bodies of theory. They are implicit in the materials of the foregoing chapters. These, like all theory, will change over time. They will change as our understanding of the world changes.

The first group of theories has to do with the blockage of individuals' strivings for goals and the consequent alienation they experience. Some of these theoretical approaches apply most centrally to violent crime; most are also of distinct relevance to property crimes. Several of the theories are explicitly addressed to homicide and suicide. While suicide is not of direct concern in this book, those aspects of the theories that apply to suicide are instructive here. Homicide and suicide are in a number of respects two sides of the same coin. Homicide is the epitome of aggression directed outward and suicide of aggression directed inward.[1]

The second body of theory pertains to subcultural conditions, roles, and behavior patterns conducive to crime. From this perspective crime is a consequence of a scarcity of role models and patterns of behavior that are socially acceptable and a prevalence of those from which criminal behavior can be learned. Several of these theories apply more to property crimes than to violence although they are of importance in an understanding of the latter as well.

The third group of theories emphasizes two related matters: The functions that crime serves, particularly as these have to do with contributing to social organization; and secondly, the social controls that society institutionalizes in order to perpetuate as well as to prevent crime. The labeling of individuals as criminal before the fact, the providing of excellent opportunities for the learning of crime in prisons and reformatories, types of punishment of offenders which lead them to aggress further—these are all examples of controls that perpetuate crime.

But to turn now to the first group of theoretical approaches: When people are blocked from achieving what they desire or when they are otherwise frustrated they become aggressive toward others or themselves. First set forth in 1939 by John Dollard and his colleagues, the frustration-aggression hypothesis held that aggression results from frustration.[2] While many modifications have been suggested and made in the original statement, the central idea remains valid. Further, aggression is heightened, takes on an added intensity, when individuals feel they have been led to expect reward and are then suddenly confronted with frustration.[3]

At about the same time that the frustration-aggression hypothesis was launched, Robert Merton explicated the relation between goals, means, and deviance.[4] Anomie is the term Merton gave to the social condition wherein there is severely limited access to the institutionalized means that can lead to widely extolled success goals. Individuals feel cut off from the mainstream of society, alienated. Widespread deviance is then to be expected.[5] Theft and violence are substitute means that arise in response to the denial of legitimate means. Through theft the material goals that spell prestige can be directly attained. And it may be possible through violence not only to retaliate against others but also to achieve a notoriety that is in itself a form of success.

As Andrew F. Henry and James F. Short, Jr. have suggested, when social arrangements are such that other persons are not blamed for the frustration that given individuals feel, then the self is blamed and aggression is directed inward.[6] Suicide is the ultimate form here. When, however, others are seen as the causes of frustration, then those others are blamed. Aggression is directed toward them. It is when others seem to the individual to block him from progress toward his goals that they become the target of violence. This is frequently so in regard to property crime as well: The victims of theft tend to be those groups or individuals whom offenders view as major sources of blockage.

Henry and Short's wider thesis has to do with external restraints placed upon the behavior of individuals by others and how those restraints are related to homicide—and suicide. These authors hold that persons of low prestige are required to conform to the demands, the "external restraints," of those of greater prestige. Persons of high prestige have much more autonomy than others. Individuals of low prestige blame those of higher prestige for the frustrating restraints placed upon them. And they may lash out homicidally—often at the only nearby targets, friends and relatives. Those of high prestige, when subjected to severe frustrations of whatever kind, have little reason to hold others responsible. If someone must be blamed, then by default it is the self. If frustration becomes great enough, the consequent violence tends to take the form of suicide.

Implicitly, Henry and Short refer throughout their argument to what Marx termed "the denial of reciprocity" that exists between the social classes. The weak and the unprestigious defer to the powerful and the prestigious. The latter do not defer in return. The strong and the elite restrain those of lesser strength and standing. The latter cannot restrain the strong, at least not in similar degree.

Reciprocity and unreciprocity are terms that will be woven through the discussion ahead. Traditionally, reciprocity has been used to mean mutual satisfaction of the needs of two or more interacting individuals.[7] Simply put, each helps the other. This meaning can be extended to refer to mutual facilitation of the playing out of social roles by two or more persons.[8] But to say that individuals fulfill each other's needs in greater or lesser degree, including needs to perform roles in socially acceptable fashion, is a half-statement. One should refer also to unreciprocity, the mutual blockage by interacting individuals of their needs and role-playing. There is much difference between simply an absence of reciprocity and some degree of unreciprocity. Active blocking of another's role performance is quite different than simply not facilitating his performance.

Straus and Straus speak explicitly of reciprocity and implicitly of unreciprocity in their discussion of homicide and suicide.[9] They refer to the closeness of structuring of a society as a function of reciprocity. The more are reciprocal rights and duties in everyday interaction stressed and enforced, the more closely structured is the society. The greater is unreciprocity in that regard, the more is the society loosely structured. Straus and Straus suggest that loosely structured social conditions give rise to homicide. An absence of reciprocity (and a condition of unreciprocity) means violence is directed toward others, those others who withhold reciprocity and engage in the blockage that constitutes unreciprocity. On the other hand, a closely structured society tends, according to Straus and Straus, to have high suicide and low homicide rates. Others reciprocate and so are not blamed for the frustrations individuals experience. The self remains as a residual target of violence.[10]

Porterfield has stressed the "well-being" of social entities as a major variable in regard to homicide and suicide.[11] He constructed an "Index of Social Well-Being" which includes measures of health, educational, and other social services in the United States. In an analysis of states in this country, Porterfield found that the lower was a state's index of well-being, the higher was the homicide rate; the greater was well-being, the higher was the suicide rate. Well-being in the Porterfield sense means that individuals arrange for the formalized and collective availability of social services, for a shared responsibility, a structured reciprocity, in everyday life. The greater that collective availability and reciprocity, the more suicide and the less homicide. The interpretation can be made that when individuals are blocked from social service and unreciprocity is high, others are blamed and those most frustrated aggress outwardly and, in the extreme, homicidally. When social services and reciprocity are prevalent, individuals may experience acute frustration because of a sense of being smothered by the social body.[12] Since there is no one else to blame, the self eventually becomes the target of aggression and suicide may result.

Arthur Wood emphasizes in regard to homicide the thwarting of aspirations for upward social mobility.[13] He suggests that homicide rates grow high the more do individuals who are near the bottom of an invidiously arranged social system believe they are deprived of movement upward while others are not. In contrast, Wood sees suicide as due to the loss or threat of loss of positions of some prestige. Here in Wood's formulation, then, relative deprivation through blockage of aspirations—a form of the Marxian denial of reciprocity—and consequent alienation are central forces in the generation of outwardly violent crime.

2. SUBCULTURES OF CRIME

Subcultures of crime develop and crime becomes institutionalized when frustrations in a society are great, widespread, and persistent.[14] More particularly, subcultures of violence and theft come into being when the denial of reciprocity is commonplace and when individuals are little bound by their roles into the social system. The group of theories now to be considered have to do primarily with subcultures of crime.

It was Edwin Sutherland, the father of modern criminology, who first set forth in systematic fashion a formulation of the criminal subculture and of the learning of crime through "differential association."[15] Sutherland conceived of two bodies of custom in any society: that

which is law- and rule-following, and that which is law-
and rule-violating or criminal. The latter contains not
only customs for explicit criminality but also those customs for breaking everyday rules as well. Thus customs
for various forms of cheating are included in the criminal
subculture although they are not violations of criminal
law.

Sutherland held that the more an individual's associations with persons who acted out customs of the criminal
subculture outweighed his associations with those who
followed the noncriminal culture, the greater was the likelihood of criminality. Thus the term "differential association." Associations varied along several dimensions and
were weighted accordingly.[16] The Sutherland theory is
meant to apply to all major forms of crime. Actually it is
especially relevant to theft, particularly patterned, routinized, "professional" theft. It is less appropriate to ex-
planations of violent crime. Much violent crime is committed by persons who have not had extensive contact
with the type of general criminal subculture that Sutherland suggests. Further, some violent crime is in considerable measure spontaneous as opposed to being purely
learned behavior. As we shall see shortly, when violence
is learned it is likely to be on the basis of a distinct subculture of violence as opposed to a generalized subculture of
crime.

Albert Cohen, using the Sutherland thesis as a point of
departure, explores the process by which criminal and delinquent subcultures develop.[17] Drawing also on the Merton goals-means formulation of deviance, Cohen's position in brief form is this: When lower-class boys have internalized middle-class goals and have been denied access to the socially approved means for achieving them
(a denial of reciprocity), a reaction-formation occurs. The
lower-class youths come to abhor the middle-class values
associated with the goals they cannot have. They take on
a value system diametrically opposed to that of the mid-

dle class and develop behavior patterns that are the antithesis of those of the middle-class subculture. The resultant delinquent subculture is, from the standpoint of the middle class, negativistic, hedonistic, and nonutilitarian.

Cloward and Ohlin refine the concept of delinquent subculture in terms of three opportunity structures that are available to lower-class youths.[18] These youths, if blocked from moving toward achievement of the goals of the middle class, may gain entrance to bodies of custom oriented toward the following: theft; retreat, meaning largely drug use; and violence, called by Cloward and Ohlin the conflict structure. But to gain entrance to any one of these is not necessarily easy. One must meet recruitment criteria and must satisfactorily learn the necessary roles. Thus access to membership in a violent juvenile gang and to patterns of assault and homicide may be highly restricted, much as is access to prestigious occupations.

In contrast, Walter Miller, an anthropologist, argues that violent and other criminal patterns are threaded through lower-class subculture. Assaultive and theft behaviors are integral parts of the way of life of persons in the lower socio-economic strata, Miller holds. While differences in the middle and upper classes are resolved largely by verbal means, in the lower classes it is common to resort to physical aggression and to stealing.[19]

The essence of a formulation by Martin Gold also has to do with differences in the subcultures of the social classes and with the socialization process.[20] Like Miller, Gold says that lower-class subcultural patterns emphasize the outward expression of aggression; there is an opposite tendency for upper-class persons to be socialized to direct aggression toward the self. Thus members of the lower class will be likely to commit homicide if they aggress violently while members of the upper class will be likely to commit suicide.[21]

Wolfgang and Ferracuti write of subcultures of violence as concentrated pockets of cultural patterns for homicide and assault.[22] While these subcultures are likely to be found in lower-class residential areas, there will be many of those areas without well-formed subcultures of violence. Such subcultures will often, although not always, be found in black ghetto-like neighborhoods. According to Wolfgang and Ferracuti, the more are patterns for violence integrated with each other, the stronger will be the subculture of violence. And the more are individuals integrated into that subculture, that is, the more do they have access to it and the more do they communicate with others who have access to it, the greater the likelihood that they will behave violently toward other persons.

The evidence to support the idea of subcultures of crime and delinquency is great. As we have seen, in the United States homicide, assault, forcible rape, and robbery predominate strikingly in lower-class neighborhoods, especially lower-class black neighborhoods. Burglary, larceny, and auto theft occur largely among lower-class youth. Yet the notion of subculture as an explanation of crime is essentially circular. A subculture of crime can hardly exist, or continue to exist, if there is little acting out of its patterns. Conversely, if there is much violence and theft within a closely circumscribed area, there will very likely develop a body of cultural patterns for violence and theft. This does not mean, however, that the idea of subcultures of crime is of no utility. It allows one to consider to what extent individual routinely learn violence and theft by following custom as opposed to the degree to which their criminal behavior is a relatively unlearned, spontaneous response.

Subcultures of crime are bodies of behavior patterns that provide ways of coping with high degrees of unreciprocity in the social system and with alienation. They *institutionalize* what was formerly explosive, idiosyncratic violence and spontaneous theft. They provide *systematic* ways of aggressing against those who appear to block role performances and thereby the achievement of success goals. They also allow patterned forms of theft that mean the more or less efficient attainment of those goals.

8. THEORY: LATENT
FUNCTIONS AND LABELING

1. THE FUNCTIONAL
USES OF CRIME

Merton has distinguished with his usual clarity between two major types of functions of social phenomena.[1] On the one hand, there are manifest functions, those which the phenomenon in question is supposed to effect and which the members of the society believe it does effect. On the other hand are the latent functions, those which occur without recognition by at least most of the society's members. Crime has the manifest function of disorganizing interpersonal relations and of costing the society much in lives, frustration, and money. It also has a number of important latent functions, now to be considered. Any system of crime prevention that does not take into account these latent functions will of necessity fail. Why that is so is discussed at the end of this chapter.

Durkheim wrote at the turn of the century of the organizing function of crime.[2] And with typical acuity Simmel discussed the necessity for both social conflict and harmony if there is to be group cohesion.[3] The law-following members of society, or at least those who give the appearance of being such, draw together in common defense against the threatening actions of criminal violators. While many other conditions lead to social cohesion and integration, the threat of crime is one. At the same time, offenders tend to organize themselves against the rest of society. Thus the law-abiding majority and a law-violating minority are each internally organized to some degree. The two groups are also organized in relation to each other through various forms of antagonistic cooperation. As an example of the latter: gambling syndicates and members of the general society must cooperate if the syndicates are to exist. At the same time there is of course definite antagonism between the public and the syndicate.

Kai Erikson, following one of Durkheim's lines of thought, has shown the ways in which the Puritans defined religious acceptability by the systematic creation of heretics.[4] They labeled individuals as heretics, *made* them heretics, and so by contrast designated themselves true believers. Similarly, criminal violations serve today as benchmarks to define varying degrees of socially unacceptable and acceptable behavior. The public drunk and the petty thief mark by their actions unacceptable but not intolerable degrees of deviance. The grand larcenist and the assaulter indicate by their offending behaviors forms of deviance that are in greater measure intolerable. Individuals who commit murder chart by their violence the outer limits of unacceptability. In part we know what is acceptable by the offenders' acting out of what is criminally offensive.

Crime also has this related function: offenders serve as scapegoats for the aggressive tendencies of many of the society's members.[5] Violators are stigmatized, imprisoned, physically and psychologically tortured, and sometimes killed in the name of deterrence and rehabilitation.[6] Through such revenge, violence is legitimized. In contrast to offenders, the other members of the society are stamped as peaceful models of rectitude while, in fact, retaliation is carried out with determination. In the process, many individuals gain vicarious satisfaction through identifying with the violator, through "living" with him the execution of his crimes and often the frustration of his punishments as well.

Coser has emphasized three functions of violence:[7] It can lead to achievement; it can serve as a warning signal of impending social disorganization; and it can be a catalyst for change. For the dispossessed and the excluded, for the outsider, crime in its various forms can indeed mean achievement. Criminal behavior well carried out can be grounds for the approval of the offender's peers and for the enhancement of his self-esteem as well. So it is with many efficient professional thieves. On the other hand, amateur crimes, particularly of violence, can serve the same general function. The individual who kills another tends to view his crime as one of decisiveness and action. While he may feel remorse, he is also likely to feel more effective. The man who commits rape "validates" his sexual prowess. In prison, violent offenders rank high in prestige; they are not "dime-a-dozen punks." And the public shows its admiration as well as its revulsion in response to crimes of violence, especially when much notoriety attaches to the offender. In the wake of widespread ambivalence, he becomes the despised hero. Identity, sometimes instant identity, is thus a consequence of crimes that, because of their bizarre or efficient qualities, arrest the attention of press and public.

Widespread upsurges in serious crimes are warning signals that social disorganization is imminent. On the one hand, crime may distinctly contribute to social organization. On the other, sudden large increases are indicative that something is seriously amiss in the social system. A great expansion of crime, particularly violence, points to increasing tension in the society that may get out of control. And such expansion of criminal activity is itself socially disorganizing.

Relatedly, increases in certain forms of crime can serve as catalysts for social change. This is especially so in regard to violence. Certainly rioting in the black ghettoes of this country in recent times and the attendant killings have been a major force behind an accelerated attack upon urban problems. Moreover, the violent tactics of southern police against nonviolent black demonstrators did much to arouse the public against southern ill-treatment of blacks. It was in part the failure of the southern authorities to reciprocate with nonviolence that caused considerable revulsion in the society at large.[8]

There is a further and very obvious use of crime in the United States. It supports an enormous enterprise: the crime control apparatus at local, state, and federal levels. Well over one-quarter of a million persons are employed in police departments in the United States. The annual cost of maintaining those departments is between one and two billion dollars.[9] As noted earlier, one-and-a-third million convicted persons are incarcerated or on probation or parole at any given time. Over a million individuals are admitted to 10,000 jails each year.[10] Nearly 300,000 persons are incarcerated in state and federal prisons on any given day.[11] Hundreds of thousands of jail and prison personnel are employed full-time. Thousands upon thousands of judges, probation and parole officers, social workers, and others swell the rolls of this vast source of employment. Crime is big business in the United States. So is crime control. It will be understandable that without conscious design the tendency is to increase crime in order to increase the need for control. Men can hardly be expected to proceed with such efficiency that they create conditions where their occupations no longer are needed.

Identity is conferred upon millions of formal agents of crime control across the land. They are seen and see themselves as crime fighters. The police are the first line of defense. The courts are the arbiters of justice for all. The prison warden is the keeper of those who would

wreck the social fabric. Executioners are professionals of
last resort. Probation and parole officers are the stern
counselors of those proven wayward. Where other than
in law enforcement and correction can a man with little
education and limited abilities gain the power, the immediate authority, and the label of defender of the right?

2. THE LABELING PROCESS

Edwin Lemert has been the leading proponent of the
idea that social control begets deviance.[12] While recogniz-
ing that deviance leads also to control, Lemert sees the
great need for placing emphasis on the opposite process,
that by which crime and other forms of deviance come to
be consequences of social controls. Controls brought to
bear upon individuals in certain ways have the effect of
inducing what Lemert terms secondary deviance. For example, parents may be unduly concerned and anxious because their child speaks slowly and seldom. Their attempts to force the child to speak more rapidly and more
often may induce in him much anxiety and so lead to a severe case of stuttering, in this instance a form of secondary deviance. Again, parents who are overly apprehen-
sive about their daughter's morals may frequently castigate her for what are actually normal forms of dating.
They may term her a slut, a whore, and the like. In so doing they may actually move the girl toward promiscuity
and in some instances prostitution. As noted elsewhere,
recent controls brought to bear on adolescents and
young adults in regard to the use of marijuana have
served to further the drug problem.

Several processes are of central importance in the generation of deviance as a result of social control. First, the
individual is likely to be labeled as a deviant. Others
then tend to treat him as a deviant. He is forced into a

position where he responds as a deviant, and thus a vicious circle of self-fulfilling prophecy is created. The quiet boy is treated as if he had a serious speech defect. The high school girl is treated as if she were highly immoral. Youths in some areas are treated as if they were on the road to becoming "hardened drug addicts."

Second, there is likely to be a spiraling interplay of unreciprocity between those who do the labeling and those who are labeled. The gap between parent and child widens. The chasm between police and youth grows greater. In some areas police and the young expect the worst of each other. Boys and young men in the black ghetto expect the police to use provocative and coercive tactics. Police expect the youths to employ violence against them. Each labels the other as dangerous. Each feels he must defend himself and so each becomes dangerous. Extreme unreciprocity becomes a reality.

Lastly, those who have been labeled as deviant band together. Their alienation from those who exert controls upon them leads them to seek support where they can—in each other. They reinforce the labels given them. They learn deviance from each other. They create deviant groups and deviant subcultures. They reciprocate with each other: they facilitate each other's role-playing as a reaction to the unreciprocity of the alien society.

It is in this light that the unconscious collusion of the public, potential offenders, current offenders, and agents of social control toward the end of perpetuating crime can best be understood. Crime has social functions that must be fulfilled.

If those functions are not fulfilled in other ways, then the well-springs of crime will remain undisturbed. Poverty in the midst of affluence will continue. There will be ghettoes beside luxury apartment complexes; strong, invidious caste and class distinctions will not weaken. For many individuals, the gap between internalized cultural success goals and the availability of legitimate means to those goals will widen. Subcultures of crime will be nurtured rather than uprooted, thus providing ready-made designs for death, injury, and theft.

If the social uses of crime are not affected by functional alternatives to crime then the society will place demands upon the formal agents of control such that crime is not on balance inhibited. Broadscale prevention measures will simply not be introduced. Law enforcement and correctional personnel will be expected to seem to control crime with efficiency while actually they will set the scene for an increasing volume of crime.

3. NOTES ON DRUG ADDICTION AND MASS DISORDER

Theory relevant to drug addiction and abuse as a form of victimless crime is not abundant. Fiddle concerns himself with analysis of the drug subculture and the ways in which the formal control process contributes to the development and maintenance of that subculture.[13] He refers to two systems that are generated by repressive legal controls, the circulatory and the survival systems. The first has to do with role relationships that make the illegal procurement of drugs possible: peddlers, pushers, prostitutes, organized criminals, and so on. The survival system involves a justifying ideology for drug addiction, a warning system for users and pushers in the local area, ritualistic patterns, the attraction of close personal relations, and a reproductive process. The last concerns the customs through which new members of the drug subculture are recruited, thereby perpetuating the over-all system.

Lindesmith is one of the few researchers who has presented a social psychological theory of addiction.[14] He places emphasis on the addict's perception of withdrawal symptoms. Lindesmith states, "Knowledge or ignorance of the meaning of withdrawal distress and the use of opiates thereafter determines whether or not the individual becomes addicted."[15]

Chein and his colleagues[16] found that addicts were reared in an unstable family setting. Fathers were either absent or disturbed. Drugs served to relieve interpersonal strains upon users and to establish distance from real-life demands. Addicts tended to have weak egos, defective superegos, poor masculine identity, unrealistic long-range aspirations, and to distrust major social institutions.

These conclusions are rather typical of social psychological approaches to drug addiction.[17] Implicit in most is an emphasis upon addiction as a form of retreat. The user seeks escape from his social environment through the use of drugs. On the one hand the drugs momentarily resolve conflict and reduce anxiety. On the other, the drug subculture into which the addict must enter provides an environment of high reciprocity and low tension.[18]

Turning briefly now to theories of mass disorder: Jerome Skolnick, author of the Task Force Report on Mass Disorder presented to the Eisenhower Commission[19] points to severe shortcomings in most past theories of "collective behavior," that is, of mass disorder and related phenomena. Mass behavior which is not aligned with the values of "the establishment," meaning members of the power structure, and with the status quo has been labeled by behavioral scientists as well as by officials as irrational, insensate, maladaptive, bizarre, and "disgusting or evil."[20] Other behavior, that which does not conflict with the prevailing power structure, has been viewed by behavioral scientists as normal, adaptive, and "therefore rational."

Skolnick suggests that, especially in behavioral science theory the *political* nature of riots and other mass disorders has been largely overlooked. Individuals who riot have social goals just as do those in power. Riots may involve quite unpatterned behavior. Often, however, there is a logic in that behavior, a degree of coordination and of patterning as well. Without conscious planning, participants cooperate in a loose fashion to burn and loot the stores of those who have overcharged them. They direct violence against those, such as police, who are symbols of an oppressive power group and who have in many instances in fact brutalized them.

Speigel in collaboration with Kluckholn sets forth what is essentially a role conflict theory of mass violence, that is, of rioting.[21] Violent rioting is a consequence of frustration, occasioned by role conflict, which exceeds a "grievance tolerance level" when alternate ways of resolving the conflict are blocked or otherwise unavailable. Spiegel recognizes that the institutional setting must be considered. Some settings involve more adequate mechanisms for resolving conflict and more penalties for aggression than others. Cultural values also play a part. Whether role conflict is experienced depends in part on those values.

Smelser presents a social structural strain formulation of collective behavior. "People under strain," he holds, "mobilize to reconstitute the social order in the name of a generalized belief."[22] Part of the Smelser analysis focuses on "hostile outbursts," meaning riots and similar forms of mass disorder.

Six major variables determine whether hostile outbursts occur. The first is conduciveness, such as the failure of leaders to relieve conditions of strain, insufficient channels for expressing grievances, and sufficient communication among the aggrieved to allow for the spread of a hostile belief. The second is strain per se as it is due to deprivation caused by organizational deficiency; as it takes the form of strain among norms or values; and as it may be a result of a failure of facilities, such as communications. Third, there must be a generalized belief that involves hostility. Fourth, precipitants must be present, ones which emphasize for participants conduciveness, strain, and the nature of the generalized belief. Fifth, there must be mobilization for action in regard to the development of leadership, organization for attack, and volatility of the hostile group. Last, there will be social control processes coming into play that attempt to counter the impending hostility.

The central thrust of the Smelser approach is placed, as we have indicated, on social structural strain. Viewed from the standpoint of the Spiegel-Kluckholn formulation, that strain mainly takes the form of role conflict. Seen in the light of much of the theory outlined earlier, strain refers to institutionalized unreciprocity in role relations.

When unreciprocity in a situation or social system is very high and when *many participants* feel the frustration of this, then there exist the fundamental conditions for a riot. The great difficulty of playing usual roles occasions a distinct weakening of individual identity. Delusion grows as attempts are made to explain the increased strain and the decreased identity.

We have considered in this and the preceding chapter a range of major theoretical approaches to criminal behavior. Frustration in its various forms is central. Especially important is the frustration that arises in those areas of the social system where individuals learn social goals, particularly material ones, and are denied access to the means for achieving them. The denial of reciprocity in human relationships, whether in regard to economic matters or otherwise, constitutes severe frustration. Alienation results.

Subcultures of crime and delinquency are the breeding sites of learned law violation. They provide role models for criminal rather than noncriminal behavior. Opportunity structures for becoming criminal exist just as do structures for becoming formally educated, for rising in a profession, and the like.

The latent functions of crime are critical to an understanding of its effective control. Crime helps to provide social organization. It provides a way of life, a meaningful career, not only for serious violators but for agents of social control as well. Moreover, the labeling of individuals as delinquent and criminal is one way of ensuring a continuous flow of law-violating deviants. What persons are construed by others to be they tend to become. When individuals are seen as criminal, they are likely to become so.

9. THE CONTROL PROCESS: I

1. SELF-FULFILLING PROPHECY

How the crime control process works so ineffectively is the concern of this chapter. The failure of control is clear. Crime increases more or less steadily in the United States.[1] As noted at the outset, two-thirds of those in prison have been imprisoned at an earlier time. Millions of petty violators are arrested time after time, year in and year out, while many who commit extremely serious violations evade apprehension.

The labeling of individuals as offenders has been discussed. Elaboration of this process as self-fulfilling prophecy is now necessary. When the highly frustrated child rebels through aggressive behavior, theft, or other forms of deviance, frequently he meets with the response that there is "something wrong" with him. Parents, teachers, and others tend to say "he's different." The formal label of juvenile delinquent is always there, ready to be applied like a brand on the forehead.

When the individual, whether juvenile or adult, is arrested, the police are likely to label him as criminal. They are expected to do so. In the police station, the detention cell, and the court, the arrested person is presumed guilty. While the legal philosophy is of course the opposite, in practice the burden is upon the accused to prove his innocence. Preventive detention, coming into vogue in recent years, is a startling example of labeling as well as a transgression of constitutional rights. The arrested individual is *presumed to be dangerous,* although he has not been convicted. He is held without bail until and during trial.[2]

During the trial, the prosecution is likely to label the defendant as criminal, "a menace to society," a "misfit who perpetuates heinous crimes," and the like. The trial judge is far from immune to using similar labeling. Judges castigate defendants much more than is realized. And at the time of sentencing they are particularly likely to hang labels officially around the necks of defendants. (Whatever a judge says in court is "official" from the standpoint of most individuals even if technically it is illegal). The man to be sentenced may be characterized by the judge, for example, as "a miserable creature who has forfeited the right to membership in the human race."[3]

As is well recognized, the mass media contribute to the labeling process significantly.[4] Newspapers, radio, and television focus much attention on "criminals." While they do not explicitly point to the person awaiting or undergoing trial as guilty they often do label him as "a man who fits the description" of "the mad strangler" or whatever. Figures of some notoriety are given names that they may or may not have had in everyday life: Johnny "The Rat" Dio, "Killer" McVidie, and "Fingers" O'Toole.

In prison most offenders receive some form of label.[5] Usually such labels designate a level of the prison prestige hierarchy. Those convicted of murder, "killers," rank high. So also do con-men and "big time" embezzlers. Forgers and assaulters are of middle-range prestige. Pickpockets and other petty thieves rank low. Still lower as a rule are those convicted of sexual perversions such as child-molesting, intercourse with animals, and so on.

Upon release from prison, the individual is for life an "ex-con." He is likely to be viewed with an ambivalent mixture of dislike and distrust and of hidden admiration. But on balance he will usually be seen in a distinctly negative light. Employment will be difficult to gain. Acceptance as a full-fledged participant in the informal interaction of everyday life will be even harder to achieve.

In cases of violent crimes, early labeling is likely to be less direct than in cases of property or theft crimes. As indicated earlier, adults who commit homicide and serious assault tend to have been quiet children who sporadically manifested sudden outbursts of violent aggression during childhood. Adults view such behavior as bizarre and often label these children as "peculiar," "odd," "maladjusted," and the like. This is what the children then gradually come to see themselves as. Labeling in cases of theft is often startlingly direct. A boy who steals once or several times and is apprehended is likely to be termed a thief. Most individuals steal at one time or another. Many are not caught and labeled. Those who are tend to be impelled toward further theft more than others because of the self-fulfilling nature of the labeling process.

It will be clear that labeling has its rewarding aspects both for those who are labeled and those who do the labeling. And this reward contributes to the process by which labeling induces crime. Labeling provides those persons with very weak identities not only with instant identity, but also with attention in the sense of notoriety as well. Identity and notoriety that are viewed negatively by the society at large are to the individual far superior to little or no identity and to inattention. Moreover, the labelers are rewarded with the belief that they are superior to those who are labeled, that they are defenders of the right against a lawless minority who would, if left unattended, through their criminal behavior wreck the social organization.

2. THE CONFLICTED POLICE ROLE

The police are the spearhead of the social control apparatus in regard to crime. They symbolize the ambivalence of the nation toward the crime problem. They reflect the manifest concern of the society with the reduction of criminal behavior. And they reflect also the latent but equally powerful preoccupation of the society with the perpetuation of crime.[6]

The police are expected to arrest some types of individuals on little or no evidence: those with no money and no power; those with criminal records and highly limited influence.[7] They are expected to avoid arresting well-to-do persons unless the evidence is compelling and the violation one that incenses the public. The police are expected by the society at large to ignore certain types of violations—much white-collar crime, for example. They are expected to bend every effort to arrest for other types of violations—drug possession, robbery, criminal homicide, and so on.

Police are charged with numerous duties that have little or nothing to do with the apprehension of criminal violators. They have the tasks of traffic control and of participating in many areas of public safety. They are often seen repairing stop-lights, painting lines on streets, and emptying parking meters. The great part of their working time is spent on duties distinctly unrelated to the control of crime.[8]

Police training is notoriously poor. While a few police officers across the country are well trained to engage in crime control, many have no formal training at all. Most others have received minimal and ineffective "dosages" of training. Monetary and prestige rewards of police work are poor. A consequence of all this is that it is exceedingly difficult to recruit educated, intelligent persons into police work. Some small inroads into this problem have been made of late, especially through emphasis on the altruistic nature of the police effort as a vehicle for the resolution of pressing social problems.[9]

As might be deduced on the basis of the foregoing, the effectiveness of the police in regard to the control of crime is exceedingly poor. This is so in three main respects: the apprehension of violators; criminal violations by police officers themselves; and the tendency for police through precipitous action to trigger crime by other persons.

It was pointed out earlier that many crimes are not reported to the police. Moreover, for a variety of reasons police do not record all reported crimes.[10] Some failures to record are due to sheer negligence. Others are in the interests of creating an improved image of efficiency. The number of arrests made in relation to the number of known crimes is one measure of efficiency. Depressing the number of known crimes necessarily raises the proportion for which arrests are made.

In any case, the percentage of recorded crimes cleared by arrests in the United States is exceedingly low. In 1970, 20.0 percent were so cleared.[11] The record was significantly better for violent than for property crime. Arrests were made for 86 percent of known murder and non-negligent manslaughter cases, 65 percent of aggravated assaults, and 56 percent of forcible rape cases. Regarding property crimes, 19 percent of recorded burglaries, 17 percent of auto thefts, and 18 percent of grand larcenies resulted in arrests. In the case of robbery, which has elements of both property and violent crime, arrests were made in 29 percent of the known cases.[12]

The percentage of arrests is decreasing. In 1967, 22.4 percent of recorded *felony* offenses ended in arrest as compared to the 20.0 percent for 1970. There was a decrease in arrests for each of the above-listed crimes.[13] This reflects the greater and greater burdens being placed on police. It reflects also the growing tendency of the society to push crime quietly under the rug while speaking with a louder and louder voice of the absolute necessity for law and order. Crime grows greater in volume; crime rates rise; criminal behavior becomes somewhat more sophisticated.[14] Meanwhile, police recruitment criteria change little; police training and actual methods of apprehension increase minimally in efficiency.[15]

A separate and yet altogether related matter: crime by the police has been proliferating and continues to do so. There are sound grounds for that generalization. Reports by the United States Commission on Civil Rights and by the National Commission on the Causes and Prevention of Violence are among those official sources that document forcefully police violence, corruption, and theft.[16] Readers will be familiar with the fact that police officers have on many occasions been implicated in corrupt practices: being "bought off" by gambling syndicates and the like. Others will be aware that in large numbers of police forces across the country "third-degree" methods of violence are used routinely to extort confessions. And they will know that police often practice brutal and illegal behavior toward poor blacks and toward poor whites as well[17]

Few will realize that actual theft by police officers is far from uncommon. The "great" Denver police theft ring of the early nineteen sixties is a case in point.[18] Over half of the officers in the Denver force were implicated in a large-scale theft ring involving millions of dollars of stolen goods. A common form of crime involved collusion of officers and store owners. Police would steal coats from a fur store, for example, with the proprietor's knowledge. The police would sell the furs, the owner would collect the insurance.

New officers in the Denver force were "trained" by old-timers to participate in illegality. They were taken step by step along the route to large-scale theft. First, they ate at lunch counters without paying, a common police practice. Then they were set to work carrying out small shakedowns, requesting and accepting small bribes for police favors, and then larger ones. Later they were moved into the major theft ring. Those who refused to participate were given undesirable beats and in many cases eventually driven from the force.

In 1970 an investigation of the New York City police force by the New York Times revealed massive corruption.[19] Police of high and low rank were alleged to have routinely accepted pay-offs for the pushing of heroin, for prostitution, and for many related activities. The Mayor of New York formed a board of inquiry. He requested that all citizens with knowledge of police corruption communicate with the City Department of Investigation. The Police Commissioner of New York City resigned.

The police officer as *provocateur* in the criminal process must be given special mention.[20] As discussed earlier, not infrequently have police precipitated riotous behavior. They have harassed downtrodden groups until explosion occurred.[21] They have arrived at the scene of minor disturbances with dogs, riot sticks, mace, and helicopters spraying tear-gas. They have expected violence; thus have they provoked it. More on this later.

But the police also precipitate in some measure violence and theft in others on an individual basis. Their stance as defenders of the established social system leads potential offenders suffering from relative deprivation to sometimes direct violence squarely at them. During the period 1961 to 1970, 633 police officers were the victims of criminal homicide per se.[22] During 1970, 18.7 out of each 100 police were assaulted, 6.6 per 100 with "significant injury."[23] More often the role of the police officer serves to elicit a response of violent or theft crime directed toward people other than police by the underprivileged. The social system symbolized by "the cop" is thereby seemingly bested. The offender feels he beats the system by assault or stealing in the face of police force.

All of this is in no sense to say that the police role should be minimized. Rather it is to say that police are the most visible symbols and focal points of societal ambivalence toward criminal behavior. And it is to say that the role of the police officer requires a thorough overhaul. This cannot be accomplished unless certain changes occur in the value system of the society. Such matters are the province of chapters directly ahead.

Without conscious awareness, society's members *use* the police to bridge the gap between the manifest aim of preventing crime and the latent aims of maintaining and generating crime. Other agents of social control are of course also "used": judges; probation and parole officers; prison and jail personnel. But the main burden falls on the police to bridge the gap between the manifest aim of preventing crime and the latent aims of maintaining and ishes on a large scale, so that its latent functions will be fulfilled, while at the same time seeming to stamp it out. The police are, that is, expected to conduct a societal-wide sleight-of-hand. They are to make it seem that what the society says it wants is what in fact it really does want. They are expected to provide the society with the latter without giving the appearance of actually doing so.

Police militancy is presently a significant weather-vane of the social pressures under which police officers find themselves. In recent years that militancy has increased rapidly. The nationwide fraternal Order of Police has a membership of well over 130,000.[24] Police strike to alter social policy as well as for economic gain. They revolt against higher authority and refuse to carry out orders.[25] In and out of uniform they take unauthorized action against those whom they consider dangerous; the Black Panthers have been a primary illustration.[26] The police of the country have developed a large lobbying apparatus. At times they attempt to tell the courts how to proceed. And they have court-watchers who make judgments as to whether their demands upon judges are being properly met. The police exercise much influence in political elections. They carry on active campaigns for particular candidates while on duty.[27]

3. THE OVERBURDENED COURTS

Our system of justice, and that of many other societies as well, operates on an erroneous view of man, an oversimplified hedonistic psychology.[28] At basis the assumption is made in legal philosophy that each person receives the same amount of reward from the commission of a particular type of crime. The more serious crimes, such as criminal homicide, are held to provide the greatest reward. It is further assumed that the deterrent value of a given punishment will be equal for all. The aim is to set the degree of punishment so that it outweighs slightly the reward value of the crime. If this is done then supposedly individuals will desist from violence and theft. Yet it is well known that the reward and frustration values of particular types of experiences vary widely for different persons. On this basis alone it is to be expected that in the United States the social control of crime will be grossly ineffective.

This is the legal philosophical backdrop under which our courts operate. And they operate under great handicaps. Judges and court personnel are extremely overworked. Court dockets have long backlogs. Trials are delayed for months. Bargain justice is the order of the day. In this form of what is in part injustice, deals are made between prosecutor and defense counsel, sometimes with the knowledge of the defendant or the judge, sometimes without the knowledge of either. The usual form of bargain justice is this: The defense counsel agrees to persuade the defendant to plead guilty to a lesser charge and to accept a trial by judge rather than by jury. The prosecutor agrees to the lesser charge and promises not to press for a heavy sentence. There being no need to impound a jury and minimal need to establish guilt the trial proceeds speedily and inexpensively. Murder trials may take no more than a few minutes when bargain justice is employed.[29]

Frequently judges have only a very limited knowledge of the law. While most are lawyers, some are not. In various jurisdictions, there are for some types of criminal courts no educational criteria associated with service on the bench. In any case, a background in law does not in any sense ensure an adequate judge. Special training is required in criminal and procedural law, in the various aspects of the total law enforcement and correctional apparatus, in relevant welfare services, in the nature of crime and offenders, in the special handling of juveniles, and in many other matters.[30] Seldom are these forms of training parts of a judge's background.

Regarding court sentences, the most extreme penalties, execution and life imprisonment, are for murder and in some instances for forcible rape and other crimes.[31] Execution has declined rapidly in the United States. During the 1950's there averaged about 70 executions a year.[32] During the late 1960's there were but a few executions per year and in some years none.[33] However, in 1972 over 600 persons were on "death row" awaiting execution.[34] The vast majority would in all likelihood escape death.

The decline in executions is a hopeful sign. Execution here and elsewhere has been a bizarre and exceptionally cruel phenomenon. Men have often struggled at the end of the rope for half an hour. Men have been "electrocuted" and found to be still alive. They have been shot and survived for a time. The reduction in these forms of state-sanctioned murder is tangible if small indication of a society's movement away from that aggressive response to crime that is both abortive and indirectly or directly begets further crime. Nevertheless, most states have retained laws that make execution a legally proper response to some serious crimes. Recently, in June, 1972, however, the United States Supreme Court ruled that execution as it is now performed constitutes "cruel and unusual punishment" and hence is unconstitutional.

For the most part, the penalties for theft grow less as the threat of physical harm to others in the course of carrying out the theft lessens and as the value of the goods stolen decreases. Thus armed robbery and nighttime burglary of residences tend to draw harsh sentences. Pocket-picking and petty larceny are likely to result in short jail terms or small fines or both. White-collar crimes, though they may involve large sums of money, hundreds of thousands of dollars, usually carry moderate or large fines and short jail sentences if any.[35] A thirty-day jail sentence for a corporation official convicted of price-rigging is considered a heavy penalty. And such a brief sentence as that is likely to be suspended. As Winston Churchill noted, one fundamental measure of a positive civilization is its effective response to crime.

Justice varies significantly by sex and race. Women are convicted less often and given lighter sentences than men.[36] Blacks are convicted more often and the penalties meted out to them are more severe than is the case for whites. One study indicates that of 409 blacks tried for criminal homicide, 81 percent were found guilty; of 117 whites, 62 percent were convicted.[37] A second study analyzed commutation of sentences. Of 147 blacks to be executed, the sentences of 11.6 percent were commuted. Among 263 whites, 20.2 percent were commuted.[38] A third study, of 821 southern homicides, found the following: in cases where offender was black and victim white, 80 percent of offenders were convicted. When both offender and victim were white, 62 percent were convicted. When both were black, 77 percent were convicted. And when offender was white and victim black, 63 percent were convicted. The percentage of convictions for first-degree murder varied greatly: offender black and victim white, 29 percent; offender white and victim black, none; offender and victim both white, seven percent; and offender and victim both black, three percent.[39]

Erroneous convictions for criminal offenses are more common than is generally thought. Two studies report that of groups of individuals sentenced to life imprisonment or death about 10 percent were later found to be innocent.[40] There is little motivation to exonerate a man serving a life sentence or a dead man. Hence the figure is no doubt higher than 10 percent. Regarding crime in general it seems altogether likely that large numbers of innocent persons are convicted. The inadequacy of arrest, pre-trial, and trial procedures are conducive to errors. There is less concern to ensure a fair trial in cases where a short sentence may be the outcome than where a harsh penalty may be the outcome.

Justice is hailed as one of the great ideals and facts of American life. Yet the police officer is asked to arrest discriminately and to use violence illegally. He is kept poorly trained and indirectly bidden to do the society's dirty work of perpetuating theft and violence. The legal philosophy underlying the judicial system is grossly unrealistic. The halls of justice are vastly overcrowded. Frequently they are run by mediocre men. Verdicts and sentences are often in error and unfair. The courts strike hard at the poor and the weak and tenderly treat the well-to-do and the strong. Thus unreciprocity is unlikely to be ameliorated while alienation tends to be increased.

10. THE CONTROL PROCESS: II

1. PRISON AND BEYOND

Generally speaking, a judge may order probation instead of imprisonment in other than capital offenses. He does this on the basis of his judgment as to whether the convicted individual's background and the circumstances surrounding the crime seem to indicate a good prognosis. Some judges use probation very widely, others in a highly limited way.

On the one hand, probation obviates the many negative effects of prison, soon to be discussed. On the other, it leaves the life circumstances of the offender largely untouched. Supposedly (that is, from a legal standpoint) the probationer must not interact with known felons, must not drink alcohol, often must observe a curfew, and must follow a variety of stringent rules. In practice, however, probation is a matter of "watchful waiting." Little rehabilitation is effected. The probationer goes about his life as he did before while the state watches and waits to see if he commits further criminal acts. Since his general life circumstances gave rise to the offense for which he was convicted, there is a considerable likelihood that they will result in further offenses.[1]

For some the stigma of prison is extremely painful. For others imprisonment is greatly rewarding: it may mean recognition for a young man who has been accepted nowhere else. It can mean a return to a position of prestige as inmate leader for an old-timer who has been out of prison, "on the street," for a period. In any case, prison provides that enduring label, that lifelong identity, of criminal, of "con."

The deprivations of prison are many. Sykes cites several major forms.[2] There is the deprivation of liberty. There is the deprivation of the right to many forms of autonomy in individual actions. There is the deprivation of goods and services that are customary in the wider society. There is of course the deprivation of heterosexual relationships and there is the deprivation of security. Prison is physically a dangerous place because of both inmate aggression and guard brutality.

At the same time, prison is an opportunity structure which provides a routinized way of life that is highly secure in certain respects although not in regard to physical attack. There is the absence of heterosexual relations but there are more or less institutionalized possibilities for homosexuality; for some this will be a decided asset of the prison. There is the previously mentioned chance to build a reputation as a "tough con," a leader of men who defy the traditional system.

Rehabilitative services in United States prisons are severely limited. Psychologists and psychiatrists are in extremely short supply in our prisons. Seldom do they carry on anything but the most limited individual or group psychotherapy. Most of their time is devoted to testing and interviewing inmates, that is, to diagnosis rather than to treatment. Moreover, the effective rehabilitation of many criminal offenders has less to do with traditional methods of psychotherapy than with experience in environments not conducive to crime.[3]

The point of interest at this juncture is *the absence in our prisons of effective rehabilitative practices.* Religious programs abound. Athletic and other recreational programs are extensive and of reasonably adequate quality. Educational programs are available although most are of low caliber. There is a considerable amount of "counseling" by untrained persons. But rehabilitation programs that get results are almost nonexistent, thus ensuring a high level of recidivism.[4]

In contrast, the prison system provides excellent conditions for learning the criminal subculture. Experts in burglary, pocket-picking, robbery, embezzlement, forgery, confidence games, and even in death are on hand. Inmates are in close interaction with each other. Often there is little to do. Much crime goes on in prison. Here is the near perfect opportunity to learn the techniques of crime and the values that underlie them, to practice those techniques and to act out those values.[5]

Most inmates leave prison as parolees. While there are numerous exceptions, generally speaking little is done to help the paroled offender locate a suitable job. In many instances, he is expected to find his own *before* he is paroled, an exceedingly difficult demand to say the least. All in all he receives a hostile reception by the wider society. Like the probationer, he is legally prohibited from associating with known felons. But with whom is he to associate? Those who are hostile to him? He is an "ex-con" and he associates with his old friends, many of whom are felonious offenders and some of whom have also served prison terms.

As is true of probation officers, parole officers are overworked and undertrained. And as with probation, parole is "watchful waiting" to see if a misstep is made by the parolee. Again one sees the negative nature of the control process in relation to the prevention of crime. The labeling as ex-con, the hostility toward him, the lack of effective guidance and help are all conducive to recidivism.[6]

2. NOTES ON THE
CONTROL OF DRUG ABUSE

It is of course common for members of the society, law enforcement officers and other citizens alike, to group together under the heading of narcotics and addictive drugs opiates, barbiturates, amphetamines, marihuana, and others. The sale or possession of these, except in highly restricted medical practices, is illegal. As we know, narcotic drugs are substances that induce sleep, reduce sense impressions, or relieve pain. Clearly, many of the drugs just listed are not narcotics. Moreover, many are not physiologically addictive. The differences between heroin and marihuana in regard to harmful consequences are enormous. Yet they are altogether too frequently categorized as similar in the popular conception and in law enforcement; there is however some recognition that heroin *addicts* are more serious problems than marihuana users.[7]

The most serious consequence of this catch-all thinking is that users of relatively harmless drugs are labeled in much the same way as are users of very harmful drugs. This tends to create true addicts out of nonaddicts. For example, the young person who tries marihuana may move to the use of heroin in part because of the *social definition* placed upon him.

The Bureau of Narcotics is the federal control agency in this country. It has traditionally taken a "hard line" on users as well as "pushers." Known users and pushers are "bought off" by the Bureau for entrapping other users and pushers. Those who cooperate are not prosecuted. State and local police frequently take a similarly hard line.[8] Moreover, persons unqualified to inform the public about drug abuse often do so. They come in many instances from the ranks of various police forces and on occasion from the Bureau of Narcotics. Harmful misinformation is not infrequently disseminated.[9]

The punitive reaction to drug use and abuse has a variety of negative consequences. The price of drugs is driven very high and opportunities are tailor-made for organized crime syndicates to move in and take charge of an enormously lucrative business. Male addicts are forced into "pushing" and theft to obtain the expensive drugs. Females turn to prostitution and sometimes theft. It will be recalled that Fiddle found that the formal legal control process served to generate and solidify the drug subculture. Customs for securing drugs are laid down as are customs for protection against agents of formal control.[10]

As is abundantly evident, then, one of the greatest problems of the control of drug abuse in this country is that efforts ostensibly directed toward prevention and amelioration are actually likely to exacerbate the problem. As with crime in the general sense, this stems in considerable measure from the underlying ambivalence about drugs that pervades the society. Many persons are frightened and repelled by drugs and their presumed or real effects. They feel that the use of drugs leads to a loss of self-control. At the same time these individuals may be attracted to that very possibility of loss of self-control. And they are drawn by the promise of escape that drugs may hold out. Thus there is much conflict over drugs. This leads to abortive, contradictory, and irrational behavior.

Moreover, drugs are now used by adults and young persons as weapons in the inter-generational war. Adults help to create juvenile addicts by labeling them such, by making drugs available to juveniles while seeming to make them unavailable. (Medicine chests are frequently the starting point for young teen-agers.) Adults may, that is, obliquely but quite definitely *challenge* the young to use drugs. The young in turn challenge the adults to stop them. The use of most drugs renders the individual relatively inactive. This is one aim, perhaps unconscious, of some adults—to neutralize the protest of youth through drugs. When youths blame adults for the drug problem, they are not without some justification.[11]

The British experience is highly instructive. For some time the British have treated addicts within routine medical practice. If the physician determines that the addict requires drugs such as heroin *as a part of proper medical treatment,* then he may prescribe and issue the drug to the addict. This policy has been in considerable measure responsible for the small size of the drug addiction problem in Great Britain.[12] While their numbers may be increasing slightly, it would appear that there are fewer than 1000 opiate addicts in Britain.[13] One consequence of this approach is that the ground is cut from under the illicit drug market. There are not huge profits to be made by organized crime through the illegal selling of heroin and other drugs.

The British plan has been widely criticized, particularly in the United States. Many feel that the drug problem is in no way resolved because addicts go on using drugs. This may be so. However, critics fail to see that the approach used in Britain serves effectively to prevent escalation of the problem. And that is a major achievement.

We turn now to present treatment of addicts in the United States. The federal government, through the U. S. Public Health Service, maintains two hospitals for drug addicts, at Lexington, Kentucky and Forth Worth, Texas. Patients enter voluntarily and are aided in withdrawal from drugs. Then a variety of services is available, including vocational rehabilitation and the like. However, there is no effective supervision once the patient leaves the hospital. The rate of success is very low.[14]

Attempts have been made to treat addicts by substituting a synthetic nonaddictive drug, methadone, for heroin. Methadone provides many of the effects of heroin but does not produce sedation or euphoria. The aim is to remove the patient from the drug subculture and to provide social rehabilitation while the patient is taking the substitute drug. The success of this approach is unclear but it does appear to have some constructive possibilities.[15]

Sheer conventional psychotherapy combined with withdrawal from the addictive drug has been spectacularly unsuccessful in producing long-term rehabilitation. This approach does not deal with the day-to-day situational problems of the addict. His social relational ties with other addicts and his integration into the drug subculture are largely ignored. There is usually an unbridgeable communication gulf between the upper-class therapist and the lower-class patient. Further, therapy attempts to ram the individual back into a social environment that causes him much anxiety. And he is expected to like that.[16]

Synanon was developed by nonprofessionals, former addicts, as a total system for rehabilitation.[17] Participants live in a large house and carry on what is in a sense twenty-four hour a day group support. Leaders are ex-addicts. Newcomers can work their way up the ranks of authority within the group. As time goes on, some members of the group go out to work during the day and return in the evening.

Aggressive confrontation is one of the major methods of treatment in Synanon. Participants meet in a group and "bare their souls." Anything less by a given individual than what others consider to be total self-honesty is jumped upon ferociously. The individual's weaknesses are explicitly brought to light. According to Synanon belief, only by "total honesty" can individuals move away from addictive drugs and lead constructive lives.

The success of Synanon appears to be superior to a number of other approaches.[18] However, it is not clear what proportion of members actually rehabilitated indefinitely. From a beginning of one house in Los Angeles, Synanon houses are now located in many parts of the country.[19]

The Odyssey House program is a new mixture of old ingredients.[20] A "house" is like a small informal hospital. Voluntary patients are aided through the early stages of withdrawal, then provided with psychotherapy by professionals. Again, there is emphasis on forcing the individual to recognize his weaknesses. However, the "reality therapy" atmosphere of an Odyssey House is considerably less aggressive than the "attack therapy" of Synanon. Odyssey House does provide a graduated and supervised release program that is missing from most other rehabilitation programs. Odyssey Houses have been in existence for but a few years and results are inconclusive.[21] It is fair to conclude that at present all drug rehabilitation programs in this country show inconclusive results.

3. RIOT CONTROL

Here again is an outstanding example of social controls worsening the problem they are ostensibly designed to ameliorate. The general social response to conditions of high tension in the black ghettoes is to tighten formal controls.[22] Repression of the oppressed becomes the *modus operandi* of the society. Thus are the frustrated and the weak forced into spasmodic episodes of mass rebellion.

As noted, many police officers are strongly antiblack. They are frequently enraged by disorder from any quarter. They tend to view the acted-out screams of protest of the oppressed as individual criminal acts against the "moral order." They are caught in the middle, between the powerful and the powerless. They are used by the power structure to maintain the status quo under the guise of maintaining law, order, and morality. They are under the multitude of extreme pressures outlined earlier.

The police tend to become provocative and violent under high tension conditions such as those in a ghetto near revolt. They and neighborhood residents expect violence from each other. Thus is the aforementioned near inevitability of riotous violence assured. Moreover, if the strain becomes too great then the police themselves riot. Many examples of this exist. The riot of the Chicago police at the 1968 Democratic national convention is perhaps the most well known of such incidents.[23] Police are like other people.

Turning to the judicial system, if the courts are overburdened in the day-to-day handling of black-collar criminal cases, they are far more so when hundreds are arrested and charged in the course of racial and other rioting.[24] Judges, prosecutors, and defense counsels are then simply in highly inadequate supply. Justice is rushed and frequently sloppy. Procedural laws for carrying through the judicial process are grossly abrogated. Everything considered, under such conditions, justice is not done: injustice prevails in the courts.

Two of the most significant aspects of the court process in regard to alleged violations of law by persons arrested near the scene of rioting are these: first, police in their frustration, anger, and insecurity often arrest indiscriminately. They arrest persons who are passing by, on the basis of no evidence whatsoever, as well as those directly involved. (In riot situations, police tend at times also to attack innocent bystanders.)[25] Second, judges, not to mention police, are all too often prone to consider those arrested in riotous circumstances as automatically guilty.[26] Some judges view anyone apprehended in the course of a riot as a severe threat to the democratic system. Those judges take the position that such persons are so obviously wreckers of the society that "justice" without due process is warranted. They may point to their city being in flames because of rioters. They throw justice out of the courtroom in the name of a higher wisdom.[27]

At this point democracy is at its greatest danger: not from the oppressed who protest and not from the wrongly accused who just happened to pass by. The greatest danger then is from within the "system": the judge, the court, who would suspend justice in the name of democracy. For a time this judge becomes "the true believer." He *knows* what is right—or so he believes.

4. PUNISHING THE UNCONVICTED

Simultaneous riots in four New York City jails during the fall of 1970 symbolized vividly the crime problem in the United States. Conditions in the jails were horrendous: severe overcrowding, guard brutality, sexual attacks, poor food, filth, lack of exercise, lack of other facilities. Those convicted of crimes and those awaiting trial were mixed indiscriminately in the institutions. The vast majority were awaiting trial and so were technically innocent. And many would later be found innocent. Meanwhile they sat in jail for months awaiting trial. They were treated like "criminals." (In practice, accused persons have very few legal rights.) They of necessity associated with others who had in fact committed serious crimes. Of those accused persons detained in New York City, fifty-six percent waited in jail over three months for trial. *Forty-three percent, almost half, waited over one year.*[28]

These inmates, innocent and guilty alike, took 32 guards as hostages and held major parts of the jails for five days. They threatened to kill all hostages. They wrecked the institutions to the point of rending large segments of some inoperable.

Many persons, including the Mayor of New York and the city's Commissioner of Corrections, admitted that conditions in the jails were in numerous respects abysmal. Guards who had been held hostages for many hours and who had genuinely feared they would be killed were afterwards often sympathetic to the inmates.

One riot ended when the Mayor promised that no retribution would be taken. As the inmates filed out of the building, guards who had not been hostages clubbed them, knocked them down, kicked them, stomped on them. This was recorded by television cameras and witnessed by reporters. Many of the guards wore no badges and of those a large proportion wore civilian clothes.

Here was the society labeling the innocent as guilty and providing them with inescapable role models for learning crime (offenders who had been convicted of serious crimes). Here was the society compounding the criminal subculture. Here was the society frustrating the unconvicted in the extreme, driving them to commit crimes of violence and property damage (in the course of their rioting). Here was the whole matter being compounded by assaultive law-breaking by guards. Thus were the inmates frustrated further. And hence was tightened further the vicious circle of control that generates crime as surely as earth, sun, and water makes possible life.

At the time of the riots, the New York State Senate Committee on Crime and Corrections had been conducting an investigation of jail conditions. In the final report, the Committee's Chairman, Senator John Dunne wrote: "A man has to be angry when he rips an iron leg from the table in his cell and batters through 3 inches of glass brick—not with the hope of gaining freedom but of merely transmitting his message of anguish and frustration to the society that imprisoned him. We must ask ourselves if the same man will be even angrier by the time he is allowed to rejoin society, and if so, how he will unleash his anger."[29]

In summary, the total process of the social control of crime and the full range of criminal behavior in many senses systematically support each other. Control perpetuates crime and the existence of crime perpetuates the control mechanisms. In numerous respects the two are mirror-images of each other. On more than rare occasions the police act criminally. The courts provide much injustice. Prisons are crime schools. Brutality is widespread in prisons and various other forms of crime flourish there. Former offenders are treated as permanent offenders. Execution, now decreased drastically, has been a striking example of violence in the control process. And so the crime problem continues. It is really not out of control at all. Rather, it is in the firm control of a system which ensures that the latent functions of crime are not threatened with extinction.

PART II
PREVENTION

11. BASIC STRATEGIES: I

1. THE DISCUSSION AHEAD

We have seen that crime and delinquency arise in large measure as responses to severe frustration, especially as that is occasioned by unreciprocity in everyday relationships. The absence of adequate role models constitutes a further form of frustration and means a lack of guidance as well. Subcultures of crime and delinquency ensure an almost automatic learning of behavior which is contrary to criminal law. The labeling of persons, especially the young, as offenders, as delinquents and criminals, serves to effect a self-fulfilling prophecy. The crime control process does much to induce and little to reduce problems of violation of the criminal law. Thus is the carrying out of the latent functions of crime and delinquency facilitated.

To reduce crime, institutionalized frustration must be lessened, particularly in regard to excessive unreciprocity in competitive activity. The availability of adequate role models must be increased. Concurrently, the availability and intensity of the criminal subculture must be decreased. Individuals must be labeled as nonviolators rather than violators. To some extent the latent functions of crime must be changed. Relatedly, alternative ways of carrying out the latent functions that remain must be found and institutionalized. These are major prescriptions for crime prevention.

A critical necessity is to communicate these matters effectively and in some detail to individuals throughout the society. Given the widespread misconceptions about crime and the ambivalence toward it as well, this is an awesome task. It may be possible at first to achieve some success in communicating with informal leaders throughout the society. This refers to informal leaders in the community, in various agencies of county and state government, and so on. As is well known, individuals who provide leadership for social change are not necessarily those so formally designated.[1] They may be persons of lesser visibility who for a variety of reasons are especially able to influence others.

Several of the approaches to prevention in the chapters ahead are very broad and will seem perhaps nearly unattainable. Others are quite specific and may appear readily feasible. Some recommendations are untried and if put into practice will certainly need to be initiated on an experimental basis. Others have been tried in parts of this country or elsewhere and found to have much promise. Again, among the types of programs and projects outlined there will be those that hold the prospect of exciting breakthroughs; and there will be those that seem to some readers quite banal. The need is for balance between far-reaching, idealistic approaches and here-and-now pragmatic programs. We must have both.

In this chapter, several central forms of required change are analyzed. Major spheres of resistance to change are assessed and ways of reducing that resistance are set forth. Chapter twelve considers formal and informal organizational mechanisms for developing and carrying out programs of prevention. Also, ways of involving individual citizens in specific action programs are explored. Finally in that chapter, the crucial necessity for close cooperation between action and research activities is emphasized.

Chapters thirteen through twenty present a wide variety of preventive programs per se. Chapter thirteen is devoted to programs of public education on a broad scale. The present condition of the lower schools does little to impede delinquency and crime and much to generate them. The schools need to be changed from places of repression to places of learning. Certainly this is at the least a challenging task and at the most a nearly overwhelming one. Related and yet distinct is the proposal to develop a series of core courses in the behavioral sciences that would be studied by the average student as he moves through elementary and high school. These courses would not be aimed explicitly at "fighting crime" or "stamping out drug abuse" or avoiding alcoholism and so on. Rather they would have the goal of providing future adults with a rational grasp of the forms and processes of social life and of the individual personality. Why this approach is considered to be so important is discussed at the appropriate time.

Also in chapter thirteen, emphasis is placed on education through the mass media. The mass media—television, radio, and newspapers in particular—can do a great deal to help the public learn the nature of crime and of its roots. The mass media may not do much of that now but the potential is there. The proof is an occasional program or article that speaks to many and speaks effectively regarding law violation and the social response to it.

In chapter fourteen the focus is on the neighborhood service center as a vehicle for intervening in the lives of children and adults who appear to be moving quite definitely toward delinquency and crime. Chapters fifteen and sixteen deal with programs for revising police and judicial organizations and methods. The next four chapters are devoted to ways in which prisons and to a lesser degree probation and parole agencies might be reconstituted so that they provide effective rehabilitation. The emphasis is on replacing prisons and jails with inte-

grated, community-based learning centers. Here, violators would have access to a variety of techniques for rehabilitation and for reentry into the wider society.

Quite obviously, the concerns of Part II of this book
constitute but a modest number of the almost infinite array of strategies for attempting to effectively control the
crime problem. One must be highly selective. On the one
hand, programs that promise results must be detailed.
On the other, any attempt to be encyclopedic in a single
volume will be abortive.

2.　NEEDS AND LATENT FUNCTIONS

If change in general is difficult, change in regard to the
prevention of crime and delinquency is formidable. As
we have discussed, there is much resistance to changing
those social conditions such as excessive competition
which give rise to criminal violation. And there is great
resistance to changing those police, legal, and correctional systems ostensibly designed to control crime and delinquency.

Social and individual change occur continuously. Yet
to bring about change in a *planned* way is usually an exceedingly difficult task. Changes are likely to run counter to the needs of individuals and to the latent functions
served by current social conditions. The first necessity is
to plan and carry out programs such that individuals'
needs are better satisfied.

Clearly, the two-way relationship between the un-
spoken needs of individuals and the latent functions of
patterned social interaction is crucial to an understanding of planned change. The processes by which a latent
function is fulfilled help not only to maintain a social system; they satisfy individual needs as well. And individuals' strivings to have their needs satisfied result in the so-

cial arrangements which bring about the latent function in the first place.

Consider one illustration of this, one mentioned earlier: crime in general and homicide in particular provide society with a means of demarcating the outer limits of socially acceptable behavior. Where homicide begins, any shred of widespread acceptability ends. In so doing the dominant group is in part defined. Those who do not commit homicide and other equally serious crimes are within the group; those who do are outside it. Identity is conferred upon various individuals: offenders, police, and so on. Other needs are also met: the offender gains a certain reward from his violence and perhaps from his punishment. The nonhomicidal citizen achieves in some cases a satisfaction through vicarious participation in the crime. He may gain a reward in seeing the offender punished. And he may be vicariously rewarded in a masochistic sense by identifying with the offender in his punishment. The police officer as protector may gain the same rewards as his fellow citizens and their approval as well. In the process he also makes a living.

In effecting change, needs can be shifted or left as they are. If they are shifted, latent functions will change accordingly. Also, patterned ways of satisfying those needs and fulfilling latent functions can be shifted or not. That is, functional alternatives may or may not be brought into play. Most planned action programs seek to change in varying degrees both needs and patterned forms of interaction. Often, however, they seek to do this in such fashion that needs go more unfulfilled than previously.

Two broad, interrelated ways of inducing change are to bring about shifts in roles and in institutionalized structures. Some roles and structures can be eliminated, some created, and still others strengthened. Institutionalized structures are largely of two types: first, there are formal organizations such as schools, certain governmental agencies, police, courts, probation and parole departments, prisons, and so on. Second, there are the relevant aspects of the traditional social institutions as exemplified by child-rearing patterns in the family, criminal law in the political institution, and competition in the economic realm.

Several examples of roles that need to be overhauled are these: the adolescent role is highly conflicted and therefore frustrating for those who carry it out. Yet the time spent in it grows steadily longer. The role of the poor black young adult male has few if any intersections with the dominant success goals of the society. Needed here most of all is the strengthening of the adult male role within the lower-class family setting so that the developing boy can model himself after it. Again, the police officer's role is a terribly conflicted one. As long as this is so, much police behavior will be aggressive and abortive, that is, abortive in regard to the effective control of crime.

Illustrative of a role that needs to be gradually eliminated is the prison guard role as we now know it. That role must be so thoroughly transformed that for practical purposes one can speak of elimination. The role of the bail bondsman, which involves lending money to the accused poor at exorbitant interest rates, must go. Lest one think that it is practically impossible to eliminate roles, consider the role of the executioner in the United States. It has, for the most part, vanished. While in recent years there have occasionally been executions, there are no more executioners.

An example of a new role that should be instituted is that of the rehabilitationist in the prison setting. Today the role is largely nonexistent although there will be many in correctional work who argue otherwise. This new role should replace the traditional guard role. Workers in a prison would serve in various rehabilitative capacities. They would have a secondary function of maintaining order to the extent that this is really necessary. Another role much needed is that of director of crime control for units of government below the state level. Those who fill this role might be paid by public funds or they might be paid by private citizens' groups. The recently instituted state crime commissions (to be discussed shortly) have directors. This is the beginning of the development of the role of director of crime control. Presently, the position of commission director is an exceedingly ambiguous and difficult one. A major reason is that the role has not yet sufficiently taken form.

Among institutionalized structures in need of much overhaul are prisons and juvenile reformatories. Most essentially these should be changed from places of punishment to places of treatment. Such changes are discussed in later chapters. Police organizations and probation and parole departments are likewise in need of substantial reorganization. While for the most part these organizations do not presently punish, their constructive accomplishments with offenders are limited. Here, too, effective treatment of offenders must be the guiding activity.

It is appropriate at this juncture to point to some examples of roles, institutional structures, values, and beliefs that should be maintained and strengthened if effective crime control in the United States is to become a reality. Despite criticisms made at various earlier points, the role of the judge is, with certain modification, adequate. We need more judges and we need them to be better trained. But the core element of the jurist's role—to ensure a fair, impartial, just trial—is valid. It *is* necessary to find out who are serious transgressors of the morés. And the role of the judge is pivotal to this end.

Regarding institutional structures, the jury system is for the most part a viable mechanism. There are things wrong with it. But broadly speaking, it is the best way we know for determining who is a violator. No one has put forth a more effective alternative. The belief that the accused is innocent until proved guilty is a reasonably valid and useful belief. To be sure, in practice this belief is often breached. But the belief itself warrants continuation and strengthening. One might quarrel with the concepts of innocence and guilt. One might wish to substitute the idea of one who is or is not *in violation* of criminal law. The basic meaning, though, that there is not to be a before-the-fact presumption of serious deviation, is sound. It is sound if we wish both to reduce crime and retain democracy.

3.   REDUCING FRUSTRATION

There is much concern in some quarters of the society that life in the United States is far too permissive.[2] Permissiveness in child-rearing, in the schools and on the college campuses, in providing welfare payments for the poor, in "tolerating" dissent—these are all seen as major sources of our most severe national problems. They are so seen by the "hard-line law-and-order" political leaders and those who agree with and support them.

As will be evident, the view here is quite otherwise. It is in large measure the sheer difficulty of life in the United States that fuels such problems as crime, alcoholism, mental illness, and many others. Major difficulties are those due to the previously discussed interrelated set of factors: institutionalized unreciprocity in, among other forms, overly fierce competition for money and prestige; one-sided competition where some are doomed to lose from the outset; physical frustrations through hunger and inadequate living conditions and medical facilities; and psychological frustrations that arise from severe child-training practices and from various forms of emotional deprivation, both relative and absolute. Put differently, severe strains in the over-all social system come to bear in excruciatingly painful ways upon many members of the society. Depending upon a variety of specific conditions, those members act in seriously deviant ways, criminal or otherwise.

To dwell upon permissiveness as the root of crime is to stand rational analysis of the problem on its head. To be sure, here and there individuals do opt for actual permissiveness, for an "anything goes" approach. This is for the most part an overreaction to the strains just outlined. However, it will not do simply to say that an upper-middle-class college student who takes part in a group protest is a spoiled rich kid who "never had it so good." He may very well have come from a terribly *emotionally* impoverished family. It will not do simply to hold that a young black who riots and loots in the ghetto should either "get out and make something of himself" or suffer the consequences. He is suffering the consequences, those of not being able to get out of the ghetto and of having no handle on social life that will enable him to make "something" of himself.

Rather than dwelling on the false issue of permissiveness, the aim should be to bring about changes in behavior patterns that lead to less frustration for society's members. In good part, then, this means reducing the extremes of unreciprocity and competition. It means reducing the excessive demands made on individuals in their playing out of their roles. It means increasing the availability of adequate role models and decreasing the criminal and delinquent subculture. Emotional deprivation will then abate somewhat. Society's members, being less frustrated, will have less need to hurt each other. And to the degree individuals are still severely frustrated, there will be less opportunity to learn the criminal subculture, that is, to learn ready-made customs for law violation.[3]

If these things can be done, some of the latent functions of crime will be largely eliminated. As examples, there will be less need for scapegoats and less need for identification with the law-violator. To some extent other latent functions will in good part remain. The contribution crime makes to social organization will be one. It will be necessary to substitute for crime and delinquency other ways of carrying out these functions. Regarding the present control process per se, obviously there will be the need to substitute for its most abortive aspects others that are not crime-inducing and that in fact help to reduce crime.

The social system is wound too tightly. However, there is little need to be concerned that loosening the strictures of competition somewhat and lessening role demands will lead to an uncompetitive and unproductive way of life. The danger of going to the opposite extreme from that which now prevails is minimal. From a purely practical standpoint, we will at best be able to ease the great strains in the social system but slightly in the foreseeable future.

4. THE COOPERATION OF AGENTS OF CONTROL

It will be necessary to persuade those already engaged in police work, in the courts, and in corrections to try new, promising approaches to the problem of effectively controlling crime. If this cannot be done then the whole effort will be seriously handicapped and very likely in fact stopped in its tracks. Workers in these fields are hardly known for their receptiveness to innovation. For reasons given earlier, defensiveness and resistance to change are great.

Agents of control must see that the rewards of change outweigh the rewards of their traditional roles—and by an amount that exceeds the frustrations that changeover will occasion. (Obviously, degrees of reward and frustration will vary from one individual to another.) Major role rewards take the form of prestige, power, altruism, and also of highly tangible items such as salary. Some of these are clearly interdependent: regarding prestige, money, and power, an increase in any one of those tends to lead to an increase in the other two.

The relationship of altruism to money, prestige, and power is more ambiguous although generally speaking it is less difficult to be effectively altruistic on a full stomach than otherwise. In any case, there is always the question of whether people do act from altruistic motives. It would seem that at times they do. Their actions here are of course tied to their own well-being. But the essential point is that many people do gain genuine satisfaction from helping others. This is not to say that altruistic rewards are necessarily to be assumed as dominant among agents of control. Neither should they be thought to be irrelevant.

More specifically, what are some of the rewards that those in the police, courts, and corrections may hope to achieve through increased effectiveness in preventing crime and delinquency? One, far greater opportunities for professional advancement and thereby for money and prestige. Two, larger scope for using initiative on the job. And three, vastly increased opportunities to help others move away from crime, delinquency, and misery.

Concerning the first, agents of control need to see that emphasis on prevention will generate whole new dimensions of their career fields. Positions will be opened up rather than closed down. (This can also be threatening, of course.) Opportunities to gain further education will open up rapidly once prevention is a serious element of the over-all crime control endeavor. Careers which in many instances are at best semiprofessional will be upgraded to fully professional levels. With these changes will inevitably come greater financial and prestige rewards. Moreover, possibilities for employing initiative and escaping humdrum routine will escalate greatly. Prevention, whether before the fact, or by the police, or in the courts, or through rehabilitation in the correctional setting, *must* involve initiative. This is inherent in the preventive process; it cannot be carried on routinely if it is to be effective.

As to the altruistic component, the potential rewards here are enormous. To take an active part in preventing people from killing and maiming each other is not to be taken lightly as a source of genuine satisfaction. To be involved in effective efforts to prevent serious theft has also its satisfactions. Why this is so regarding theft may be less clear than in the case of violence. The fact is, we have a money economy. And the latent functions of theft notwithstanding, everyone loses when that economy is badly disturbed by crime. Everyone loses not only money but is likely to suffer some degree of psychological frustration as well. To see that justice is fairly done, then, has its intrinsic rewards.

Helping those who have seriously violated the law *rehabilitate* themselves is perhaps the area where altruistic rewards are most self-evident. While there are for many offenders real satisfactions in committing crime, broadly speaking men long for acceptance by the in-group. Men want to be well thought of, respected, held in some esteem, considered to be honorable and trustworthy members of society. Crime is second best. There may be esteem in the criminal world and in the prison. But those of the criminal world are outsiders not because they choose to be but because circumstances have compelled them to be. They want fundamentally to be insiders. The basic problem with crime is that it splits people off one from another. Life is difficult for all. Although crime is one way of resolving problems, on balance it makes life more difficult. Crime makes strangers of brothers. To help the greatly frustrated, the rejected, the spoilers, is not an ignoble endeavor.

Finally, a word about standards of success in regard to crime prevention. It is extremely important for all concerned to have a realistic view of what constitutes degrees of success and failure here. There is a tendency in the United States to assume that true success inevitably means something close to one hundred percent success. We assume that a ' oy who receives "A"s in all of his courses and who consistently avoids any hint of wrongdoing is a success. A boy who passes some of his courses, does well in several and "poorly" in many, and who is apprehended a few times for violating school regulations is hardly viewed as a success. He is in fact likely to be seen as a failure. At the same time, there are startling exceptions to this general view. A surgeon may have many of his patients die and yet be considered a great success.

Success should be measured in terms relative to what has gone before. We have delineated the great scope of the crime problem in this society and the growth of that problem. If in this country we could in the decades ahead swiftly arrest the increase in the crime rate and maintain the rate at the present level, that would be a very large accomplishment. If we could actually reduce it by but several percent that would be a near miracle. Given the fact that very little even in the way of attempted rehabilitation takes place, if we could help significantly toward the rehabilitation of but one offender out of every ten or even every hundred who are incarcerated we would be making a tremendous start.

Assuming allowance is made for changes in reporting and recording crime, comparisons of rates of homicide, various forms of theft, and so on, for various population groups are good indicators of success or failure of crime prevention programs. Yet in individual cases one should not assume that commission of a crime is flatly a sign of failure. Progress may be made in moving an individual away from crime and yet he may commit a crime. For example, a person may be substantially less violent than formerly and yet still commit a violent act. Moreover, an individual may be largely rehabilitated and yet carry out a crime; he may be thrown into unusual crime-inducing situations where many persons would also act criminally.

12. BASIC STRATEGIES: II

1. ORGANIZATIONAL MECHANISMS FOR CHANGE

We shall discuss briefly now several major types of mechanisms that presently exist for introducing changes in the social system, changes that can lead to effective preventive steps. Two broad categories of these are private and governmental. In the private realm, formal organizations, either national or local, are fitting vehicles for the prevention of crime. These can be organizations similar to those which have the purposes of advancing mental health and reducing mental illness. They may be foundations that have as one of their specific aims the prevention of crime. Apart from formal organizations, there are the possibilities of different types of informal citizens' groups which have the purpose of decreasing crime. And there is of course the single individual acting alone. The use of these private mechanisms for preventive programs is referred to at various points in the discussion ahead.

In the governmental sphere, there may be agencies that are the result of federal, state, or possibly local legislative action. Funds for the operation of these agencies may derive solely from the federal government, the federal government in conjunction with state and local units, or any governmental unit acting autonomously. There may be study commissions organized at the federal or lower levels. And there may be action commissions established at any level for the direct purpose of instituting preventive programs.[1] Any one of these—agencies; study or action commissions—may initiate particular programs.

The federal government's Law Enforcement Assistance Administration in the Department of Justice is the primary governmental mechanism for the development of crime control programs and for the dispensing of funds to support these programs.[2] Annual block grants go to the various states partially on the basis of population. Additional grants are available for special projects. These funds are administered by a Commision on Crime and Delinquency (or Criminal Justice or similar title) in each of the states. Regional offices of the Law Enforcement Assistance Administration coordinate the states' efforts.

Members of the commission of a given state are appointed by the governor. They include jurists, police officials, probation, parole, and prison administrators, mayors, county commissioners, and sociologists and psychologists specializing in the analysis of crime and delinquency. Also within most states are a number of area or regional councils on crime and delinquency. They are composed of professionals in law enforcement and correction and laymen interested in the resolution of the crime problem. These councils can be viewed as local arms of the state commissions.[3]

Each state commission has a chairman and an executive committee authorized to make basic policy decisions in some instances and to recommend policy to the full commission. Grants for planning and action programs are made to local units of government—cities, towns, counties, and so on. As examples, grants may be for the purpose of increasing the efficiency of communications facilities of police departments, for providing counseling for inmates or staff in county correctional institutions, or for instituting an experimental program in the rehabilitation of drug addicts using as treatment personnel ex-addicts who are specially trained within the program.

To a limited extent the commission can itself conduct programs without making grants to local governmental units. Whether programs are carried out by the commission directly or by local government, federal laws are presently such that a wide range of projects is possible. One state might stress "law-and-order" projects aimed largely at increasing the effectiveness of the police to apprehend violators. Another state might emphasize prevention and rehabilitation programs. Many states attempt to do both.

Federal funds must be partially matched by state funds. When the commission makes grants to local units of government, those units must supply partially matching funds also. These latter can in many instances be "in kind," that is, can consist of the provision of space, equipment, personnel, and the like.

This system of state crime commissions and area councils within states is one that is likely to be in existence for many years. It can be an exceedingly useful vehicle for the institution of some types of preventive programs. Other programs will be better effected by private organizations or by different governmental arrangements. In any event the state crime commissions appear to be here to stay and cannot and should not be ignored in planning programs of crime prevention. Their effectiveness will depend in large measure on the individuals appointed to the commission by the various governors. If tradition-oriented law enforcement and correction officials dominate the commissions, then the crime problem as it presently exists will be perpetuated. If innovative individuals knowledgeable about crime and society are in considerable supply on the commissions, then prevention of crime may be facilitated. There is the promise here, then, of new and viable roles and organizational forms.

2. CITIZEN INVOLVEMENT IN ACTION PROGRAMS

Involvement of many citizens in a wide range of meaningful prevention programs is the most effective way of educating the general public. Such an educational process should be so constructed that participants are made aware of and are able to keep in mind the larger social context in which they and preventive programs exist. They should develop a constructive empathy with offenders or potential offenders. They should grasp what social controls, both effective and ineffective, are really like. They should attempt to comprehend the social meaning of crime and some of the sociological and psychological forces leading to it.

Here are examples of programs that lend themselves to such involvement: Citizen boards to determine police fairness and legality in dealing with suspects. Service on grand juries where the juries are made instruments of justice rather than committees that "rubber-stamp" the state or local government's decision to prosecute. Participation in recreational and educational programs in correctional institutions. Citizen teams, whether they be chess, debating, weight-lifting, or baseball teams, that compete against inmate teams. Dramatic and other hobby activities can be carried on jointly by inmates and by other citizens who go to the institution to take part. Arrangements can be made for citizens to enroll with inmates in education courses in prison. In other words, some adult education programs can be prison-situated.

Citizens can serve as volunteers to assist police, courts, prison, jail, and half-way house personnel and probation and parole officers in many phases of law enforcement and corrections. In all of these activities persons of varying age groups can and should be engaged. The young and the old provide rich resources. The fervor for reform of the young can find true challenge here. The need of the aged for meaningful ways of contributing to the social good can be fulfilled. And female volunteers should be called upon to the fullest extent possible. Apart from their obvious relevance to female offenders, there is much they can do to help directly in relation to male offenders. There is also the sheer fact that participation of females will lend an atmosphere of some normality to situations that are otherwise heterosexually sterile. (Obviously the reverse also holds true: male volunteers are needed in female institutions.)

Described below is one extended illustration of how citizens can involve themselves constructively in problems of crime control. By taking part in such a program they can contribute in the short-range sense of achieving rehabilitative results. They can contribute over the long-range by gaining an increased understanding of the over-all crime problem; and through that understanding by affecting other citizens constructively. In some respects it would be advantageous to delay discussion of specific action programs until later chapters. However, it is useful at this juncture to show clearly how citizens can take part in a particular program and through that participation become better educated.

The program to be considered is one in which parolees or prison inmates and other citizens discuss in depth how the offenders' crimes occurred and the social reaction to those crimes. (This program is currently being carried out on an experimental basis at the University of New Hampshire.) Assume that a group is composed of five parolees and five other citizens. Three or four of the parolees might be males and others females; the same might be true for the five other citizens. Of the latter, one might be a garage mechanic, another a housewife, one a small businessman, still another a student, and so on. (The reason for the lesser proportion of women is that there are far fewer female than male parolees.) The group could meet one evening a week for, say, twelve weeks on a rotation basis at the homes of the participants. This means of course that one week they might meet in a middle-class suburban home and the next in a single tenement room.

There must be a discussion leader trained in helping others to generate meaningful dialogue. The discussion leader says little but what he does say and do, the verbal and other cues he emits, have much to do with the success or failure of the enterprise. (Programs can be devised wherein discussion leaders train parolees and other citizens to be leaders.) *The focus of the discussions is on how offenders can "go straight."* This leads to the exploration of many aspects of the crime scene: psychological motivation for crime and social forces that generate that motivation; the roles of the offender, the parolee, the average citizen, the police officer, and so on.

While these should not be construed as confrontation groups, there will be much forthright give-and-take. Parolees will question the complacency of citizens in general, the self-righteous attitude toward crime of much of the public. Nonparolees will point out the parolees' tendency to want quick acceptance in the community and to have unrealistic expectations as to financial and prestige rewards that may come to them.

Because of their make-up—a combination of parolees and nonparolees—these groups will have inherent interest for both. Further, the groups will have also a built-in middle-range degree of reciprocity. There will be disagreement and moderate unreciprocity by virtue of the differing roles participants have. At the same time, tension need not run unduly high during discussions. It is the leader's major task to see that these conditions prevail. If he is able to accomplish that, constructive dialogue will flow readily. Nonparolees and parolees alike will gain wide educational benefits in the form of increased understanding of the nature of crime and related social problems. Parolees will over the months experience an invaluable form of rehabilitation. Here again, new roles are created. A traditional organizational form, the age-old discussion group, is given new meaning. For the parolees any effects of the criminal subculture are diffused. Very likely the labeling process will be positive rather than negative for all concerned.

This approach can be used to much advantage with other types of groups. Series of discussion sessions among the following will be highly useful: police officers and juvenile offenders; everyday citizens and police officers; prison guards and administrators and inmates; judges and offenders; behavioral scientists and prison officers (to decrease prison resistance to treatment); mentally ill inmates and prison officers; probation officers and probationers; parole officers and parolees; and many others. Some of these have been tried on a limited basis and with considerable success.[4]

3. CATALYSTS

A small proportion of individuals possess the unusual ability to serve as catalytic agents for social change. Put more precisely, some persons can serve as such in certain kinds of situations. Particular confluences of personality and situation catalyze change. Potential catalysts for social change tend to be flexible, relatively secure, and highly verbal, although not verbose. While they do not seek rebuff they are not greatly distressed by it. They have stable self-images, identities as persons who get things done, as persons who are able to solve problems well. They have high tolerance for unreciprocity and conflict.

To illustrate: prisons are notorious for their resistance to adequate training programs for guards and other staff personnel. The catalytic individual will be able to draw together the disparate motivations in a prison and focus them in such a way that decided movement is made toward an adequate training program. He will transform resistance to a training program into a situation conducive to its development. He will then bring the program into being. One of the methods he may use is to convince a significant proportion of the custodial staff, especially the younger men, of the following: training is a major prerequisite to success in the field of correction, the way to better jobs, to promotion, both in the present institution and elsewhere.

There will be individuals who on a part-time basis can serve as valuable catalytic agents. They may do this for salary or purely as volunteers. For example, a person who is himself a volunteer may help to develop an ongoing program of volunteer aids for probation officers. Individuals in various walks of life can spend several hours a week assisting overworked probation officers in a variety of tasks. Being relatively unofficial members of the social control apparatus, they will in some instances serve as useful buffers between probationers and probation officers. They will on occasion be able to communicate with probationers more effectively than probation officers. The catalytic individual will in this case overcome the resistance of probation officers to the proposed program, mobilize volunteers, and see the program put into effect.

While catalytic individuals are obviously self-reliant, they cannot be expected to be magicians. Particularly will this be so in regard to their own initial entry into the field of social change. It is too much to expect individuals solely on their own to grab hold of the enormous complex of social system conditions that give rise to crime and other social problems and unilaterally to take catalytic action. This does on rare occasions happen. But it can hardly be relied upon day-in and day-out.

What is needed are state, regional, and national organizations to "catalyze" potential catalytic agents of change. No doubt many of us would rather see less proliferation of formal organizations and more immediate action. But in a very large, multi-faceted society, organizations are not only facts of life but up to a point necessary ones. Such organizations will act as clearinghouses for persons who want to aid in the resolution of crime and related social problems and who have the capacity to do so. They will bring together situations and persons such that changes toward the desired ends are likely to eventuate.

To illustrate: in the chapter that follows, the program for teaching the behavioral sciences in the elementary and high schools will be outlined in some detail. Such a program will serve to increase the public's understanding of various social problems, including crime, and will contribute to the development of a more effective public stance toward those problems. It will also move young, developing individuals away from, instead of toward, crime and other forms of deviance. Such a program will require teachers who have a knowledge of the subject matter and are catalytic individuals as well. There will be much opposition to the introduction of such courses into the school curriculum. Teachers involved will need to neutralize that opposition and to the extent possible convert it into a positive force.

The necessity is to bring catalytic teachers and appropriate school situations together. Behavioral science courses should be introduced where resistance is not great. Catalytic teachers will not have any systematic way of knowing which schools are appropriate. Moreover, they may not even have thought of the matter of teaching the behavioral sciences although their background is in those academic areas. One function of a state or national organization could be to make possible the matching of teachers and schools. These organizations would match individuals with many varied skills to appropriate segments of the social system. The organizations would be something akin to nonprofit employment agencies, with special emphasis on catalytic persons and social change.

The over-all suggestion, then, is to create the role of the catalytic agent. Once created, this role, through suitable organizational means, will be injected at strategic points into those institutions that severely impede the effective control of crime and delinquency. This will apply not only to schools but also to economic, political, and other institutions.

4. RESEARCH IN RELATION TO ACTION

Certainly the eternal cries for more research have been heard so often that not infrequently they fall on deaf ears. Nevertheless, the most central finding of the President's Commission on Law Enforcement and Administration of Justice is the pressing need for research on crime: "the greatest need is the need to know."[5] The Commission points out the paucity of funds allocated for research. Of the over four billion dollars spent annually on criminal justice, only a small fraction of one percent is spent on research. In startling contrast, fifteen percent of the Defense Department's huge budget goes for research. Most industries make significant investments in research, far outreaching that in the field of crime control.[6]

The Committee's formal recommendations are these: "Criminal justice agencies such as state court and correctional systems and large police departments should develop their own research units, staffed by specialists and drawing on the advice and assistance of leading scholars and experts in relevant fields."[7] Further, "substantial public and private funds should be provided for a number of criminal research institutes in various parts of the country."[8] And "Universities, foundations, and other private groups should expand their efforts in the field of criminal research. Federal, state, and local governments should make increased funds available for the benefit of individuals or groups with promising research programs and the ability to execute them."[9] Further, "A National Foundation for Criminal Research" should be established as an independent agency.[10]

As the Commission well phrased it, research is an instrument for reform of the criminal justice system. Needed are data that are much improved in both quality and quantity as to characteristics of crimes and offenders and of the crime control system. Equally needed is research on ways of implementing action programs. Moreover, *evaluative research to gauge the effectiveness of old and new programs has an urgent priority.* Ongoing "pure" research on the causes of crime is also of high importance. Through these various forms of research, continuing progress toward the effective control of crime can be made with regard to prevention before the fact, to controls exerted at the time of criminal behavior, and to rehabilitation.

Some useful steps have been made since the Commission's report in 1967. A National Institute of Law Enforcement and Criminal Justice has been established within the Law Enforcement Assistance Administration of the Department of Justice. A number of centers for criminal justice have been instituted across the country. Programs for funding research projects now exist within the Law Enforcement Assistance Administraation and within some subdivisions of the Department of Health, Education and Welfare. Research projects of the broad types noted above are being carried out in the various regions and states on a vastly greater scale than ever before.

Nevertheless, most planning and action programs are set into operation without the necessary relevant data and without evaluative research. It is true that action cannot simply be put on the shelf until research is fully adequate. Pressing problems of crime and other forms of deviance loom larger every day. The building momentum of public interest in problems of crime control must not be lost. Thus action must be taken.

However and fortunately, research and action programs can be carried on simultaneously and in conjunction with each other. Not only can they but in many instances it is advisable that this be done. Research leads to the formulation of action programs which are redesigned in the light of further research. The results of action programs lead to the reformulation of theory. Thus research and action serve as checks on the validity of each other.

Here is one illustration: research on the role of the probation officer and the probationer can lead to experimentation in effecting changes in both roles. Further research can evaluate the relative effectiveness of the various types of changes. Such a program might of course include female and juvenile offenders. But assume for the sake of simplicity that only male probation officers and adult male probationers in a state of small population come within the scope of the project.

First, it will be necessary to determine what probation officers and probationers do, how they spend their time. How much of the working week of the officers is spent in keeping records, in traveling, in collecting from probationers funds for the support of their children and estranged wives? How much time do officers spend checking on the activities of probationers and in obtaining for them various services of probationers and in obtaining for them various services of social welfare agencies? How much time do officers spend counseling probationers? (Very little, in all likelihood.) How do officers do what they do? To the extent that there is counseling how is it carried out? What are the educational and social backgrounds of probation officers? Personality characteristics? What are their attitudes toward crime, offenders, the law? What are their attitudes toward probationers and themselves? Regarding the latter how do they conceive of their role as probation officers? How are these matters related to the effectiveness of the officers?[11]

Turning to the probationers, how is their time spent? With whom do they interact? What characterizes their social backgrounds and present personalities? What is the specific nature of their interaction with probation officers? What are their attidudes toward the following: crime, the law, probation officers, other offenders, themselves? And how do they conceive of their role as probationers? How are all of these data related to their success on probation?

What are some possible ways in which the roles of both probation officers and probationers might be altered such that the probability of effective rehabilitation is increased? These are matters to be determined in the light of the above kinds of information and in view of sound theory about crime, social control, interaction, rehabilitation per se and so on. Should the bookkeeping and money collection duties of probation officers be largely delegated to others? Should officers spend most of their time counseling probationers? Should they first receive greater training in counseling? Should individual counseling be set aside in favor of group therapy? Should there be a combination of both? Should officers be largely administrators who run the office and who have lesser-trained assistants and volunteers who work directly with probationers? If this is done, which of the numerous ways of working with probationers are to be followed?

Should the probationer's role be changed such that he is subject to far fewer external restraints? Should he be placed in various types of group situations to which he now has no access? If so, which types of situations? Should he be given heavily increased responsibilities, moderately increased ones, less responsibilities? Should he receive greater monetary and prestige rewards? If so, to what degree? How will this affect the general response of the wider community? How will it affect the officer-probationer relationship? Any change in one role means change in the other role.

Decisions have to be made in the context of existing knowledge as to which of all of these changes are to be carried out. And in what ways they are to be carried out. By whom and where? By all probationers and officers or some? What of control groups against which to measure the outcomes, the rehabilitative consequences of the changes? What are the many complex procedures to be used in the evaluative process? At a still later point, how can the knowledge gained through the various forms of action and the evaluation processes be channeled back into the ongoing probation situation so that further changes, in roles and otherwise, are made such that the effectiveness of rehabilitation is increased? This is then, one instance of the way in which research can play a meaningful part in planning, effecting, and evaluating specific action programs.

13. PUBLIC EDUCATION

1. CONCERNING THE YOUNG

As we have said, the first prerequisite toward the goal of reducing crime and delinquency is the creation of mechanisms that will facilitate the satisfactory introduction of action programs. Given that, many of those programs oriented toward prevention will be aimed at the young. To be sure, broad educational programs for various segments of the adult population, programs aimed at prevention before crime occurs, will also be of great value. But much effective preventive activity will be directed toward the young simply because they have not yet gained sufficient age to be in a position to commit large amounts of crime and delinquency.

On the one hand it is important that much effort toward prevention directly involve children. On the other hand it is a great mistake to make rigid distinctions between young and older persons in regard to any social problem and its resolution. The young are not terribly different from older persons. After all, they *are* people. While there may seem to be generations, they do not in fact exist. People are born every day in about the same numbers. Births do not come in massive waves every twenty or thirty years. The fact that life is a process of aging from birth onward is overlooked with startling regularity. And the young are seen, and often see themselves, as if they will always be on the threshhold of adulthood.

There do remain certain important differences between youths and adults. One major difference is simply this: as people age they become more skilled at working within the "system." They gain intuitive or consciously rational insights into the prevailing system and how to live with it and at times to change it. The young often have flashes of insight that penetrate to the core of the drawbacks and limitations of whatever system prevails. But they seldom know how it works and how to work with it.

The young disdain the system not because they are more pure in heart than their elders. Their disdain is a result of their lack of understanding of the system. They turn to violence because they are at their wits' end as to how to cope with a system they find frustrating. And having had little experience with violence, they are less aware of its consequences than others.

It has been indicated that prevention of crime before the fact necessitates certain changes in social values and the implementation of functional alternatives to crime. In one way or another, many of these impinge upon the young. Examples to be detailed later in this chapter are shifts in patterns of child training, clinics for mother and child, identification of children who are moving toward serious crimes and remedial help for these children. The police and the courts will do well to avoid labeling young persons as violators. And certainly it will be necessary to make some special provisions for adolescents who must be incarcerated.

The final report of the President's Commission on Law Enforcement and Administration of Justice set forth a substantial array of broad social action programs that presumably will help to reduce crime through early prevention.[1] Recommendations concerning the family included these: guaranteed minimum family income (since enacted into law although for an extremely low level of income); ensure availability of birth control information;

provide assistance in problems of domestic management and child care; and expand greatly facilities for counseling and therapy.

The Committee recommended that ways be developed for involving youth in community activities; that young people be employed as "subprofessional" aides; that there be established Youth Service Bureaus to make available and coordinate programs for the young; and that local residential treatment centers be provided for those youths in need of treatment. Regarding the schools, major recommendations were: ensure adequate financial support for teachers and facilities; improve the quality of teaching; reduce racial and economic segregation in the schools; compensate for children's inadequate preschool preparation; develop more effective means for "dealing with behavioral problems"; use instructional materials of more relevance to urban life; encourage able students to pursue higher education; revise programs for students not going to college; expand job placement activities of schools. Apart from the schools, the Commission advocated the elimination of irrational barriers to employment; the creation of new job opportunities; and the increased accessibility of employment information.[2]

2.   MAKING SCHOOL MEANINGFUL

We now consider several preventive programs per se, beginning with those of a broad educational nature. It is well established that the public schools have little meaning for many white and black children from the lower socio-economic reaches of the society.[3] The "orderly" activities of the middle class are alien to these children. The contents of the curricula, with their emphasis on verbal and quantitative precision and their reflection of middle-class values, are incomprehensible to children from a quite different social world.

Needed is the understanding that education is a many-sided process, that what is useful for some is not for others. In a large technological society such as ours certainly basic reading, writing, and arithmetical skills are essential. Beyond those, however, much diversity in educational programs is possible and probably desirable. Present curricula in the public schools are mainly of two types: college preparatory and vocational. There are many poor children with little understanding of the benefits of college in schools that emphasize preparation for college. The vast majority of vocational schools are stigmatized as second rate and lower class.

All of this means that many children find school an exceedingly frustrating environment. Rather than finding avenues to success goals opened, they find institutionalized blockage to those goals. They find a microcosm of the system that oppresses them. In this way the public schools actually induce in some children, particularly those from lower socio-economic families, that rebellion that is the underlying hallmark of much serious crime.

The possibilities for revamping public school curricula are vast and exciting. Within a school of any size there can be a considerable variety of programs. Courses of much intellectual weight can exist side-by-side with courses that are equally demanding in other respects, for example in physical alacrity and coordination. Courses in vocational subjects and in the traditional academic disciplines need not be mutually exclusive. Above all, what is taught must be meaningful to the student in relation to his general life circumstances if he is to learn effectively. Stories in reading books about the fluent and affluent middle class seldom make sense to children from the ghetto.

Of great importance in the public schools is to help each child gain a positive identity as a person who can cope with his social environment. This means assisting

him in learning skills with which to gain further coping
skills. Most males want a "respectable" job, respectable
being what society holds to be respectable. Most females
want their husbands to hold those jobs. Most individuals
feel, at the conscious level at least, that they need the
ability to get along with others without severe altercations.[4]

To accomplish these ends, changes in the school as a
social system and in the roles within it must be effected.
In some schools there is much strain and high tension;
many pupils find it exceedingly difficult to perform well.
In others, there is near stagnation and students are chal-
lenged little if at all. Seldom are there conditions between
these extremes, conditions conducive to effective learning.

The basic concern should be with active inquiry by students and teachers about the world in which we live. Currently there is little of this. Either high standards of
precision and near rote-learning are set for students or
low standards that involve little more than sporadic at-
tendance obtain.[5] Student and faculty roles need to be
shifted so that there is a questioning by both the child
and the teacher as to "what is going on out there" in the
total environment. To do this there must, among other
things, be changes in the role of the principal, a role
which tends now to be somewhat similar to that of a
high-level and rigid police officer. The principal ordinarily sets the tone of the school. Schools must become
places where reasonable questioning by individuals of
the environment and of each other is a way of life.

We are talking here about all manner of inquiry: about
the physical environment, the social environment, the individual. How an automobile engine works and how to
fix it is as relevant as the histories of highly industrial-
ized nations. Physics in the usual sense is as relevant as
how to raise children so that they are not psychologically
crippled by the time they reach adolescence.

3. TEACHING BEHAVIORAL SCIENCE IN THE PUBLIC SCHOOLS

The President's Commission on Law Enforcement and Administration of Justice emphasized in its 1967 final report that "the most effective way to prevent crime is to assure all citizens full opportunity to participate in the benefits and responsibilities of society.[6] This is a valid enough statement. The implementation of it is an enormous and nearly impossible task. The Commission did make several hundred specific recommendations and we shall consider a number of them in the pages ahead.

But it will be well to heed also the warning of the National Advisory Commission on Civil Disorders (the Kerner Commission). In its final report of 1968 that body stated its position clearly: "Our basic conclusion: the need is not so much for the government to design new programs as it is for the nation to generate new will."[7] Certainly specific programs are a necessity. But the "new will" of the nation is mandatory if that new will is translated to mean an enlarged understanding by the general public of the nature of social problems and of crime in particular. It is mandatory if the social control process is to be effective in reducing crime rather than inducing it.

A variety of forms of social education will be useful. One having a very high priority involves instituting in the curricula of the elementary and high schools across this country education in the behavioral sciences of sociology, psychology, and cultural anthropology. Such a program would have benefits not only in regard to crime. It would have much positive effect with respect to a wide variety of other social problems: mental illness, drug addiction, alcoholism, divorce, and so on.

The program would embrace most children, all those

who go to elementary and high school. Only a minority attend college despite a popular belief to the contrary.[8] And only a minority of those complete college. Further, to begin learning behavioral science at age eighteen or nineteen is too late. Knowledge of human behavior needs, so to speak, to seep down into the bones of the great bulk of the society's members.

The ultimate aim is to provide practically all individuals in the society with a sound grasp of the forces that shape human behavior. These would not be how-to-do-it courses, not courses in how to choose a mate, how to avoid drug addiction, and the like. Rather they would involve broad principles of behavioral science. The learning of those principles would, however, be tied to concrete life experiences. While a few such courses may be taught here and there in this country, there does not now exist any sustained program that extends over most of the child's years of formal education.

The program could very well begin in the first grade and span the twelve years of lower schooling. Certainly there would in some communities be much resistance. This could be overcome in a variety of ways. In the early years of its inception, the program might start at the beginning of junior high school rather than first grade. Those who would teach the courses must be well trained in the subject matter. They should also be catalytic persons of the type discussed earlier, people who can induce change effectively and gain reward from doing so. In any case, the program should be tried on a limited, experimental basis and only after some years of feedback and modification should it be used on a broad scale. Initially, federal government or foundation grants would finance the project. Later, continuous funding by federal, state, and local governments combined would be appropriate.

As to actual content of the curriculum: the program could begin in the first grade with psychological learning principles, perception and the like. In the later elementary grades the focus would be on considerations of personality. Sociological principles of group processes and the analysis of the social system can be studied in the junior high school. The senior high school years might be devoted to cultural anthropology. Here the student would gain insight into the nature of culture and the behavior of the members of his society in relation to societies around the world. Certainly this sequence could be reversed: one could well begin with cultural anthropology and move later to sociology and finally to psychology.

All of the material taught over the years could be vividly and rewardingly presented. For example, learning principles could be shown in action in the classroom through the use of rats, mice, hamsters, and other animals who would learn to run mazes, operate simple machines, do tricks, and so on. Learning principles could also be demonstrated in relation to the child's own learning. He would chart his learning progress and see how his efficiency rises when he follows certain principles. (Most persons go through ten or twelve years of school and some many years more without any understanding whatsoever of the learning process in which they are engaged.) Group dynamics can be explicated in the classroom in equally interesting ways. So can aspects of the varying cultures of literate and nonliterate peoples around the world.

It is not necessary in the teaching of this material to create undue resistance as has sometimes been done in the past. It is not necessary the first day of class to have the sixth grader write an essay on "Which Parent You Dislike the Most and Why." It is not necessary to have children rate the prestige of other children's families. It is not necessary to show "Why Sweden Is Better Than the United States." Some sense of proportion and concern for the feelings of others must inform any successful project. So it is here. The emphasis should be on the ideas of the behavioral sciences and their use for understanding the world in which we live. The focus should not be on evaluative matters of who is best and who is worst, what is good and what is bad, and so on.

While the relation of behavioral science principles to crime and other social problems would not be ignored, the thrust of the program would be toward laying a groundwork for preventing and working with those problems. Knowledge well grasped and then consciously set aside is often a prerequisite for dealing effectively with a complex problem. Take by analogy the artist as he paints at his easel. Almost all able artists are well schooled in the techniques of drawing and painting. Whether self-taught or otherwise, they have mastered the principles of their art. Once they are at the easel, however, most artists set aside any conscious concern with principles and technique. They paint in a flowing and by definition artful fashion.

So it could be with the average person approaching the problems of everyday life. Admittedly he or she can perhaps not be considered fully analogous to the artist at his easel. However, the young mother, informed in a general way by education in the behavioral sciences, would be in a far better position to interact constructively with her small child than her present-day counterpart. Without following any particular rigid rules of child-rearing she would be able to channel her behavior and her child's behavior toward creative outcomes and away from the generation of serious problem behavior.   The beginning police officer, so educated, would be more suitably equipped than is now the case to cope with the conflicts and difficulties of his role and to avoid that overreaction that so frequently fuels criminal behavior by others. The teenage boy confronted with several opportunity structures, some legitimate, some illegitimate, would be much more able to advance his career in ways that will not culminate in serious criminal endeavor.

A word regarding the drug problem and public education. As has been emphatically stated in different terms, drug abuse is a serious social problem that has been created largely out of thin air. There were few addicts in this country 15 years ago and the problem of the abusive use of nonaddictive yet potentially harmful drugs was relatively small. These problems have spiralled upward with enormous rapidity. This has been due in no small measure to overreaction and ambivalence: repressive controls; labeling of a small problem as a huge one; hidden desires of some of the most militant antidrug individuals to themselves experience the escape of drugs; love and hate between younger and older persons.

Drug abuse educational programs for children, juveniles, and adults have been promulgated on a large scale. Many have been harmful. Scare tactics used by police and other lecturers have alienated the young and caused panic in those older. "Cute" educational tactics have "turned off" the young by the millions; for example, films that show in melodramatic terms the "horrors" that result from marihuana usage. Moreover, much "education" in regard to drug abuse has been of the "how-to-do-it" variety: literally teaching how to use and experience drugs under the name of prevention.

Now, in any event, we do have a considerable problem of drug abuse. Sound, effective educational programs are in order.[9] These will best be presented outside of regular school curricula. While it is manifestly unwise to turn those curricula over to courses dealing *explicitly* with crime, mental illness, alcoholism, drug abuse, homosexuality, prostitution, and so on, programs of continuing education for both adults and the young can be instituted. Often they can be held in the public schools in the evenings. Qualified persons will lecture and hold discussion workshops on the drug problem. The content of these sessions will emphasize rational, unemotional non-scare approaches. It should always be borne in mind that the need is to inform properly rather than to attempt to pressure individuals to avoid drugs.

4. EDUCATION THROUGH THE MASS MEDIA

The debate over whether television is a vast wasteland or a glutted toy and candy shop for the moronic will no doubt continue into the foreseeable future. The fact remains that television possesses enormous promise for the resolution of pressing social problems. It has great potential for helping citizens to gain some understanding of what constitutes these problems. It is an educational device and there are a number of ways in which it can be effectively employed in this regard. This is true of both commercial and "educational" television.

The use of television to be emphasized here is that of a public forum for the consideration of crime and other related social problems. This has of course been done on a limited scale and can be expanded and refined greatly. Discussion of the issues involved in the causation and control of crime can be the central focus. Informational segments of programs can be interspersed with panel discussions and questions and comments from a live audience and by telephone from the home audience. On a limited yet substantial basis, the federal government or private foundations can fund programs on public affairs for prime commercial time. A weekly series of programs related to, say, the role of the police in the crime control process could extend over several months. Other series could revolve around different aspects of the control process and around various forms of causation of crime.

The programs must be of wide general interest. There is a workable way to make them so. They must simply "tell it like it is." They must show the processes by which crime is created. They must document the services provided the society by crime. They must show how the young are made criminal through labeling, that is, how the innocent are made guilty. They must document the processes by which the social control apparatus perpetuates crime while seeming to move against it. They must describe vividly ways of effective prevention. If television does this, it will not only contribute to the understanding and the eventual resolution of a most pressing social problem; it will also make money in the process.

Presently, of course, the television networks devote each week many hours of programming to violence and other crime as means to success goals and as ends in themselves. There is some possibility of exerting sufficient influence on the networks to decrease those programs. Private citizens' groups in conjunction with the Federal Communications Commission and other branches of government have the power to bring about these changes. The fact is that many adults *are* concerned about the harmful effects upon children's development of programs that implicitly advocate or applaud violence and crime in general. That concern can be translated into effective action fairly readily. Interest groups must "lobby" with the networks directly and with relevant government agencies and officials.

When one turns to another of the mass media, the newspapers, a quite different social response prevails. The newspapers label individuals as criminals and play up the macabre aspects of offenses and offenders (and of arrestees who are nonoffenders as well). Overall, the public is little inclined to bring pressure to bear upon the newspaper. The present crime reporting satisfies widespread needs for the creation of scapegoats.

However, there is an avenue toward crime prevention that can be explored in relation to the newspaper. Documentary articles and series of articles regarding the generation of crime, the abortive control process, and the creation of criminals can be run successfully in many papers. As with television documentaries, the content of such articles has intrinsic interest for many. The fact that these articles can be run side-by-side with misleading reporting of crime is ironical. More important, that fact is in itself a commentary on the interrelation of crime and everyday social life in the United States.

Increasingly there is a demand for books about social problems and how to resolve them. These can be misleading and help to bring about abortive action. Others can be useful. Clear discussions in everyday language—without jargon—of the nature of crime, of the forces that result in crime, of the functions of crime, and of the social control apparatus and its functions can do much to educate the public.[10] There is little doubt that whether the medium be television, newspapers, or books, the "tell it like it is" documentary approach now has wide appeal and is educationally effective.

14. THE NEIGHBORHOOD SERVICE CENTER

1. THE NEED FOR SERVICE CENTERS

Adults and children alike must have some place they can go for help when they need it. They must be able to get help in coping with a wide variety of otherwise insurmountable problems. They must be able to do this by having access to organizations and individuals prepared to assist rather than to criticize, ready to offer whatever aid is needed rather than to moralize. It will be obvious that if a boy or girl or parent in trouble seeks help and is subjected to a lecture he will be unlikely to return.

When those in the middle and upper socio-economic levels require psychological or social services—and in some instances financial services—they go to the appropriate organizations or individuals and purchase those services. They enter private hospitals, they pay psychiatrists and clinical psychologists. If necessary, they borrow money at the prevailing interest rate. It is only infrequently that those in the lower socio-economic strata can do these things. They quite obviously do not have money. And in any event they are unlikely to know how to make use of such services. They do not know how to contact a psychiatrist in private practice. Often they do not know how to make a bank loan. If they do know how to do these things, they will tend to feel out of place, uncomfortable, and embarrassed doing them.

Seldom will friends and relatives be able to provide help when persons with little money and prestige are in difficulty. Friends and relatives have few resources and often possess similar problems. When beset by severe difficulties, individuals at the lower end of the socio-economic scale have four main choices. They can do nothing and bear the illness or the onset of deviance. They can grow more ill, watch their children learn delinquency, become addicted to drugs or whatever the case may be. They can turn to illegitimate means: medical and psychological quacks, loan sharks, prostitution, drug-pushing, theft. Finally, they can appeal to public or private state and community welfare service organizations. These organizations are supported in considerable measure by persons in the upper and middle classes through taxes or donations. These organizations' policy-makers, the advisory board and executive board members and the higher administration, are members of the upper and middle classes. Most of the work of the organization is done by full-time middle-class employees.

Such organizations, then, whether parts of government or of the private sector, are dominated by middle- and upper-class men and women. They tend to believe in self-determination, hard work, and "high" morality. In general, members of the higher socio-economic strata may not actually determine their life courses greatly. They may work less than they profess and they may fall far short of their own moral standards. But they believe in these things. They believe they are right. And especially do they believe in them for the poor. All too often, they do not see that many of the poor are so beset by myriad frustrations that they are all but immobilized. They do not see that the poor are unlikely to have had access to role models who could provide patterns for overcoming obstacles, for "success" as the culture defines that. They do not see that the poor possess a somewhat different morality. They do not see that their insistence on the poor following the dictates of middle-class morality if they are to receive aid is a form of totalitarian control. And they do not see that, over time, that control backfires. The poor resist and as a consequence are fixed in the deviance and illness they seek to avoid.

The need is for youth and family social service centers that take the individual on his own terms and provide effective assistance without insisting upon extensive value change. Effective assistance cannot result if such change is insisted upon. It is one thing to want to help a girl addicted to harmful drugs. It is quite another to act as judge and guardian of her purely private sexual life. It is one thing to help a boy to move away from theft. It is another to insist that he take a bath every day.

Private, highly informal, centers for aid have been springing up here and there across the country. They point the way to what needs to be done. In some smaller communities there have developed "group living centers" for youths with serious delinquency problems. A family will open its home to a few teen-agers who would otherwise very likely go to a reformatory. Authorities unofficially recognize these as "living-in" houses of probation. In the ghettoes and in other depressed areas of large cities one now occasionally finds residential self-help centers. These are manned largely by neighborhood residents. In some instances persons of low income background who have gained appropriate professional skills offer their part-time services.

As might be imagined, both these and the private group living arrangements in the smaller communities are, for the most part, inadequately financed shoe-string operations. Some constructive practical results are obtained because the persons providing the help are motivated, dedicated, and relatively uninterested in changing private morality. But they can achieve their aims on only a very modest scale because of the shortage of funds. Yet when money comes from government or private donation there is a strong tendency for the strings of enforced middle-class morality to be attached to it.

2. ORGANIZATION OF THE CENTER

Two major questions are these: How might adequate funding and staffing of these youth and family service centers be effected while avoiding the resentment that comes from the attempt to dictate moral matters? Second, what are the services that these centers should provide and how should they do this?

Regarding the issue of relatively value-free funding, there is no doubt that most of us push our values to some extent. But there are vast differences in degree and in the ways this is done. The federal government is not as prone to insist in practice upon the carrying out in specific programs of a political ideology as many would believe. The federal administration and the Congress (and state administrations and legislatures) may take fairly definite public positions on such sensitive and potentially explosive matters as crime, delinquency, criminal justice, welfare, and other social services. An administration may be on record as, say, strongly in favor of "law-and-order," of strict enforcement of the criminal law, of harsh punishment, of "no mollycoddling of wrong-doers," of a guaranteed minimum income, and of the legal requirement that all able persons receiving welfare assistance do work of some sort. An administration may stress very little in its official statements the need for prevention of crime before the fact or for effective rehabilitation. But this does not at all necessarily mean that in practice federal and state funds must be used solely or largely for "law-and-order," "crackdown," and "get tough" programs. And it is not likely to mean that forward-looking preventive programs are ruled out. As long as the laws pertaining to the use of funds are observed there is much room for a variety of programs. Seldom does the law state that a particular kind of program cannot be funded and carried out. Which programs are effected and how they are carried out depends much more on the nature of the individuals directly involved at the local level than on political party ideology in Washington and in the state capitals.

However, the more local the unit of government, the greater the probability of attempts to enforce rather specific forms of ideologies and morality. Some programs are funded largely or solely by county, city, or town governments. And most federal programs become in good part local programs. Since local governments usually pay part of the bill, in practice they have much to say about what is done. Additionally, private individuals are hardly known for a hands-off attitude when they donate for purposes having to do with the supposed resolution of pressing social problems.

Still, there is a partial way out. It will be possible to employ innovative, catalytic people in a wide variety of programs. But even here there is a danger. Some catalytic persons with forward-looking ideas regarding crime prevention will seek to coerce others to follow whatever is their particular brand of belief and morality just as will some of the middle- and upper-class leaders and workers in social welfare. Their belief and morality systems may be quite different. Yet the catalytic individual may be just as zealous in pursuit of strict adherence to his "party line" as any of the others. However, he is not likely to be very catalytic when he does so in the capacity we are discussing. For he too will create resentment. Yet in other endeavors he may be quite effective as a catalyst regardless of his emphasis on his form of morality. For example, a man who insists on cleanliness may not be able to work effectively with the poor. But he may be able to bring about significant changes in police departments; he may be able to institutionalize effective crime control methods in the most tradition-encrusted departments.

The second question posed earlier was this: What are the services that youth and family centers might provide and how would they provide them? Put differently, what services will individuals need and how can they be most effectively made available? Persons who need help may require what can be termed ordinary goods and services of various sorts: food, clothes, living quarters, furniture, electricity, heat, transportation, medical treatment. Alternatively, persons in distress may require counseling broadly construed: advice of various sorts, light supportive counseling, various forms of psychotherapy in depth, group therapy. It may be necessary for the center to refer individuals to particular organizations or professionals either for therapy or for other purposes.

There is no reason why a service agency should not make referrals from time to time. This is not necessarily a passing of the buck. Not everyone can do everything; specialization is altogether necessary. But it will not do simply to refer, simply to tell the individual where to go. Often he must be guided to the proper place, introduced, taken back again, made to feel sufficiently comfortable. If financial costs are involved he will probably need assistance with those. And of course if a service center becomes merely a referral agency then it is no longer what is meant here by a service center. There is a place for the referral agency. But we are concerned here with centers which, while they may occasionally make referrals, in the main provide direct services. The concern is with centers that give the individual not only what he needs specifically but a sense of security as well.

The individual must feel that there is a place of last resort where he can gain help without questioning of his motives and without exacting changes in his value system in exchange for assistance rendered. He must feel that he and members of the service center are entering with mutual respect into a common endeavor to help individuals in distress (one of whom happens to be he). He must be given the opportunity later to enter the process of helping others.

Some readers will raise questions about certain deviant individuals who seek help. What, for example, of the inveterate check-passer who is down on his luck and seeks money to buy clothes and who will then be able to make a good appearance and cash more bad checks? Certainly there is no need to help individuals commit crimes. But what people say they want and what they actually need are in many instances quite different. As discussed in an earlier chapter, the persistent check-passer is beset by an array of situational and personality problems. He may need clothes but he needs more the support of others to get him out of the vicious circle of passing bad checks and out of the life style and interactional patterns that create that vicious cycle. It is one thing to avoid legislating private morality for others. It is quite another to abet and condone by implication public illegality.

While the center will provide services for children, youths, and adults, there will be few distinctly separate *channels* for doing so. This is a neighborhood or community service center. Whole families or individuals are aided without excessive attention to age, sex, race, and the like. There will be times of course when common-sense distinctions must be made. In general, however, the emphasis will be on people as members of a neighborhood whether they be eight years old, forty-eight or eighty-eight, black or white, and so on.

The center should be located directly in the given neighborhood, in surroundings that are not threatening to lower-class parents and children. An abandoned store in the local area would often be ideal. The center will be staffed by both trained professionals and neighborhood residents without formal training. As indicated earlier, it is absolutely essential that staff members be relatively free of that missionary zeal which seeks to convert those in need of help from one private morality to another. Psychologists, psychiatrists, sociologists, social workers, and physicians will be major figures in the professional staff. One or two will be full-time. Others will serve part-time, some with salary, some on a purely volunteer basis. Untrained persons will be recruited to work with individuals in need of help and to learn on-the-job. Most will be neighborhood members in need of funds and will be paid, although some may be volunteers.

3. THE SERVICE CENTER AND THE CHILD

On the one hand, it is necessary to have children who are moving toward delinquency make use of the neighborhood service center. On the other hand, there is the very real possibility of labeling the child as one with problems, as "a delinquent," and of so creating a self-fulfilling prophecy. The neighborhood service center aside for the moment, in the wider sense this is a recurring dilemma. Potential violators should be identified and helped to avoid delinquency and crime. Yet the very process of identification can readily worsen the problem one is attempting to remedy.

Programs for identifying and treating in the public schools children who are potentially or actually delinquent have been proposed from time to time in recent years. The reaction to such proposals tends to be extreme. Either they are met with much favor or they are abhorred.

There is considerable reason to think that the school is not the most suitable place for identification and treatment. Of course students are now informally labeled delinquent in the schools and given no treatment. But to institutionalize and formalize such labeling can make matters worse. In all but the smallest villages, the schools are bureaucratic organizations which represent the prevailing community power structure. Labeling children as delinquent is an attempted form of social control. It is a way of punishing those children, usually lower class, who do not seem to reflect the value system of the power structure. Formal mechanisms in the schools for identifying and treating delinquency-prone children are likely to be used for this end rather than for the children's benefit.

The neighborhood service center offers a viable way out of the dilemma. In a somewhat informal fashion, potentially or actually delinquent children in the area can be identified and treated. The service center *is* a neighborhood creation. It is not bureaucratically organized. It is not pushing the value system of the prevailing power structure. Hence the neighborhood service center is less likely than the school to punish the child who needs help.

After the service center has been established for some time, workers at the center will know the families of the neighborhood reasonably well. By sound if informal means they can identify those children who are moving toward serious delinquency and who are most in need of assistance. The signs of impending delinquency and crime frequently show early in the developing child. Much unreciprocity and thus high tension in role relationships between child and family members is a primary indicator. Regarding potentially violent offenders, sporadic outburts of sadistic aggression constitute another indicator. Children who are likely to commit homicide or assault later in life tend to be quiet, repressed children.[1] Their withdrawn demeanor is punctuated with sudden attacks on other children or animals. Frustrated in some way, the child may smash a younger child's head against the pavement. He may throw a rock at a passing automobile. He may cut up a cat.

As we have said, the prevailing power structure controls the schools. And the children who do not reflect the values of the power structure are those most likely to be mistreated by the schools. At the same time those children who do most poorly in school, whose grades are low, and possess a history of truancy, and so on, are those most likely to commit delinquencies outside of school. The power structure makes the laws and enforces them. If the child cannot achieve legitimately within the system that is the school, then he is unlikely to achieve legitimately within the larger social system that is the society. And his failure within the school embitters him and alienates him from the power structure and its code of ethics which are embodied in the criminal law. Thus, as numerous analyses have shown, failure in school is a good predictor of delinquency.[2]

Once a child has been identified as potentially delinquent, a central problem will be that of inducing parent and child to go to the center. A staff member of the center should go to the home, explain the center, and invite the parent or parents to come with the child for an initial session at some time in the near future. The staff member can then return to the home at a later time to escort the family members to that session. In some instances to have fathers attend will not be feasible. Many will be away from home, some will have deserted the family.

To illustrate: assume that there is a family of four. The father and mother are at serious odds most of the time; the fifteen-year-old boy has been in juvenile court several times for theft; there is also a three-year-old boy. The mother and three-year-old attend the center. The mother did not want the second child. She is exasperated by her environment in general, by her husband, and by her teenage boy. She displaces much of her consequent aggression to the small child. He in turn is a "difficult" child; he cries readily, wants his way at every turn, is destructive and has temper tantrums.

The basic aims of the center in this case are to help the mother better understand her total situation and to provide the mother and the child with opportunities to create new and more constructive relationships with each other. A variety of techniques would be used to achieve these ends. At the center mother and child would see another mother and her child interacting in a warm, communicative fashion. The second mother and child would be of a similar socio-economic status as the first mother and child. Mother and child would under expert guidance engage in role-playing sessions with others and between themselves. Various forms of counseling and psychotherapy in some depth would be available (the fifteen-year-old boy would of course not be ignored in all this; nor would the husband).

Given the kinds of progress outlined above, one of the most workable avenues to easing unreciprocity between mother and young son involves the shifting of certain fundamental child-training patterns. As has been demonstrated, mothers and sons, especially when the sons are potentially violent offenders, tend to get into interactional binds, to become at loggerheads with each other. To the extent feasible, patterns of training children in regard to eating, toilet matters, and the control of aggression should be liberalized so that the child is less restricted.

It is exceedingly difficult for mothers, especially defensive, anxious, and resentful mothers, to see that restricting a child unduly often has the opposite effect of that intended: he tends to become difficult and fundamentally rebellious. It is the conventional wisdom to think otherwise. Moreover, these mothers may well have underlying motivations to get into interactional binds with their children, particularly their sons. They are likely over their life histories to have repeatedly gotten into such binds with males—fathers, boy friends, husbands. They are now used to it, "addicted" to it.

If custom can be shifted somewhat, so that it is accepted procedure to be less restrictive in the areas of child training mentioned, then the interactional situations between mother and son will be eased at least slightly. This will open the way for further easing of the child's frustration—and to some extent of the mother's as well.

Whether children or adults are treated, the neighborhood service center will be a new organizational form in the community. The center will provide new roles for neighborhood members, both those who are treated and those who work part-time there. It will aid in reducing unreciprocity both in the community and in the family. In the long run the center will serve to crowd out much of the delinquent and criminal subculture. It will provide positive role models for the young.

In numerous ways, the center will ease the frustrations of everyday life, especially for the poor. It will make possible a viable opportunity structure through which the family and the individual can come to grips with pressing problems. In so doing it will to some degree open up to those in the lower socio-economic strata the traditional educational and occupational opportunity structures.[3]

15. CHANGING
THE POLICE

1. THE POLICE AND
THE COMMUNITY

We shall now begin to consider the several components of the formal control process as it affects crime. Those components are the police and the courts; prisons and jails; and probation and parole systems. What changes might be effected in those such that prevention is increased and the crime problem decreased? That is the guiding question.

Turning first to the police: One of the great necessities is to reduce conflict in the police role and hence to decrease the police officer's feelings of frustration.[1] This can be done in good measure through clarifying the public's expectations for police and by introducing greater specialization into police work. Professionalization of the police role must occur in significant degree. And the police officer should have a far greater understanding not only of his society but of the nature of the criminal offenses he confronts.

The central function of the police officer is to apprehend those suspected of violating the criminal law.[2] This the public does not clearly see. The need is for the members of the society to understand that this function is primary. Such understanding collides of course with the latent desires of many members of the public to have crime proceed unimpeded. Nevertheless, it will be possible through efficient community relations efforts to help large segments of the general society to see that a highly professionalized police force is a great public asset. Professionalization is the pivotal idea for increasing community support, reducing police role conflict, and increasing police effectiveness.

As the final report of the President's Commission on Law Enforcement and Administration of Justice makes clear, police departments in all large communities should have adequate machinery for carrying on effective community relations programs.[3] In smaller communities, several police forces can combine to have a single community relations effort. The President's Commission points out that ill feeling between minority groups and police is at the heart of the police community relations problem. Some police and some minority group members have mutual respect and trust. Frequently, however, that is not so. Minority groups see police as the spearhead of a repressive system. Police see members of minority groups as threats to their authority, as abusive and disrespectful. Seldom do police understand the attitudes, aspirations, and problems of minority groups.

Dramatic evidence of minority group feelings toward police is shown in the results of a national opinion poll.[4] In answer to the question "Do police do an excellent job? 23 percent of whites as compared to 15 percent of nonwhites said "yes." Seven percent of whites and 16 percent of nonwhites responded affirmatively to the question "Do police do a poor job?" To the question "Are police almost all honest?" 63 percent of whites and only 30 percent of nonwhites said "yes." The question "Are police almost all corrupt?" yielded one percent white affirmative answers and 10 percent nonwhite.

Police and minority group members should participate in community planning. Citizen groups that act as advisory committees to the police should be formed, especially in minority group neighborhoods. Much more active recruitment of minority group members into police forces should be carried out, particularly in communities where minority groups predominate. Thoroughly adequate grievance procedures should be instituted for citizens who have complaints against the police.[5]

Through widespread education of the general citizenry in regard to problems of crime in a free society, vastly increased financial and other resources for the police can be realized. Such increased resources will be of no avail unless alternatives to the latent functions of crime and of the formal control system are found and effected. Otherwise, those latent functions will simply be compounded by police forces which contribute increasingly to the growth of crime.

Given workable functional alternatives, the following kinds of increased resources and improved conditions are especially needed: More thorough and active recruitment of police officers. Emphasis should be placed upon recruiting youths in their late teens to serve as apprentice policemen and to attend college during periods of leave. Gradually movement should be made toward the requirement of a baccalaureate degree for police officers. The role of the police officer is an extremely complex and sophisticated one that requires considerable relevant formal education as well as on-the-job experience.[6]

Salaries need to be raised substantially so that they are competitive with positions in business, industry, the various agencies of government, and so on. Not only are carefully planned and carried out training programs for new officers crucially needed, but also in-service yearly training programs for all police are a necessity. Promotion should be based on merit rather than seniority; the opposite is now generally true across the country.[7]

Laboratory facilities must be greatly improved. Efficient detection, apprehension, and prosecution in cases of serious offenses often depends on the availability of appropriate laboratory equipment, techniques, and personnel. Centralized data processing units that handle information regarding violations, offenders, and related matters are required. Further, each police department of moderate or greater size should have available a legal advisor. The police must deal constantly with problems of law but are not trained in it. Hence they must have such a resource person at hand regularly.

Police must guard against corruption and other illegitimate practices within their ranks. A major mechanism for accomplishing this is an internal investigation unit; thus can police police themselves. There should be units outside the police as well, the aforementioned citizens advisory groups and formal governmental bodies as well, to inquire into possible police wrongdoing. Nevertheless, self-regulation is indispensable.[8]

2. PROFESSIONALIZATION

We have spoken in general terms of the resources needed by the police. These will help to provide the police role with professional stature. But more is required. Specialization by police is essential to professionalization and to the lessening of the ever-present and highly debilitating role conflict that now exists. One basis for specialization is that outlined by the President's Commission on Law Enforcement and Administration of Criminal Justice.[9]

The Commission envisions three major categories of police: community service officers, police officers, and police agents. The community service officer would be a young apprentice. He would carry on patrol and investigative work under supervision. He would perform a variety of service duties for the public and at times be available at community service centers, and so on. He would wear a distinctive uniform and he would carry no arms. The police officer would perform routine duties in the areas of law enforcement, apprehension, investigation, emergency calls, and so on. The police agent would handle the most complex and demanding tasks of police work. He might be involved primarily in juvenile work or community relations. He might specialize in investigation of homicide or of narcotics offenses. He might be a specialist in patrolling high-crime neighborhoods or those where tensions are at a given time especially great.

Readily apparent in this plan is the considerable specialization of function. One can go further. There can be auxiliary police forces whose work will have to do with essentially noncriminal matters: traffic direction, calls for assistance that do not involve problems of law violation, and desk jobs now performed by police officers. The three categories of police officers recommended by the President's Commission plus this auxiliary category would in themselves serve to reduce role conflict. The public would tend gradually to expect competence in the carrying out by the officer of the responsibilities in the given specialized role. An auxiliary who directs traffic would not be expected to handle explosive, potentially riotous situations. An officer who handled those situations would not be expected to patrol regular beats and empty parking meters. While some overlap of function and knowledge is inevitable and necessary, a specialist in homicide investigation would not need to be especially able with regard to most juvenile problems.

It will be necessary for small police departments to effect a high level of cooperation and in some cases to combine if the specialization required for reduced role conflict is to obtain. Resistance to this by community officials and police officers is well known. They fear loss of power and autonomy. Yet some useful starts on both the combining of forces and full-scale cooperation of forces have been made. Little in the way of adequate police work can be accomplished without funds. And there will be a shortage of funds unless a police force or group of forces numbers several dozen men at the very least and services a moderate-sized community. The town or small city with a police force of a few officers retains its full autonomy in law enforcement at the price of having no actual power. It is a hollow autonomy. Moreover, cooperation brings a new kind of autonomy; it brings a measure of meaningful, specialized autonomy toward the accomplishment of reduction of the crime problem.

Jerome Skolnick, author of *The Politics of Protest,* a task force report to the National Commission on the Causes and Prevention of Violence, makes two suggestions of special importance[10]: He urges that a National Service Academy be instituted for the training of police officers, social workers, and persons in related occupations. These would be somewhat similar to the present service schools: the U. S. Naval Academy, Military Academy, and Air Force Academy. Students would earn the bachelor's degree in the process of practical training. They would intern on-the-job during the summers. Potential police officers would be educated in an atmosphere conducive to ideas that transcend police work per se. While most police, social workers, and so on would not be educated at this academy, presumably its graduates would have a constructive catalytic effect on police work in general.

Skolnick's second suggestion is that there be lateral transfer among police departments. At present it is next to impossible for a police officer to move from a given rank in one department to a higher rank in another. Promotion is almost solely from within and largely on the basis of seniority. The one exception is chiefs of police. They are frequently brought in at the top. Skolnick's suggestion would increase competition among officers. It would also increase competition among forces to recruit able men at all levels. Thus would salaries and efficiency be raised.

3. SPECIFIC OFFENSES AND THE POLICE

For reasons set forth earlier, in the United States police effectiveness in regard to the crime problem has seldom been high. However, the police have been least ineffective in dealing with "black-collar" offenses of homicide, assault, rape, robbery, burglary, and larceny. It is these crimes with which they have some familiarity. It is these which they, like the general public, think of as "real crime" (plus certain others such as kidnapping, arson, skyjacking, and drug abuse).

Regarding crimes of violence, homicide and assault in particular, equipping police with modern medical facilities of a mobile nature can do much to reduce the results of violence. On-the-spot medical treatment and fast transport to hospital emergency wards can avert many homicides and reduce the injurious consequences of assault. In large forces, the police should have medical teams of their own. In smaller forces, they can work in close cooperation with hospital teams.[11]

Some communities now have emergency domestic quarrel teams composed of social and psychological specialists to intervene in serious domestic altercations. (Many assaults and homicides result of course from such quarrels.) Police now send an officer along with these teams to protect team members. Greater integration of police and social and psychological specialists will increase positive results here.[12]

Taking crimes against the person together—homicide, assault, forcible rape, and armed robbery—it is fair to think that when high rates of these obtain there may be a violent subcultural condition in the given area. Police should scientifically determine which the areas of high personal crime, when these crimes are most likely to occur, and which conditions are likely to precipitate them. Police can then intervene in some instances to block violence, in others to apprehend offenders.[13] As has been stressed at earlier points, police must be careful to avoid precipitating violence themselves.

Moreover, police can cooperate with the aforementioned neighborhood service centers to avert violence. Those centers can constitute a national organizational focus for constructive police efforts. While the community center personnel should obviously avoid becoming spies for the police, they could at times refer seriously dangerous persons to the police. Conversely, the police could, for example, refer incipient juvenile "gang" problems to the center.

There is a growing tendency for citizens to act as the eyes and ears of the police, reporting trouble-spots. This can be helpful or damaging. If the process sets citizen against citizen, raises the level of suspicion, then it will be of incalculable harm. If it does not have those adverse characteristics, then it can serve to noticeably reduce violent and other crimes.

As time goes on, small two-way radios, similar to wrist watches, will become usual. Citizens will use them for a variety of purposes including calling the police in case of attack or the witnessing of crime. Also, there is the possibility of police-controlled television scanners in high-crime areas. These would be mounted high above the ground and relatively impervious to destruction. They would scan given blocks and be monitored at police precincts. The possibility of "big brother" watching is certainly a real one here. This must be balanced against the possible effective control of incipient crime that could be gained.[14]

It will be remembered that Cameron observed the following: When amateur shoplifters are apprehended, severely warned, and then released without booking and labeling, there seems to be a salutory effect. This is not likely to be the case with the more habitual and professional larcenist. Here swift apprehension, trial, and incarceration appear necessary. Treatment can then be carried on in community-based learning centers (prisons) soon to be discussed. Much the same applies to check forgers and confidence men. The offenses involved—larceny, confidence games, forgery—may not necessarily be compulsive activities. However, they are certainly in cases of the professional and the semiprofessional offender deeply ingrained habits that can hardly be expected to abate because of a warning.

White-collar crime presents a special case for the police officer. Much of such crime varies only slightly from ordinary business behavior. That is, it is just over the line and illegitimate rather than just on the other side of the line and legitimate. Frequently the police officer does not understand the distinction and may in fact stand in awe of the generally affluent milieu in which white-collar violations occur. One possibility here is to have segments of large police forces which specialize in apprehension of white-collar offenders. However, as noted previously, many business concerns do not like to have the police involved because of adverse publicity, because crime within the organization is thought to be a sign of failure and to be bad for the morale of employees as well. Nevertheless, there must be police who are capable of apprehending white-collar violators when called upon to do so. This can best be accomplished by having small specialized groups of police specially trained for the task.

In the areas of victimless crimes, especially drug abuse, prostitution, and homosexuality, the police lack a fundamental understanding of the problems involved.

Certainly the police are not alone here. The general populace also lacks that understanding. Yet the police will be dealing with suspected offenders. Therefore they need some capability to proceed effectively. The drug problem, as we have said, triggers highly emotional and ambivalent responses in individuals and is in part triggered itself by those responses.

Special units of police or, in smaller forces, single individuals can be trained to have some understanding of the differences between drugs and their effects. They can be trained to gain some idea of the social and personality forces that combine to create problems of drug abuse. They can learn something of treatment methods. The police should not themselves be involved in carrying out treatment. But they should have some knowledge of the total series of social and psychological processes connected with drug abuse. The one area where the police currently have substantial knowledge is the drug distribution network.

When police forces are not especially large, it may be wise to have the same officers specialize in the apprehension of offenders engaged in a variety of victimless crimes such as prostitution, homosexuality, and abortion. Regarding all of these offenses, police should have a rudimentary grasp of the ambivalence inherent in the social response to them. Often the police find themselves pressured to make arrests of offenders in these categories only to see the cases handled by the courts in such a way that the offender receives a token slap on the wrist. A week later he is back at his old activities, arrested again the following week, back "on the street" the next week and so on.

The police need to understand at least to some degree the conflicting feelings in the society regarding those offenses. They need to grasp that in many instances they, the police, are not actually the intended targets of the aggression that follows upon that ambivalence. If through proper training programs, selected police personnel can achieve these understandings then their resentment of much of the public will to some degree abate. Their major task of effective apprehension of suspects will be made that much more efficient.

In a general way, the police understand the nature of organized crime. No one in the society has a full-scale knowledge of the "organization" and practices of organized crime in the United States, including major figures in organized crime itself.[15] But the police do understand quite well the implicit hand-in-glove realationship between organized criminals and the "law-abiding" public. Some government officials and some police as well must cooperate with organized criminal violators if the public need for illicit services is to be met. That is to say the police understand corruption on a large as well as a small scale. There is little that local police can do with respect to organized crime. Special units of the Federal Bureau of Investigation and of state police forces may be able to gather some incriminating evidence on organized criminals. Local police forces are hardly in a position to do this. If organized crime exists on a considerable scale, then the police are implicitly prevented from taking effective action by "legitimate" forces in the society which in effect cooperate with organized criminals.

4. RIOT CONTROL

The great need in riotous mass disorder situations is for the police to lower tension. The inclination of the police is to raise it. Interestingly and fortunately there has been some recognition of this by government officials and police themselves in very recent years.[16] There has been some grasp of the highly conflicted role of police officers which tends to lead them to seek aggressive encounters and to protect themselves. There has been some awareness that police force in a mass situation tends to label that situation a riot, that over-reaction begets over-reaction, and that if police and protestors *expect* violence from each other then self-fulfilling prophecy is highly likely.

There has been some understanding that police find it exceedingly difficult if not impossible to see that mass disorders are qualitatively different from disruptive action by a single person. There is awareness that police simply do not understand the underlying dynamics of racial and university protest. And there has been some recognition that police feel extremely threatened by hippies and by females who shout obscenities at them; both disturb violently the police vision of an adequate world. Finally there is some public knowledge of the fact that as a consequence of all these misunderstandings and cross-pressures, the police at the scene of a riot very frequently arrest indiscriminately. As noted earlier, often innocent passers-by are thrown into jail because they are mistaken for "hard-core dissidents."

The first step toward adequate police action in riotous situations is education of police so as to reduce ignorance and misunderstanding. Segments of police forces which will form "disorder patrols" need to learn that over-reaction escalates conflict; that there is a large *political* element of motivation in most mass disorders; that dissenters are not necessarily critical of police although they may seem so; that stereotyping of individuals (e.g., long hair means violent tendencies) is misleading and dangerous; and that citizens' rights must be protected by police at the time of disorders as well as at other times.

Given these newly acquired understandings, the special police disorder patrols will need sound training in deescalating high tension riotous situations. Broadly speaking, the police need to do whatever is possible within the law to reduce unreciprocity in the immediate situation. At the same time, they need to be able to apply force selectively toward individuals who become explicitly violent. Admittedly these are not easy tasks. However, they are not as irreconcilable as some may think. *Some* implicit force behind attempts at reconciliation is usually a positive factor in achieving that reconciliation. If well-trained police move quietly into a tense situation, without obvious display of force yet with the clear implication that sufficient force is present to back up ameliorative action, then they can be maximally effective in preventing the wildfire spread of riots.

Effective leadership of on-the-spot police disorder patrols is an absolute necessity for the prevention or deescalation of riot conditions. The able leader will have the full confidence of his men and vice versa. This means that the patrol leader must not be a higher-ranking officer who is suddenly thrown in charge of the "riot squad." Leaders and their men must train and work together regularly if there is to be sufficient discipline to transcend the vicissitudes of mass situations. Trust must be built up, developed over months and years or it will not exist at all.

The leader must understand something of the nature of crowd behavior and of the forces that generate unrest. He must communicate to his men a sense of certainty, certainty that what he orders is best for resolution of the situation. This is the core characteristic of leadership: *the communication of certainty.*[17]

Members of police disorder patrols must have had sustained practice in handling themselves under threatening crowd conditions. Given excellent leadership, only in this way can they come to feel secure in their immediate role. First-class equipment that is not provocative is essential: sophisticated mobile radio facilities; helmets with flip-down, see-through face-masks; tear-gas and similar chemicals if absolutely needed; collapsible shields for individual officers that can be spread and employed as necessary; fire-arms as last-resort items of equipment. Police dogs should be used very sparingly if at all; the provocation they arouse usually far outweighs any effective control functions they can perform.[18]

Through all of these measures regarding both riots and the various forms of traditional crime run the threads of police specialization and professionalization. Fortuitously, effective police work requires specialization, the upgrading of skills and equipment. As earlier noted, this in turn means greater professionalization and less role conflict. Thus can the police role and subculture be changed significantly. Thus can police work provide an opportunity structure for rewarding occupational careers and for effective reduction of the crime problem as well. Thus can violence by the police toward the general public and false and unnecessary arrests by the police be eliminated.

5.   A PROMISING PROGRAM

The neighborhood police team is a recent innovation that has shown decidedly promising results.[19] A typical example is as follows: A team of about 30 police officers—several lieutenants and sergeants and two dozen patrolmen—are selected to handle virtually all law enforcement matters in a high-crime neighborhood. They are expected to operate *as members of the community.* They are to get to know the residents, old and young alike, to provide them with protection from crime and a variety of social services.

The men take part in a one- to two-month intensive training program before going on duty in the selected neighborhood. This program stresses the human relations aspect of police work: how to interact in a constructive fashion with the public. Much attention is given to ways in which the usual police functions—patrol, questioning bystanders, handling various types of emergencies, and so on—can be so carried out that public cooperation and goodwill are gained rather than lost.

Sociologists and psychologists familiar with police work play a major part in planning and conducting the training program. A number of neighborhood residents, both adults and youths, are included in this training phase of the project. Their advice is sought as to both training and the actual operation of the police team. In this way the community learns of the project and participates in and contributes to it from the outset.

While training is in progress, a centrally located abandoned store is taken over to serve as the police station. Informal efficiency is a key characteristic of the entire operation. The store does not look like the usual police precinct headquarters. Yet the equipment within is up-to-date and in sufficient supply. Officers wear blazer jackets rather than uniforms. They drive ordinary cars rather than marked cruisers. They take part in neighborhood life and as professionals provide help such that the community gradually gains greater protection from violence and theft.

Usually the program is initiated for a one-year period with plans to continue it in following years. Training continues throughout the program with two-day sessions every other week. Also, regular meetings between police and residents are held to discuss assets and liabilities of the project and to institute changes in it. Periodic scientific evaluations as to degree of success or failure are made by outside, disinterested research organizations.

This approach emphasizes quite the opposite of the trend toward specialization of the police officer's role discussed above. The members of the neighborhood police team are generalists doing all manner of police and so-

cial service work. When problems requiring special expertise arise, such as the detection of homicidal offenders,
they call upon the central police force. Other than in such
instances, the neighborhood team is equipped to handle
a very wide range of problems.

This illustrates the frequent necessity in social change
of looking in several directions at once. As here, often
roles need to be made more specialized and yet it may be
necessary to counterbalance that with greater emphasis
on its opposite. It can truly be said that the role of the
member of the neighborhood police team is one of specializing in being a jack-of-all-trades.

Moreover, the police officer on the neighborhood team
and the resident identify with each other. They work in a
common cause rather than against each other. Their
roles become more similar rather than increasingly dissimilar. Their subcultures to some degree merge. Labeling of police and everyday citizens as "enemies" of each
other is to a significant degree avoided.

16. CHANGE IN THE JUDICIAL SYSTEM

1. THE LAW

Until recently, it was usual in the United States to look upon criminal courts as sacred institutions that could do little if any wrong. Not so any longer. The inefficiency of the courts and the irrelevance to daily life of much of the criminal justice system have changed that.

The major problems of the criminal judicial system have been indicated in chapter nine: antiquated and unrealistic laws and procedures; an insufficient number of judges, many of whom have inadequate training; a shortage of other related personnel, prosecutors and defense counsels in particular; and limited physical facilities. These deficiencies result in a great backlog of criminal cases. They result in "bargain" justice which is half justice and half injustice at best. The court system does little to deter; in some instances it in fact induces crime.

Our laws, and here we are concerned with criminal law, can be legitimately overhauled only by legislative action. And legislative bodies are generally notoriously slow to react. Law is piled upon law and there develops a haphazard structure that all but topples. Certainly citizens can do much here by impressing upon legislators the immediate need for legal reform. Particularly is this so in regard to victimless crimes.

The general need in regard to criminal law is to effect changes such that the law makes sense in relation to everyday life. It was foolish several decades ago to institute laws against serving and drinking of alcoholic beverages. Too large a proportion of the population drank regularly. As is common knowledge, those laws were flagrantly violated. And this led to the violation of other laws. Eventually it was necessary to repeal "prohibition."

The necessity is to abolish laws that are violated regularly and *en masse*. Ludicrous examples are laws against sexual relationships on Sundays. Conversely, it is of the greatest importance to institute laws that deal effectively with seriously disruptive behaviors of various kinds. These include white-collar crime. And special bodies of law need to be developed regarding participation in mass disorders. Mass looting during a riot may be behavior that cannot be positively sanctioned. It may be that looters should be brought to trial. But it is ridiculous to indict housewives who loot once under the same laws that apply to burglary (breaking-and-entering) and grand larceny.

There are presently attempts to legislate abortive "tough" laws in regard to the gathering evidence and the treatment of suspects. Laws to enlarge wiretapping by police, search and seizure, household entry, and the like are being passed. Laws to allow judges to detain without bail or recognizance those suspects deemed dangerous—preventive detention laws—have much support. These are for the most part laws contrary to the Constitution. These are laws which, passed in the heat of anger over violence and disorder, will undermine still further our shaky legal structure. They are "illegal laws" being given a temporary stamp of legitimacy. This inevitably weakens the judicial process.

Moreover, public backing of harsher penalties for criminal violations is increasing. This goes so far as to include in some areas the advocacy of the death penalty for selling relatively harmless drugs such as marijuana.[1] The problem here is that the same erroneous course is being followed that has prevailed for decades and centuries: the assumption that all persons experience the same reward from particular types of crimes and the same frustration from given forms of punishment. The battle between the supposedly noncriminal majority and the criminal minority is joined. The majority sees the violator or potential violator as more dangerous than before. The violator views the majority as more repressive and vengeful. Each becomes a target for the other. And some simply masochistic persons are directly motivated to commit crime in order to gain the punishment that supposedly will deter.

Laws relating to publicity by the mass media about trials, defendants, and prosecution are frequently highly ambiguous. The need is to reconstitute the law so that the rights of the defendant are as fully as possible protected; so that the effectiveness of the prosecution is not limited by publicity; and so that the image of the court as a place of justice is not demeaned. Regarding the last, injustice in the court should not be hidden. But neither should the judge nor the jury be made to look like fools. The public's right to know must be balanced against the practicalities of a fair trial. It is especially important that political leaders be prohibited from commenting on criminal trials pending or underway. A useful start on this problem can be made by the appointment of still another federal commission to study and recommend guidelines regarding the press, political leaders, and due process.

2. REORGANIZING THE COURTS

It is necessary to increase the *efficiency* with which *justice* is dispensed by the courts. This means justice, not injustice. Court organization and procedure must be made vastly more efficient but that efficiency must lead to greatly increased justice. Presently a double-standard exists in the courts, as elsewhere. Other things equal, the poor and the powerless are treated harshly, the well-to-do and the powerful leniently.

Detailed studies of the judicial systems in the various states should be undertaken at the outset.[2] We know the courts are inefficient; we know the judicial process is poorly administered. But we do not know as clearly as we should the points at which the greatest problems arise. We do know that the time between apprehension and trial must be shortened drastically. As noted earlier, it is not uncommon for the accused to sit in jail for six months or even a year or more before his trial begins. One proposal is to set by law strict time limits on the period between arrest and trial: If the accused is not brought to trial within two months from the time of arrest, then the charges against him must be dropped. While this idea has some merit, it will simply be unworkable unless a variety of changes accompany such a law. There must be more judges and other court personnel, more courts, more physical facilities, and so on.

Certainly there is need for a court administrator, similar to a hospital administrator. Presently the administration of the court is done informally and often haphazardly as well. While there are exceptions, in many courts the clerk is an untrained person who holds his position because of political reasons. He confers with one or more of the justices or with none and he administers the court. Professional programs for training court clerks should be instituted in the universities. And recruitment for the position should be put on a sound civil service basis with as little political intrusion as possible. Also judges, prosecutors, and others require specific training for their jobs. This will be discussed in the next section.

The exceedingly critical shortages of court personnel must be relieved. Especially is this so in regard to judges, prosecutors, and defense attorneys. It may be incomprehensible to some that there is a scarcity of defense attorneys. Certainly there are many lawyers across the land. The vast majority, however, are involved in civil rather than criminal cases. Moreover, most defendants have low incomes and cannot afford counsel. And those attorneys willing to do an adequate job when the state pays them a very modest fee to represent the accused are few.

There is a great need for more judgeships, larger prosecutor staffs, and proper payment of defense counsels by the state. Judgeships must be doubled. The practice of electing judges by popular vote must be abolished. Judges should be appointed either by local governmental units or by governor and council. They should be appointed for long periods, at least ten years, to reduce the degree of effective political influence over them. At the same time, reasonable mandatory age limits for retirement should be set.

Physical facilities of the criminal courts must be expanded drastically. While some courts are little used, most jurisdictions need additional court buildings. Many courts presently meet in back rooms of police stations, and so on. Necessary facilities and conditions, not the least of which is privacy, are woefully lacking. Relatedly, some judges are required to travel from one court to another and are away from home much of the time. Generally this is undesirable. A significant increase in the number of judges and a doubling of court facilities would balance out conditions so that few judges would travel to any extended degree. Moreover, experts in business management should be called in to advise on ways of restructuring the court's activities so that maximum efficiency is obtained or approached.

All of this quite obviously requires large sums of money and legislative bodies will be reluctant to make the necessary appropriations. Massive educational efforts directed toward the general citizenry and legislators in regard to the crime problem will be the single most effective way of making inroads here. One countervailing possibility: Many of the lower courts, inferior and local magistrate courts as they are often called, can in effect be dissolved. These courts, which try only misdemeanant cases, were once necessary in small, relatively isolated communities. They have outlived their usefulness, however. They can often be fused with the superior trial courts where felony cases are heard. Resentment of vested interests will of course be one consequence. But money will be saved and efficiency increased. In any case this has been tried with some success.[3]

Put bluntly, the bail system is a national disgrace. Reform is a pressing necessity. Private wealth should not determine whether a person is held in custody during the time between apprehension and trial. Those of limited means either borrow from a bail bondsman who is likely to charge an abnormally high interest rate or they remain in jail. One major step toward reform is to increase radically the use of personal recognizance—the promise of the accused that he will return to stand trial. In most instances the judge now has the option of using recognizance or bail. Many judges do not know they have that option, or do not in fact know the meaning of recognizance. If a judge does employ recognizance, he is likely to do so with well-to-do individuals. The poor pay. In any event, the vast majority of accused persons will return for trial. Other than where the most serious crimes are involved, there is seldom need to hold the accused in custody or to require bail. The judge should retain the right to set appropriate bail in unusual cases.

The whole process of "bargain" justice should be abolished.[4] That process, earlier described, involves a "deal" between prosecution and defense. Usually the accused agrees to plead guilty and to accept a trial without jury. In return, the prosecutor agrees to reduce the charge—from second-degree murder to non-negligent manslaughter, from rape to assault, and so forth. Essentially, any agreement between prosecution and defense should be formalized, out in the open, and effected with the knowledge of the judge. It is particularly important that the judge explain to the accused what his rights are and what may be the consequences of the several choices open to him.

Two related matters are of special significance: First, it is imperative that there be a sociological and psychological investigation of the accused before sentencing. This is done, if perfunctorily, in juvenile courts. It should be carried out with professional competence in both adult and juvenile courts. Properly trained social workers would gather data about the defendant's life history and present personality. These data should be of particular relevance to sentencing and treatment. If the accused is guilty, what within the limits set by law would appear to be the optimal sentence? Would the individual benefit most from probation or imprisonment? What types of treatment are indicated?

Second, behavioral science panels to advise judges in regard to particular cases should be instituted. These panels would be composed of psychologists, psychiatrists, sociologists, and social workers on a part-time basis. They might meet with the presiding judge one afternoon a week. They would review with him the social background and psychological data just mentioned of those who are presently before the court and charged with serious violations. They would advise on treatment possibilities. The judge would retain all the authority he now possesses. He would simply have the benefit of expert advice. Government or private grants can make possible experimentation with these panels on a trial basis.

The entire matter of sentencing requires a review and revision. Presently it is usual for judges to sentence within maximum and minimum periods as prescribed by law. For example, the law may read that for a given violation the minimum sentence is five years imprisonment and the maximum is ten years. The judge may sentence for any period within that range such as five years, or ten, or five to ten, or five to seven, or seven to ten. Greater flexibility is needed so that in a given case a shorter sentence is imposed and in another there is the possibility of a longer sentence. If a violator rehabilitates very quickly then it should be possible to release him. If this is not done, he will retrogress over the additional years in prison and he is likely to learn or relearn the criminal subculture. Conversely, if with appropriate treatment an individual does not rehabilitate, he should be incarcerated indefinitely. There will be many failures in the course of rehabilitative attempts. It may be extremely unwise to put back into the general society those violators who continue to be physically dangerous or otherwise seriously disruptive. As things presently stand, in many states an inmate must by law be released by parole or otherwise upon having served a certain number of years. This is so even when all relevant knowledgeable persons agree that he should not be released.

Finally, witnesses and jurors should be better treated during their periods of service. They are often held in cramped conditions, jurors in hotel rooms and witnesses sometimes in jail. (Witnesses who are deemed unlikely to appear for trial and who cannot post bond may be held for months in jail prior to the time of trial and their giving of testimony.) Both jurors and witnesses should be financially compensated for their services. Presently, many are forced to miss work for lengthy periods and suffer severe financial loss in the process. One way to resolve this is to ensure that witnesses and jurors are compensated by amounts equal to the average income level that prevails in the given state.

Programs for the adequate training of judges and other court personnel will now be discussed. These programs, together with attainment of the changes outlined above, will go far to increase significantly the efficiency of the courts. More important, they will do much to ensure the accused a greater degree of justice. It is not difficult to see that few conditions erode a society more than injustice parading under the guise of equal justice for all.

3. TRAINING OF JUDGES AND OTHER PERSONNEL

Rigorous training beyond the law degree is a necessity for judges, prosecutors, and defense counsels. Each will require a different curriculum. And the court clerk should also receive proper training, especially in regard to the aforementioned administration of the day-to-day business of the court. Few training programs for any of these personnel now exist. There are some schools for judges, usually offering sessions of several weeks during the summer, that are relevant. But they are few in number and only a very small percentage of judges ever enroll.

Judges (and prosecutors as well) should serve apprenticeship periods of a year or more. During that time, in addition to on-the-job work under an experienced judge, they should be required to spend several months in formal training programs. For the sake of practical convenience, this might be done during periods of four or six weeks each over two consecutive summers. The curriculum for trial court judges should, for example, stress both procedural and substantive criminal law. The rights and obligations of defendants, prosecution, and judges should all be carefully considered. Instructing of juries and sentencing are matters of special importance. There should be not only the usual classroom work, but also closely supervised role-playing in mock court-rooms.

Here judges would try out the ideas, approaches, and techniques studied in class. And there must be special training for juvenile court judges. Laws pertaining to juvenile courts are considerably different than those applicable to adult criminal courts.

A further aspect of the problem is this: judges, prosecutors, and defense attorneys understand some aspects of crime well, other aspects poorly. Broadly, they understand *how* criminal behavior occurs. But they do not understand why it occurs or what is its meaning. For example, they tend to understand that homicide occurs in the course of an altercation between two persons who know each other. But many follow the conventional wisdom in believing that the offender is vicious, evil, deranged (yet sane enough to stand trial), and so on. They seldom understand adequately the part played by victim-precipitation in homicide, assault, and rape.

Judges and others are unlikely to grasp the resentment that drives much property crime, both white- and black-collar. They are more likely to think such crime is carried out largely for profit. Few will have a fairly objective view of drug use or homosexuality. Sex crimes of various sorts are often seen through emotional, irrational lenses, as is true for the general populace as well. Organized crime tends to be viewed as more consciously organized into a vast national network than is actually the case. Riots are perceived all too frequently as a collection of individual acts of irrational, "senseless," "insensate" mayhem. Rioters are sometimes seen as agents or dupes of a communist or other conspiratorial operation.

The need is for selective education of judges, prosecutors, and defense attorneys regarding these matters. In addition to the summer courses mentioned above, intensive courses can be offered for judges and separately for prosecutors and for defense attorneys. Universities and colleges are frequently equipped to provide such courses.

The curricula should stress the social and psychological forces that give rise to the various forms of crime. Emphasis should be placed also on the meanings and functions of these forms of crime for the offender, the victim, and the wider society. Finally, attention should be paid to the kinds of preventive steps that can be usefully undertaken—before crime occurs, during the court process, and in rehabilitation.

The courts are charged, so to speak, with replacing unreciprocity with reciprocity in human affairs, or at the least with reducing the degree of unreciprocity. Not by any means do they always accomplish this. Changes in the role of the judge, in court organization, and in the criminal law as described above would go far toward gaining this goal of reduced unreciprocity. If in the courts there is not justice and something approaching reasonable reciprocity then in the streets there will be violence and something approaching total unreciprocity.

4. NOTE ON GUN CONTROL

The question of whether to institute strict laws limiting greatly the possession of firearms is a controversial and important one. Patrick Murphy, Commissioner of Police for the City of New York, has said that we must disarm our citizens.[5] A progressive police officer, Murphy believes gun control is an important step toward the prevention of serious crime. The National Rifle Association strongly disagrees. Criminologists range from those who rather favor gun control to those who believe it is either impossible to effect or will have little bearing on the crime problem.

There were as of 1970 over 90 million privately owned firearms in the United States.[6] Twenty-four million of these were handguns, 31 million were shot-guns, and 35 million were rifles. About half of all homes in the country have at least one firearm. Sales of rifles and shotguns doubled over the period from 1962 to 1968. Sales of handguns increased four times during those years. Fifty percent of sales are of secondhand guns.[7]

Three thousand persons die annually due to firearm accidents. Twenty thousand suffer accidental injuries. Forty percent of the victims are children and teenagers. Firearms were the weapons in two-thirds of the criminal homicides in the United States in 1970. One out of four aggravated assaults involved firearms. Almost two-thirds of known armed robberies were committed with guns.[8] The handgun is the principal type of firearm used by criminal violators. While handguns constitute one-quarter of the firearms in the United States, they are employed in three-quarters of those homicides where firearms are involved.

The Task Force on Firearms of the National Commission on the Causes and Prevention of Violence states the following: "State and local firearm regulation in the United States is a patchwork quilt of more than 20,000 laws, many of them obsolete, unenforced, or unenforceable. Serious efforts at state and local regulation have consistently been frustrated by the flow of firearms from one state to another. Attempts to establish uniform state and local firearms laws have failed.

". . . The Gun Control Act of 1968, which followed the assassinations of Dr. Martin Luther King, Jr., and Senator Robert F. Kennedy, commits the federal government to support state and city gun control laws by reducing the interstate flow of firearms which has long frustrated local control efforts. Proposals for a federal system of screening firearms owners have not been enacted."[9]

A central conclusion of the Task Force on Firearms is this: "Since handguns are the major problem, a nation-wide restrictive licensing system for handguns promises a more certain and more substantial reduction of gun violence in this country than a permissive system."[10]

If in fact the numbers of firearms are reduced modestly, little will be accomplished. Many will remain available for those who wish them. It is erroneous to think that licensing and similar practices will somehow mean that those who may be dangerous will not have access to guns. If many firearms exist in the country, there is no way to ensure that they will not be turned to violence.

If, however, it were possible to decrease drastically the number of firearms in the United States, to remove most from circulation and to control closely many of the remainder, that would be another matter. Violence might well be significantly reduced. A major reason we do not do this is because we *are* a violent society. The forces that contribute to violence contribute to the maintenance of "a gun culture."

This of course is not to say that those who favor relatively free access to firearms are necessarily potentially violent. But those social forces in the social system behind both violence and the massive distribution of firearms are similar. If those forces were altered, the problem would fall of its own weight. Put differently, in the United States the numbers of available firearms provide a useful index of the extent of our ever-ready potential for violence.[11]

17. CORRECTIONS: TRAINING PROGRAMS

1. PERSONNEL

Corrections is usually taken to refer to probation, to the incarceration in jails and prisons of convicted persons, and to parole. We shall in this and the chapter which follows discuss various specific changes that can be effected in those three areas. We shall then go on, in Chapters 19 and 20, to an extended discussion of the possibilities of community-based correctional institutions, here termed learning centers.

We begin with the assumption that all convicted persons should have access to reasonably adequate rehabilitation facilities whether on probation, incarcerated, or on parole. Presently little rehabilitative assistance and guidance is available anywhere. And parole itself, even without rehabilitation, is too frequently nonexistent, not a part of the process by which the individual moves from within to without the correctional institution.

In corrections, as with the police and the courts, one matter of the most urgent priority is to increase the quantity and quality of personnel.[1] As noted earlier, caseloads of probation and parole officers are extraordinarily high. Guards in correctional institutions are in sufficient supply; other personnel areas are severely understaffed. Large sums of money are required to rectify the situation.

The federal government can and is helping here. Federal funds for new positions are available on the basis of matching funds by state or local governments. After some years the state, county, or municipal government must take over full responsibility for funding the positions. But the match-funding during the first years is a fairly effective inducement to the lower levels of government to add positions.

The competence of probation and parole officers and prison and jail personnel is in general not high.[2] Low levels of education and intelligence abound. With these come ignorance and reactionary views of the crime problem. (To be sure, the latter can also be found in intelligent persons with much education.) But, again, to change this, to raise the level of competence, requires money.

Much more than money is necessary however. The very real challenge of a correctional career must be made clear to potential workers. So must the greatly increasing opportunities for professional advancement. Any adequate account of the crime problem and the abortive attempts at control that characterize the social response to it will by implication show the challenges and the opportunities in the correctional field.

Above all, what is necessary is individuals who can help those who seriously violate the criminal law avoid further crime. That is, probation, parole, and institutional personnel who are effective rehabilitationists are crucially needed. Those who successfully engage in rehabilitation must be persons who are adequately trained in the formal sense—there will be some exceptions here—but who also can communicate well with others and bring about change in those others.

To assist in the various rehabilitative and other responsibilities of correctional personnel, it is extremely important that part-time persons be used. Some of these will volunteer their services at no salary; some will be paid. Some will be highly trained and of wide experience; some will be without training or relevant background; others will fall between those extremes. Enormous pools of man-power and talent exist ready to be tapped. These include retired professionals, housewives with and without for-mal training, and graduate and undergraduate students.

One body of opinion holds that these individuals will be most effective when they are "pure volunteers," that is to say, unpaid. Another view is that they should be paid a salary commensurate with the work they perform. While much can be said on both sides, the latter view has perhaps greater merit than the former. The fact is, most people who are willing to provide useful services also need additional income. Moreover, in a money culture like ours, payment for work done puts an official stamp of seriousness of purpose on the endeavor. At the same time there is no need for excessive rigidity: programs can be designed so that those who so wish can "turn back" their salaries. And standards of selection can obviously be as high as necessary whether or not volunteers are paid.

Take as but one example a program to provide assis-tance for probation officers.[3] Under the best of circum-stances overworked probation officers will not have their caseloads sufficiently reduced in the immediate future. One way to ameliorate the situation is to provide them with part-time volunteers. These volunteers will assist mainly in these ways: First, gathering information about the life circumstances of the accused person. This information is used by the court in making a decision whether to place the accused, if convicted, on probation. It should be made use of also by probation officers in car-rying out their rehabilitative function. Second, volun-teers will assist in routine duties which consume so much of the probation officer's day. Foremost here are record-keeping and the collecting of funds from probationers who are paying damages or helping to support families from which they are separated. Third, volunteers will assist in counseling probationers. Some of course may be well-qualified counselors in their own right. Most will not, however, but can be trained to carry out light counseling *under supervision.*

As we have said, volunteers need not necessarily be highly trained. They should, however, be able persons who have some catalytic characteristics, who can learn rapidly, and who do not resent playing a secondary role to the probation officer. There must be an effective recruitment effort at the start of such a project. And it should be coordinated with the probation department and individual probation officers who are to be affected. The aim should be to have the probation officers involved in planning the program and in the recruitment process. Thus they will not be suddenly confronted with the fact of an assistant and a program foreign to them. Others such as judges with whom the probation department works closely should also be a part of the planning and recruitment processes.

The recruitment net should be thrown wide—to cover retired professionals, housewives, students, and so on. The major outlines of the program should be made clear. Information as to a single individual who can be contacted should be disseminated. It is important that the potential volunteer be able to call or visit a *person* rather than an organization.

Turning now to the operation of the program, assume for purposes of illustration that funds are available for a small probation department of 30 officers to be supplemented by 12 half-time volunteers for at least one year. One of these is a retired clinical psychologist; two are housewives with social work training. The remainder are about evenly divided among adults in various walks of life, graduate students in the behavioral sciences, and undergraduates majoring in one of the behavioral sciences.

The retired psychologist will serve as advisor on the development of a rehabilitation program which the department of probation does not now have. The program is to combine counseling with role therapy—the latter being the placement of the offender in roles designed to reduce the probability of future crime. The two women with social work experience will assist in coordinating probation activities with those of various service agencies and institutions (hospitals, mental health and drug clinics, employment bureaus, and so on). Graduate students will assist in counseling and in program planning. Undergraduates will help in a variety of ways including record-keeping. Apart from the psychologist and two social workers the volunteers will number nine, each of whom will work with one probation officer.

Training of volunteers and evaluation of results must be built into the venture. Volunteers should initially be enrolled in a concentrated orientation and training program. The program could extend over two weeks, half-time; most volunteers will be paid for their participation. Probation officers, especially those who will work directly with the volunteers, should be brought into this program although on less than a half-time basis. They too must have the benefit of training—particularly in how to work with volunteers. On-the-job training will begin after these first two weeks and continue indefinitely. Obviously one or more capable persons must be available to conduct training.

As in all experimental endeavors in the crime prevention field, evaluation of the program should be a continuing effort. At various stages, the effectiveness of the venture can be objectively measured. While we will not dwell on detail here, one approach will be to compare this probation department with another of similar size and general characteristics, one which does not utilize volunteers. What is the effect on probationers of the volunteer effort? What proportion of those guided by one department as compared to the other avoid further crime over a given period of time? Evaluation cannot be done by those directly taking part in carrying out the program. They are too involved to be reasonably objective. Competent outsiders must do this job.

There is an enormous reservoir of talent and motivation in this country waiting to be tapped to provide help in the correctional field and in other areas directly related to the crime problem. These persons must be provided with adequate opportunity structures to participate. If this is done, the benefits will be great. Apart from their direct contributions, such individuals will indirectly serve to educate the wider public about crime and the offender. They will communicate the fact that constructive approaches are finally being taken. And they will transmit a sense of optimism that with these beginnings much more can be accomplished. This is no mean prospect.

2. TYPES OF TRAINING PROGRAMS

We turn now to the wider questions of training of correctional personnel.[4] What are some major, effective approaches to training full-time workers? There are a number of important questions to be considered. Are the individuals to be trained persons already on the job or are they potential workers? Are they to be trained in the organizations in which they work or otherwise? If not in those organizations, then in technical schools, academies, colleges, universities? What distinctions are to be made among training programs for probation work, for parole work, or for service in correctional institutions? What further distinctions are to be made between the training of those primarily to be involved in rehabilitative efforts and other personnel?

Ordinarily probation and parole officers can receive much the same training although certain distinctions must be made. (Parole work quite obviously requires skill in helping the offender who has been incarcerated to readjust to the wider society in a way that probation does not.) Various correctional personnel can usually be trained in the same programs. While all should receive training in at least understanding the rehabilitative process, some should be trained in depth in this and others should not.

We cannot here discuss in detail all of these possibilities. We shall, however, consider three illustrative types of programs. The first has to do with training prison personnel who have been on the job for some time. The second involves training in colleges and universities for young persons who expect to become professionals in the corrections field. The third is an intensive one-year professional degree program for individuals planning a career in any one of several areas of the over-all criminal justice system. As to the first, most men and women working in prisons have received little relevant training for their positions. Exceptions may be prison psychologists, supervisors of work programs, chaplains, some white-collar clerks, and so on. We will stress the training required for officers and guards. Special programs will be needed for wardens and deputy wardens; here it will be advisable to design programs whereby these individuals from several institutions train together at some convenient locale. At this juncture in the discussion it is well to emphasize the point that training in corrections should be an on-going and never-ending process. Those with training adequate for a given time need to absorb in a systematic way new knowledge and new techniques as these develop.

Assume that in a given institution there are 500 custodial personnel—guards and officers charged primarily with maintaining security. Few have had any formal training at all; several have taken an occasional week's course here or there. Therefore, one program will suffice for all. There will be logistical problems. Most of these men cannot participate simultaneously in a training program. The prison must be properly manned at all times. Moreover, if all or most men were at a given time involved in a training program tension would spread throughout the institution. Prisons are authoritarian organizations dedicated to the status quo. Training programs, however well-conceived, are threatening to those committed to the ideology of a "total institution."

There can be four series of training sessions, each lasting thirteen weeks and following each other over a one-year period. From a hundred to a hundred and twenty-five men will be enrolled in each. Care should be taken that in each series some constructive officers and informal leaders in the guard ranks are enrolled. The first series should include a disproportionately large number of innovative, catalytic, forward-looking men. They will help to transmit to the others a positive feeling about the program.

Three-hour sessions will be held one day a week, in the morning, afternoon, or evening. If possible, training should occur outside of working hours, outside of whichever of the three shifts the men are on. Ideally, the men should be paid additionally for participating in the program. Many prisons are so organized that this cannot legally be done. If such is the case, then the men can at some later point be granted time off equivalent to the hours spent in the training sessions and in studying for the sessions.

Instructors should of course be suitably trained persons who can communicate well with prison personnel.

There should be a training director and several assistants. Outside speakers with special knowledge of the topic under consideration could be brought in from week to week. The format of a given session would be this: trainees would have been provided a week previously with study materials, readings relevant to the given topic. These materials should not be lengthy or overly technical. In general the men will not be used to much reading and will be demotivated by large quantities of material.

There would be a brief lecture of twenty minutes or so by a visiting speaker. This would be followed by a period of questions from the trainees and answered by the lecturer. There would then be a break for coffee. The second third of the session would be used for various techniques of involvement in the learning process, role-playing being an example. During the last third of the session the men would meet in groups of twenty-five and carry on discussions of what had transpired. The training director and his assistants would serve as the discussion leaders. The visiting lecturer would move from group to group, taking part for ten minutes or so in each. At the end, the visiting lecturer would summarize the session.

But what of the content of the program, the curriculum? How is it to be designed? What will be its major components? One fruitful approach is this: establish a planning committee to construct in broad outline the curriculum. The training director and his assistants will work within that framework and put the program into action. This approach has been tried with significant results.[5]

The planning committee will be composed of about nine persons. Three will be correctional officials and professionals with talents for this task. For example, an administrator in the state's central office for corrections, a prison psychologist or sociologist, and the warden of the prison where the program is to be carried out. Three will be educators who are conversant with the problems involved. And three will be men who will be directly involved with the program: the training director and an officer and a guard who will later be trainees in the program. Those nine individuals will meet weekly for ten or twelve weeks. Making use of their experience and of published materials, they will design the program in basic outline.

One illustrative type of curriculum that might result is in the barest skeletal form as follows:

Week 1:   Relationships between the Correctional Institution and the Wider Society

Week 2:   Relationships Among the Correctional Institution and Other Components of the Criminal Justic System (Police, Courts, Probation, Parole)

Week 3:   The Internal Organization of the Correctional Institution

Week 4:   The Functions of the Correctional Institution

Week 5:   Basic Principles of Human Relations

Week 6:   Further Principles of Human Relations

Week 7:   Human Relations in the Correctional Institution

Week 8:   The Nature of Rehabilitation

Week 9:   The Role of the Guard in the Rehabilitative Process

Week 10:   The Nature of Authority

Week 11:   The Role of the Guard in Maintaining Order

Week 12:   The Correctional Institution and Positive Community Relations

Week 13:   Integration and Summary

The second type of program to be discussed is that offered for the college undergraduate who might wish to follow a career in corrections. The first two years would be much the same as for any Bachelor of Arts program. The third and fourth years would involve a major in either sociology or psychology with special concentration in the analysis of deviant behavior and social control. Courses especially relevant are: General Sociological Theory; General Psychological Theory; Methods of the Behavioral Sciences; Theories of Deviance; Theories of Social Control; Criminology; Delinquency; Abnormal Psychology; Psychological Testing; Formal Organization. During the summers following the sophomore and junior years the student would intern in a correctional organization of one type or another. During the senior year the student would under close supervision carry out a small applied research project. This would require half of the student's time during one semester. Examples of suitable projects are these: a survey of the educational needs of the inmates of one institution. (Contrary to general belief this vital information is often not available.) Characteristics of successful and unsuccessful probationers or parolees as these might be later used to develop predictive instruments. A survey of the dockets of one or more criminal courts to ascertain the extent of undue delay in the hearing of cases.

College and university programs for students who plan to enter correctional work should include some practical experience. But they should also include courses in theory—that much misunderstood word that is so often erroneously interpreted to mean impractical, ivory-towered, and so on. As noted earlier, without adequate theory there can seldom be effective control or prevention. And programs should also include training in how to gather factual data in reasonably objective fashion. This is extremely difficult to do and it cannot be fully learned in a few courses. However, progress can be made. The student can at least learn to recognize the shortcomings of improperly conducted surveys. In general the aim is to provide the opportunity for the student to learn something about the nature of crime and its control and analysis in a systematic way. Even under the best of conditions he is unlikely ever to have that opportunity after he embarks upon a career.

3. THE ONE-YEAR PROFESSIONAL DEGREE

One especially promising training approach is the one-year professional degree. There is no fundamental reason whatsoever why professionals in the field of justice, corrections, and the like, cannot receive the major portion of their formal training in one year's time. To be sure a liberal college education takes much longer. But the concern here is with a professional education. In one year, a person can learn a great deal about the correctional and police professions. This can be supplemented later with on-the-job training. In this way experienced, properly educated men and women will flow steadily into the criminal justice field. Two-year associate degree programs exist at a growing number of institutions and in general are of much value. Here, however, we are concerned with a new, experimental one-year program.

The armed forces have had much success with intensive training programs. Among the best examples are the Air Force's flight training schools. In from seven months to a year men have been trained to be competent and in some degree experienced pilots and navigators. The first necessity in these programs has been a selection process that distinguishes those most likely to do well from others. Other necessities have been: an exceedingly well planned curriculum that involves actual "doing" as well as classroom learning; an able instructional staff; considerable but not excessive competition among students; and following-up with what amounts to further on-the-job training.

Drawing upon the Air Force experience, a one-year criminal justice academy can be instituted on a trial basis. Before the academy actually becomes operative, several years should be spent planning the curriculum and related matters such as the selection process. As to selection, it is necessary to determine the social background and personality characteristics of individuals who are now especially effective as probation, parole, prison, jail, and police officers. These men and women will not, however, have passed through intensive educational programs. Hence it will be necessary to select persons who in addition to having proved themselves effective have also the capacity to learn rapidly the types of material to be included in the curriculum.

During the first years of the operation of the academy, analysis should be made of the predictive accuracy of the selection process. Two types of trainees should pass through the curriculum: experimental groups composed of individuals chosen, by the best selection processes available, from among those who make application; and control groups made up of random samples of all who apply. (Care should be taken to publicize the academy and otherwise ensure that a wide range of persons apply.) Over the years following graduation, track should be kept of trainees' effectiveness and ineffectiveness in their jobs. This should be related to differences in the original selection process. Did the experimental group on balance prove to be significantly more effective than the control group? Which individuals in the experimental and control groups did well on the job and which poorly? How do those who did well differ in background and personality characteristics from the others? In the light of this data, how should the selection process be modified so that the proportion of effective graduates is steadily increased? And how should the curriculum be modified to provide still more suitable training?

Let us turn now to the initial development of the curriculum. The one-year program can be envisioned as composed of three segments. The first, an orientation phase, will span two months. Here, materials of general relevance to criminal justice will be learned. Stress will be placed upon familiarization with several subsystems that constitute the over-all criminal justice system: the criminal law, the courts, the police, probation and parole, jails and prisons. *Major emphasis will be given here to learning how to learn.* Trainees must learn how to retain accurately large amounts of written and spoken material. Trainees can practice efficient ways of learning in the course of studying the criminal justice subsystems just mentioned.

The second segment of the curriculum, the intermediate phase, will cover four months. This is essentially a continuation of the first phase: more detailed and complex materials about the various subsystems of criminal justice are learned. Some of the trainees' learning will occur on the spot, that is, wherever these subsystems actually operate: in the legislative halls; in the courts; in the police precincts; where probation and parole officers and violators meet; in the jails and prisons. The first segment is devoted largely to orientation and to getting the trainees in a position to learn well. The second segment involves intensive learning about the criminal justice system as a whole.

The third segment of the curriculum requires six months and is one of specialization. A trainee will pursue one of three curricula: One, correctional institutions; two, probation and parole; and three, police. (In certain academies, training for work in courts as clerks, and so on, can be added as a fourth specialty.) Intensive study into all major aspects of the professional worker's role in any one of these three specialties will be the focus. Much attention will be given to dove-tailing classroom work with "live" experience in the field. That experience must, however, be closely supervised by members of the academy's faculty.

Thus if a dozen trainees spend half of each day for two weeks working with the detective squad of a nearby police department, they will be directly under the supervision of an instructor who is a specialist in detection. It will be the instructor's responsibility to effect maximum coordination between classroom and field efforts; to facilitate communication between trainees and detectives; and to ensure that the time is spent in true experiential learning and not in standing around and waiting.

All instructors, classroom as well as field, must be chosen with great care. They must have a thorough knowledge of the area of specialization from both the textbook and "real life" standpoints. *They must be effective teachers.* Knowledge alone will not suffice. They must be able to stimulate and to motivate trainees as well as to transmit knowledge.

The year's course of study must be challenging. The trainees' minds must be stretched to the fullest degree consistent with not being overwhelmed. There must be considerable competition in the academy. This means that some trainees will fail the course and be dropped. Others will be recognized as outstanding students. The jobs they move to upon graduation will be determined in part by success in the program. Too many training programs in corrections and related fields have proceeded on the basis that all who are present are judged to be successful in approximately equal degree simply because they are present. This depresses learning and creates apathy.

When trainees complete the course and take on fulltime positions, there must be close follow-up activity for at least a year. The academy's field coordinators will work with the former trainees and their supervisors.

From time to time, perhaps monthly, trainees will be brought back to the academy for two-day workshops. These workshops and the efforts of the field coordinators will be designed to ensure two things: that what was learned in the academy is applied on the job; and that what is learned on the job is related to what was earlier learned in the classroom.

Individual rehabilitative programs to cover the first year of the three-year period will be worked out for each man. Broadly, two related forms of treatment will be used: weekly discussion sessions regarding the roots of violence and individual light counseling sessions. The discussion sessions will bring together the twelve men and a well-trained discussion leader. There will be some readings on the nature of violence; these will be non-technical and brief for most of the participants will have had little education. The discussion leader will seek to help the men to understand the problem of violence in general and of homicide in particular. They should grasp something of the social and personality forces that generate violence; the social controls that come into play in response to violence; and those forces that help effectively to counteract violence. While there are elements of group therapy here, the emphasis is on discussion in the sense indicated. The aim is to help the men gain a general understanding of the problem. Self-insight will come later.

Concurrently the men will meet individually twice a week with a therapist who is familiar with the discussion sessions. He will carry on light psychotherapy with each man, the focus being on how each can avoid future violence. Whatever problems of any type that the men face can be discussed. As the year proceeds the men will in these individual sessions and in the group sessions help to plan their rehabilitation program for the coming two years. It should be clear that where individual conditions require, the program for a given man will be altered. One offender may be psychotic and unable to enter into the above forms of treatment. He may need quite a different program, one that emphasizes individual psychotherapy in depth.

Again, speaking broadly, the second year will be devoted to group therapy sessions that build upon the previous year's discussions. Parallel to these will be individual psychotherapeutic sessions that are of somewhat greater depth than previously. The aim is to help the offender gain insight into his violent behavior, into its relationship to the cultural, social, and personality forces considered during the first year.

The third year will have a two-track program which issues from and builds upon the earlier years. Those offenders who are most emotionally disturbed will in the main follow track one although they will to some extent participate in track two. The others will follow track two. The first track involves highly personalized intensive psychotherapy three or five times a week. The second track utilizes role therapy; this requires explanation.[6] Role therapy consists of helping an individual to take on certain roles and eliminate others. It means creating opportunities for learning appropriate new roles and for putting them into action in everyday life. Mock role-playing sessions can be helpful at the outset. As the program continues, however, there must be opportunities to play the actual roles in the usual situations in which they are found.

Often the offender is not really able to play any occupational role. He can learn in the prison setting. Not only is it likely that he will be inexperienced in any line of work, but he may very well lack experience in how to go about getting a job and in related matters also. He can learn an occupation in prison and in role-playing sessions he can practice the ancillary skills. Later, he can go out into the wider community and work, returning to the prison for the night. The offender can try out or discard various other roles: recreational, religious, political. But he must have help both in deciding which to try or discard and in finding situations, mock or otherwise, in which to practice.

A major problem of the male homicidal offender very frequently is the inability to play the masculine role in regard to females and to tolerate frustration in so doing.[7] This of course creates an exceedingly difficult rehabilitative problem. The offender is likely to be ultra-sensitive about his lack of ability here—even after two years of more or less general discussion of various sources of violence. He does not want to admit that playing the male role is a problem for him. Moreover, he exists now in a one-sex institution, a condition which allows him to avoid coming to grips with this problem and thereby perpetuates it.

In the typical prison little can be done regarding the sex problem. However, through the use of female secretaries, volunteer women's auxiliary activities, female teachers, discussion groups that involve inmates and both males and females who are not inmates and who come in from the outside, and so on, a small amount of practice can be provided. When the offender leaves prison more opportunities obviously present themselves.

Transition from prison life to the larger society is the concern of a later section. However, the following should be noted at the present juncture: If the offender is rehabilitated years before his legal time for release, the only recourse frequently open is to seek a commutation of sentence by governor and council or whatever body considers commutations. If he remains in prison, he is likely to regress.

3. TREATING CHILDREN WHO STEAL

We turn briefly now to the second illustration of rehabilitative programs. Assume that approximately twenty boys aged twelve to fourteen years have been incarcerated for repeated thefts. Some readers not directly involved in criminal justice may think it highly unlikely that children of so young an age will have engaged in

serious theft—theft beyond the petty pilfering stage—
and have been incarcerated. Actually there are considerable numbers of young adolescents (and even children aged eight or ten years) who carry on in gangs or as
individuals theft on a persistent and significant scale.
Moreover, there are occasionally young people involved
in adult professional theft rings. Here they perform a
variety of tasks: acting as look-outs, as messengers,
entering the theft sites through small spaces, e.g., tran-
soms, where adults cannot go.

In any case, all but the smaller states will have more
than a few young people, mainly boys, so incarcerated.
We will assume that twenty boys are incarcerated in a
juvenile institution and are thus available in one place
for rehabilitative treatment. As with adults, only more
so, a great need is to counteract the negative effects of incarceration. Labeling of the boys as delinquents, as
thieves, is to be counteracted. So is the usual possibility
that close interaction among offenders will serve to increase and harden patterns of law violation. One can say
of these boys, "as with adults, only more so" because
the young, developing rapidly, probably are more sus-
ceptible to the effects of labeling and of acculturation to
that body of behavioral patterns that constitute the
criminal subculture.

What does one want to achieve here? One wants to
label positively rather than negatively. One wants to
have the boys share their problems in order that each
may come to a greater understanding of himself and his
behavior. Yet one wants to avoid having the boys learn
criminal behavior patterns from each other. One wants
the boys to avoid delinquent and criminal acts.

Let us say the program will extend over a six-month
period. The young are seldom in a correctional institution for years and so treatment must be concentrated. As
with the adult men just previously discussed it will be

best to have each boy involved in both group and individual rehabilitative programs of a closely related nature. Weekly discussion sessions will be held over the six months. Three groups of six or seven boys each will be optimal. The young, even more than adults, need small group situations if they are to proceed effectively in discussions. The discussion leader must be highly skilled with the young. He must help them to label themselves as good bets for a special program. He must help them to understand what are the underlying causes of theft. He must help them to find new legal ways of achieving what they want.

In the individual therapeutic sessions there will be discussion of what the boys cannot bring themselves to talk about in the group sessions. Individual and group forms of treatment must reinforce each other. Between the two the boys must come to see that they are not freaks, that they need not perpetually be outsiders to the society. They must discover ways of achieving legitimate goals and have opportunities for trying out these ways in the correctional setting. Role-playing will be one useful approach. The taking on of actual new roles in the institution will be another.

Group discussions, individual psychotherapy, and role therapy will go far toward neutralizing the criminal and delinquent subculture, toward ensuring that the boys' patterns of law violation are not spread among them and reinforced. Most essentially, through these approaches the boys must come to see that legitimate behavior is more rewarding than illegitimate behavior.

Practically everyone wants a place in the sun, wants "to be somebody," to be well thought of. One condition especially and quite naturally favors the choosing of rewards from the legitimate system: that is where most of the people having the greatest social approval to dispense are to be found. But there must also be *opportuni-*

ties for success in legitimate areas. And the individual must have the ability to make use of those opportunities. In the final analysis, successful rehabilitation of offenders, young or older, is largely a matter of education. As we have said, through discussions, dialogue with a therapist, and so on, the person must be able to learn how he can achieve more in the legitimate than in the illegitimate world. And relatedly he must have available sustained situations for trying out, learning in practice, those "hows." When he finds that he can achieve more prestige through lawful than unlawful means, then he will become lawful. Even in cases of psychotic violators this will be so. It is only that here the requisite learning may well be more difficult.

The problem with correctional institutions presently is that they simply do not at all accomplish this. They do the opposite. They provide prestige for being especially adept at crime. In the main they provide neither opportunity nor approbation for legitimate success. Thus we turn to consideration of how a correctional institution might be so designed that these conditions are reversed.

19. THE CORRECTIONAL LEARNING CENTER: I

1. GENERAL CHARACTERISTICS

The President's Commission of Law Enforcement and Administration of Justice wisely and forcefully stressed the need for greater integration of correctional services into the community structure.[1] To be effective, those services must be parts of the community rather than isolated from it. This provides some degree of normality as a setting for rehabilitation. It facilitates movement of offenders into the wider society. Conversely, it facilitates movement of nonoffenders, citizens from various walks of life, into correctional institutions and organizations.

There is at the outset the complex problem of whether to attempt to merge local jails, whose inmates now are largely misdemeanants, with state prisons where felons are incarcerated. Ideally, these would be merged. Seldom would a misdemeanant actually be incarcerated. In most of the less serious violations probation would serve well. The occasional misdemeanant who cannot safely be placed on probation could be sent to the same institution as felons who are not on probation. However, as discussed earlier, there is at present much reluctance in many parts of the country to allow the jails to go out of business.[2] Vested interests support these county and municipal institutions. In many instances the local correctional institution is a part of the domain of the sheriff or chief of police. These institutions provide an array of quasi-political jobs. The jail may be a source of considerable financial gain. In some jurisdictions the jail-keep (sheriff or police chief) receives a certain sum of money per day per person incarcerated to administer his institution. Controls on him may be minimal. Thus he is in a position to pocket the funds not spent. And the larger the population of the jail, the more funds to be pocketed.

The heart of the rehabilitation effort should be the community-based, integrated learning center. This center would in certain respects embrace probation, imprisonment, and parole. In large metropolitan areas it might be situated directly in the urban core. In other instances it would be located between the urban center and the surrounding suburbs. For purposes of illustration, assume that the learning center is located in a small city. A former estate on the outskirts might be purchased. The manor house would serve as the central administration building. The carriage houses and the like would be used to house motor vehicles, and so on. Dormitories, eating facilities, classroom buildings, and other necessary structures would be constructed. These need not be stone monuments like most prison buildings of the past. Wooden structures will suffice.

The maximum security learning center will have an electric fence around the perimeter of the grounds intended to prohibit escape. In purely practical terms, it makes little difference whether or not there are walls, fences, guardtowers. A very small percentage of inmates escape regardless of security precautions. In the learning center described here, one would expect the proportion of escapees to be lower because of improved programs. However, it will be some decades before the public in the United States accepts the idea of minimum security for those who have committed serious felonies. Therefore it will be necessary to have some tangible form of security: a wall of electric fence.

The electric fence will be preferable for it is less obtrusive than the traditional prison wall. Those incarcerated will of course know it is there. And yet they will not daily be faced with a wall that literally and symbolically separates them from the larger society. Given the public demand for rigid security provisions, the electric fence will be in keeping with the tone of the learning center: Within the limits that the society allows, there will be as constructive a posture toward the offender and toward his rehabilitation as possible.

Ideally the institution would house two or three hundred offenders. Programs could then be run without undue impersonality. However, the per capita cost would be quite high. To reduce cost it may be necessary to have a population as large as five hundred. Many overhead expenditures are fixed and amount to little more for five hundred than for two hundred. Some impersonality may have to be accepted in the interests of economy.

There is the extremely vexing problem of how to provide security personnel, that is, guards, without causing undue damage to the ongoing life of the institution. While it is changing slightly, the prison guard subculture is predominantly antirehabilitation in its orientation. It embraces an extraordinarily conservative value system that cherishes the status quo, the conventional wisdom, "the way things have always been done," at all costs. If significant remnants of this subculture are imported into a learning center of the type being described and advocated here, much harm can be done.

One of the great advantages to the development of learning centers is that they are new institutions, unfettered by the encrusted beliefs of traditional prison life. Under the best of circumstances the early years of a learning center will be trying ones for staff and offenders alike: there will be much ambiguity as to how things are to be done, as to what are the contents of the various roles involved. There will be excitement in such a venture, to be sure, but there will also be much uncertainty. To introduce elements of the old guard subculture into such a situation is to invite serious trouble. For some of the more uncertain and anxious staff and offenders will grasp the values and customs of that subculture as reference points. They will pit themselves against other offenders and others of the staff who maintain a more innovative posture.

But how to resolve the problem? It will be possible to choose a dozen or so men with guard experience who are not imbued with the guard subculture. Careful selection will turn up a core group of experienced men who do not share the conventional wisdom of the traditional prison. In addition to these there must be recruited young men with no guard experience. These should be individuals with some bent for innovation who hope to make a career in corrections and who will find the guard position a valuable stepping-stone. They will receive adequate training prior to the opening of the institution. All of the guard personnel, experienced and inexperienced, will to some degree be a part of the over-all rehabilitation effort. How they take part will be explained at later points in the discussion.

The names, the labels, placed upon institutions and participants in them bear of course, sometimes quite significantly, on the everyday accomplishments of those institutions and individuals.[3] The phrase "learning center" is a good one. What are offenders to be called? It will not do to use the words such as offender, inmate, and the like which have the old connotations of individuals to be punished. And it will not do to call adult offenders students for this rings falsely as a forced euphemism. Trainee may be suitable. In any case if the institution is to be effective, there must be mutual respect between staff and offenders. If there is respect, it will be reflected in verbal usage. Mature men incarcerated in the learning center should not be routinely referred to by their first names or nicknames. Generally Mr. (or Mrs. or Miss) will be suitable. But there should be latitude for whatever natural forms of salutation develop among various members of the learning center.

2. PROFESSIONAL STAFF

A board of trustees will oversee the workings of the center much as such a board now has over-all responsibility for one or more prisons. The learning center may be a state institution or it may be a part of a local governmental structure. In any case, most members of the board would be appointed by appropriate elected officials: governors, county commissioners, or mayors. It would be well if a plan were developed whereby trainees and staff of the center played a part in the selection of at least several of the board members. While the board would have something of a political complexion, one of its major functions would be to provide a buffer between the institution and politics as usual. Prison boards of trustees now perform this function reasonably well. For the most part members are men and women of accomplishment who do their job with little direct attempt at political machination. There is every reason to believe this tradition can be maintained and even made more apolitical.

The full-time staff internal to the center would be headed by an executive committee of five highly trained professionals. These would be a clinical psychologist, a social psychologist, a psychiatrist, a sociologist, and a cultural anthropologist. Some although not necessarily all of the five should have had experience in correctional institutions. They should not have become imbued with the outmoded elements of the traditional prison subculture.[4] At the same time the possession of some experience in corrections by several of the senior staff members is crucial. Many of the trainees will have served prison sentences and will bring with them segments of the inmate subculture. The staff must have a first-hand understanding of that subculture. In the new institution, it is crucial that the effects of the usual inmate subculture be neutralized and that customs and values compatible with rehabilitation develop in place of that subculture.

One of the five senior staff members will serve as director of the learning center. The director will be selected by the Board of Trustees and will have direct responsibility for the day-to-day operation of the institution. He and the other four senior staff will form the executive committee. The director will take the advice of that committee explicitly into consideration in making decisions. Generally it is unwise for one individual to serve for a long period as director of a correctional institution. He tends gradually to become excessively defensive because of the pressures of the position and to cling tenaciously to ways that worked in the earlier years of his administration and are unsuitable now. The director should serve a three- or four-year term with the possibility of renewal for a second term. He should not serve more than two consecutive terms.

Several psychologists, ten to fifteen social workers and a similar number of elementary and high school teachers would comprise most of the remaining professional staff. There would also be directors of kitchen and laundry facilities and of various work programs within the center. Probation and parole personnel would serve in roles directly related to the center but might be considered as members of different organizational units. The functions of probation and parole officers will be discussed in the next chapter.

The learning center is treatment oriented and research oriented. While the central thrust is toward rehabilitation there will be a decided attempt to encourage research by all staff members. In some instances this will be related directly to treatment programs and will be designed to enhance them. In other instances, only a very indirect relation will obtain. For example, a high school teacher of history might be encouraged to carry on historical research although it bears no direct relation to the rehabilitation of offenders. The central point is that a spirit of inquiry will pervade the learning center. The director and the four other senior staff members will conduct original research. So will the social workers and teachers. Where feasible, employees will do so as well. Trainees will be encouraged to take part in these inquiries. In some cases trainees might serve as subjects for research. Care must be taken, however, to ensure that trainees are not put in a position where they take on the central role of "subject."

This spirit of inquiry will provide an innovative environment for the rehabilitation of offenders. It will keep the staff intellectually alive. Rather than, say, a teacher teaching his subjects routinely day in and day out, he will attempt to create knowledge as well as to convey it. About one-quarter of the staff's time will be devoted to research. This will be a great asset in attracting innovative people to the center. It will discourage those with opposite tendencies.

Graduate students will play a significant part in the operation of the institution. Students pursuing graduate study in the behavioral sciences at nearby universities will intern at the center. (It may be possible to provide internships for advanced undergraduates as well.) At any given time perhaps a dozen graduate students will serve as part-time workers at the center. For example, an advanced student in clinical psychology might under guidance of a staff psychologist carry out testing of trainees and some limited counseling. This he would do half-time. The other half of his time would be spent on the research and writing of his dissertation. He would receive the usual graduate stipend.

Not only will graduate students be trained. In a very real sense all staff as well as all offenders will be continuously in training. The atmosphere will be one where the staff members are always learning. And it will be one where regular evaluation of staff as well as of trainees is considered a necessary and constructive part of effective activity.

20. THE CORRECTIONAL LEARNING CENTER: II

1. OPERATION

Trainees will live in dormitories housing about fifty each. While there will be adequate facilities for unduly obstreperous trainees, most will live two to a room in these simple houses with no locks or bars. Each dormitory will have a head resident, a trained counselor who is responsible for the conduct of the dormitory. Resident counselors will take part in the treatment program and will constitute important elements of the institutional staff.

Trainees will follow a split-shift schedule. Treatment, including rehabilitation, will occur over the morning hours for some; in the afternoon they will work. For others the opposite schedule will obtain. It has been usual in United States prisons to set inmates to work at whatever needs to be done. At the learning center, trainee and job will be matched for maximum effectiveness in the rehabilitation of the trainee. Given that, ordinary forms of work in a place of incarceration can be highly useful. In most western societies, certainly ours, individuals need to work. They are more or less used to it and most tend to stagnate without it. Moreover, most trainees will be individuals who have held or will hold skilled, semiskilled, or unskilled positions.

Some members of the society feel that offenders have little to offer the work force. Others go to the opposite extreme and somehow believe that great occupational advances should accrue to incarcerated individuals. (Not everyone who seriously violates the law is going to be "rehabilitated" such that in the process he becomes an atomic physicist or a surgeon.) There is nothing whatsoever wrong with some individuals performing as janitors. There is not necessarily anything wrong with instances where individuals chip paint all day. Some like to chip paint. Some do excellent jobs as janitors and are not suited to operating complex machines. Others will need jobs both in and out of the institution that require considerable intellectual ability. The main point is that the job should fit the individual rather than vice versa. Given that, there will be many trainees suited to fill the regular housekeeping jobs of the institution.

The system of financial responsibility required of trainees is highly important. Presently most prison inmates have no financial obligation to their families, to the victims of their offenses, or to the state. They are paid some very small sum for their work, often 25 cents a day. Out of this they are to buy such items as toothpaste, razor blades, and so on, and if they smoke, tobacco. In most institutions, all inmates earn the same small wage; there are no promotions and no wage increases.

In the training center advocated here trainees would be paid an amount approaching a normal wage. The least skilled jobs might have a wage of fifty dollars a week. Trainees could work their way up to a maximum of perhaps one hundred dollars a week for highly skilled or supervisory jobs. An explicit promotion system would be used. Various charges would be deducted from the trainee's salary. Twenty-five dollars a week might be deducted for his room and board. In appropriate instances he would be required to indemnify those who suffered because of his offense.[1] He would be required to help support his family. We live in a society that is highly conscious of money. It is only sensible to align the institutional system with the system in the larger society to the extent possible. Moreover, the trainee will gain some sense of self-respect by earning a realistic salary and paying his way. This he cannot do on a wage of twenty-five cents a day.

Trainees will in certain respects operate in two-person teams. Two men will hold the job of, say, pastry cook in the kitchen. One will work in the morning, one in the afternoon. The first will have his afternoons devoted to treatment, the second his mornings. As trainees gradually leave the institution and merge with the wider community this split-shift arrangement will continue for a time. More on that later.

It will be noted that treatment, except in the highly informal and indirect sense, will not occur in the evenings. Treatment should take place during part of the regular work-day, not following that, when people grow tired. Too often at present whatever little treatment does occur in prisons is pushed into a secondary place in the evening hours. Evenings should be largely free for individual pursuits such as watching television, reading, hobbies, and so on, and for such group activities as dramatic clubs, team sports, etc. Certainly some of these have therapeutic value but, as will now be discussed in some detail, treatment per se will usually occur during the morning or afternoon.

A wide range of treatment programs will be instituted at the learning center. There will be individual psychotherapy in depth, psychotherapy in less depth, and light counseling in various forms. There will be group therapy. There will be psychodrama and role-playing sessions. There will be a variety of types of discussion groups. For example, there will be the series of discussion sessions among offenders and nonoffenders mentioned in an earlier chapter. Under guidance four or five trainees and an equal number of other citizens from the surrounding community will meet in the institution once a week for twelve weeks. Their aims will be to explicate the forces that led the offenders to commit crimes; to discuss what can be done regarding their rehabilitation; to educate both offenders and nonoffenders as to the nature of the crime problem. For probationers and parolees such groups will be carried on outside the institution.

Members of the wider community will be encouraged to go to the institution for a variety of reasons: adult education classes, amateur dramatic groups, chess, bridge, and so on. Women can form a learning center auxiliary and help trainees with a range of everyday problems. Specialists in different activities will lecture on their specialties. For example, a man who runs an employment service might talk about how to get a job. A man who owns a nearby manufacturing company and who welcomes trainees as workers could discuss opportunities in his company. The local congressman would talk about governmental problems. Apart from lectures, a former semiprofessional baseball player might be "drafted" as unpaid coach for the institution's baseball team. A singer would give voice lessons. All of this will serve to provide the institution with some degree of normalcy. It will serve also to prepare the trainee for his emergence into the general society.

Overnight visiting facilities for trainee's families will be important. A man's wife and children will be able to spend certain weekends with him in a cottage located within the institution yet removed from the mainstream of activity. The staff will need to determine at what stages in the trainee's progress such meetings among family members will be beneficial for all. These visits too will help to provide a sense of normality. In some cases they will serve to keep families intact, families that might otherwise become permanently fragmented because of the husband's incarceration.

The educational program will provide the core courses of the elementary and high school curriculum. If there are a dozen or so full-time teachers, others can be recruited for a course here and there to round out the curriculum. The aim is to provide trainees with as much education, up to the high school diploma, as time allows. Twenty percent of those who presently enter prison are functionally illiterate: they cannot read or write an average paragraph.[2] Few have a high school education. Much can be done in the learning center to remedy these deficiencies. Trainees with considerable education will often be given jobs in the institution as teacher's assistants or as instructors per se.

A word about the manner in which new trainees are to be integrated into the institution: directly upon arrival, the trainee would be interviewed by one of the five members of the executive committee. Rather than being held in isolation during his first weeks of incarceration as is now customary in our prisons, the trainee would on his first or second day be placed in the ongoing life of the learning center. On the basis of the initial interview, the senior staff member would make the following tentative decisions: Choice of an experienced trainee who would serve as a guide for the new trainee during the first weeks of incarceration. Obviously many factors of compatibility would have to be taken into account. Assign temporary living quarters. Select a temporary job for the new trainee. Devise a limited, highly temporary treatment program. This might involve, for this initial period, daily discussion with a counselor and enrollment in certain obviously needed educational courses.

During the first weeks of incarceration the initial steps of the classification process will be carried out properly, not in the haphazard fashion now usual in most prisons. Careful diagnosis of the new trainee and the development of an optimal plan for treatment are the major processes. The plan for treatment and the work assignment will then be implemented. A more permanent assignment to one of the living units will be made. From time to time the trainee's progress will be carefully evaluated. Changes in the individual's over-all program will be effected as needed.

There will be regular meetings of all members of the learning center, trainees and staff alike. These will be sessions to review progress of the center and to discuss problems. Members will break up into discussion groups. In a given group will be a number of trainees, a number of professional staff, one or more of the staff who oversee work programs, several guards, and one or several graduate student interns. The focus of the discussions will be on developing ideas for the increased effectiveness of the institution. These ideas will be considered for implementation by the senior staff. Genuine attempts will be made to make constructive use of the ideas so generated.

2. LEAVING THE CENTER

The discussion turns now to the steps by which a trainee who shows marked rehabilitation progress will be gradually integrated into the surrounding community. Assume that two trainees have been working on a split shift (each one-half day) as janitors in the learning center. They are now ready to participate on a limited basis in life outside the institution. A social worker will arrange that the two men take on a job as janitor in a nearby business concern. One will work there in the morning, the other in the afternoon. Each will spend the rest of his time at the learning center and will continue his half-day treatment there. The social worker will from time to time discuss with the trainee problems of adjustment to the larger society.

When the men are ready for the next step they will move their living quarters from the institution to a de-

tached learning center. The two will not of course necessarily take this step simultaneously. The detached learning center will be similar to what is often termed a half-
way house. It will be a house out in the wider community
where a dozen or more trainees live under the guidance of
a social worker who serves as director. The name half-
way house is unfortunate. It connotes what may be a
fact: that residents are half-way between the institution
and the general society. But individuals do not like to be
labeled half-way. Hence the term "detached learning center" or some other suitable phrasing.

During their first months at the detached center the
men will continue with their half-time positions as janitor. They will return to the main learning center for treatment each morning or afternoon. They will have the evening meal and sleep at the detached center. Eventually a
given trainee will no longer return to the main center. He
will at this point take on a full-time janitorial position.
He will continue to live at the detached center. Appropriate treatment, often group therapy, will be carried on
there.

At still a later stage the trainee will move from the center to living quarters of his own. He may live by himself
or he may live with his wife or with his parents. He will
continue with his job and return to the detached center or
to the main center occasionally for whatever treatment
is required. He is now on parole. He will be under the direct guidance of a parole officer who will cooperate closely with the social worker under whose guidance he was
previously. If he is to live with his family and they are
not nearby and cannot readily move, then he may be
transferred to the parole district where they reside and
given help in obtaining a position there.

The department of parole, and of probation as well,
will be closely tied to the major learning center. Parole officers and learning center personnel will have a clear
idea of what each other do. In some few instances the

same person may play both roles. For example, the social worker who arranges for the trainee's first position outside the institution may be a parole officer. Whether the department of parole will be a subunit of the learning center remains to be seen. Probably it will be best if it is. In this way the possibility of two organizational structures at odds with each other, with the trainee the loser, will be minimized.

Whatever the organizational structure, it will be necessary to have a parole board that determines when the individual is to be released. This can take several forms. Presently parole boards are largely composed of part- or full-time persons, paid or unpaid, who have little knowledge of the crime problem and of the field of corrections. Ideally the five-man board of directors of the learning center would serve as the parole board. It may be, however, that efforts to change the law so that this is possible do not succeed. In that event it will be extremely important to see that those appointed to parole boards in the future have at least a rudimentary working knowledge of the problems with which they deal.

The probation situation is somewhat different. Probationers may or may not have been imprisoned at some earlier time. In any case, as probationers they have been assigned by the courts to live directly in the general community rather than at the center. And it is of obvious importance to avoid the implication that they will later "end up" as trainees at the center.

At the same time, a close working relationship between the department of probation and learning center is essential. To the extent possible the center should not be thought of as something "bad" for the offender and probation "good." Weekly group therapy sessions carried on outside the center will be one major form of treatment for probationers. Nevertheless, it may be that in some cases probationers will come to the center for treatment services more complex than probation officers can provide. The main point is to create an atmosphere where the learning center is seen as a basic constructive rehabilitative resource for a variety of offenders, whether or not they are incarcerated.

In the larger states it will be well to design learning center complexes that involve several major units: a center for adult male trainees and one for adult female trainees; a center for juvenile males and a center for juvenile females. All four will be located adjacent to each other. Attached will be probation and parole services for adults and, separately, for juveniles. Also related to this complex although physically removed will be a series of appropriate detached learning centers, some for adults, some for juveniles without parents or from excessively disorganized homes. Central diagnostic services and certain treatment facilities can serve all segments of the complex.

Will it be necessary to have special institutions for those trainees who do not respond to treatment? Special institutions may not be necessary. The rehabilitative spirit of the learning center should overcome a number of obstacles to effective treatment. The center is likely to help trainees with especially severe and prolonged problems more than they are likely to endanger the work of the center. No one is beyond the possibility of rehabilitation. Moreover, much can be learned from treatment efforts that fail. And renewed efforts can be made: one can try again.

3. SPECIAL TYPES OF OFFENDERS

The learning center will be most effective in the rehabilitation of those who have violated the major categories of criminal law, those that apply to violence against the person and to theft. In these offenses there are victims involved. Special attention must be given to the possibility of rehabilitative facilities for persons who carry out victimless offenses, for offenders who are members of organized crime groups, and for those who engage in mass disorders.

There is in fact some question as to whether the first and last of these types of offenders require rehabilitation. In the case of victimless crimes, is it largely the laws that need to be changed? In instances of mass disorders, is there such a broad political dimension to the technically offending behavior that one faces the problem of rehabilitation becoming enforced political indoctrination or reindoctrination?

Granted that some change in the laws will be necessary in regard to victimless crimes, there will in all likelihood remain drug, prostitution, and homosexual offenses that the society considers seriously criminal. These are especially likely to involve the "pushing" of harmful drugs, the possession of hard drugs such as heroin, public solicitation of customers for prostitution, and homosexuality between adults and minors. Of further concern is the operation of organized crime in relation to certain of these offenses.[3]

The suggestion here is not that these offenders be lumped togehter in some removed rehabilitation institution and treated alike. Rather, the necessity is to make clear that problems of treatment for them are likely to vary significantly from those of offenders who have engaged in violence and theft. Specialized treatment units, perhaps attached to the learning centers described earlier, are indicated. While some offenders should and will be placed on probation, there will be needed a residential treatment facility for compulsive drug-users, one for those who repeatedly engage in prostitution and come to the attention of the police, and one for adult males who have been convicted of homosexuality with minors.

Those females who engage in prostitution tend to have an aversion to close relationships with men. Moreover, they have been labeled prostitutes and are likely to have internalized an identity as such. Treatment here should involve a reversal of that labeling process and the availability of viable opportunities to establish "normal" relationships with males.

As noted earlier, adult males who carry on homosexual relationships are highly likely to feel extremely insecure in close relationships with women of about their own age. While psychotherapy may in some instances be useful, generally speaking it has in regard to homosexuality met with a most limited success.

One possibility is to have those who are chronic prostitution and homosexuality offenders join in common rehabilitation programs. They would obviously live in separate quarters but come together daily for treatment sessions. Each group has in common an aversion to the other sex. Each needs above all opportunities to develop relationships with those of the other sex. These opportunities are under ordinary conditions very difficult to come by. For one labeled as a prostitute or homosexual to initiate the development of a "normal" relationship with a person of the other sex is almost prohibited by the anxiety he or she experiences in the process. The treatment center unit can provide this opportunity and help trainees to bridge the crucial initial problem of anxiety blockage.

The usefulness of this proposed form of treatment can only be ascertained by actual implementation on a pilot program basis. Whether it is workable remains to be seen. If it is in a general sense viable, then specifics of the process must be worked out in what is in the best sense of the word an experimental program. Certainly, putting together for mutual treatment individuals of quite different characteristics who in a broad way share common problems has in some instances shown marked positive results. So it may be here.

The two most crucial problems in the rehabilitation of those addicted to harmful drugs are these: To aid the individual in effecting withdrawal from the drug; and to ensure that he does not return to the drug subculture. It is the second that is exceedingly difficult. During the recent times of his life, most of the individual's group support has come from members of the drug subculture. If he returns there, it will be all but impossible for him to avoid the harmful use of drugs.

At the beginning of treatment of addicted persons, a modified version of the Synanon plan will be optimal. Those attempting to break the addictive pattern will live together in a house and under the guidance of professionals talk out their problems. There can be some aggressive interchanges, some confrontation situations, but these should be kept at a somewhat lower pitch than is usual at Synanon. In attempting to escape the low tension conditions of drug usage, Synanon members engage in a reaction-formation: They create through amateur "reality therapy" high tension. In a word they overdo it. A modified Synanon approach will mean that reciprocity is *decreased* and tension *raised* without going so far as to induce abortive high tension.

The next necessity is to have the individual move out of this Synanon-like house and into nondrug-using walks of everyday life. These must be environments that are sufficiently rewarding to overcome the pull of the drug subculture. This is exceedingly difficult to accomplish; the former addict is not especially likely to receive a warm reception in other circles. The solution lies in getting former addicts caught up, highly involved, in relatively complex social situations of a quite different sort than those of the drug subculture. For example, it would be approaching the ideal to enlist former addicts in coping with disaster problems: the human consequences of floods, earthquakes, tornadoes, forest fires. Drugs will then become for the most part irrelevant. There are clear tasks and goals at hand. The needs of the moment for the disaster victims become the focal point of all activity. The former addict, is, so to speak, taken outside himself. The drawback here, of course, is that one cannot perpetually deal with disaster.

Two rather unrelated types of offenders are now considered: those who engage in organized crime and those who take part in mass disorders. The major common thread between the two is the fact that for reasons to be discussed both are rather unsusceptible to rehabilitation. Regarding organized crime it will be well to allocate most resources to prevention before the fact. It will be necessary, that is, to realign to some degree the social system such that organized crime does not flourish. With respect to all forms of crime this is in general a wise priority. But it is particularly apt regarding organized crime. Once individuals become functioning parts of organized crime systems it is enormously difficult to effect rehabilitation. They have taken on full-scale a rewarding way of life. That way of life has many built-in protections against their apprehension and rehabilitation. Still there will be in the foreseeable future some who engage in organized crime and who are convicted. What to do with them.?

Organized crime offenders can be divided into two broad groups: lesser workers in the system and those of greater power and prestige. The lesser workers will generally be more amenable to rehabilitation than the others. As with confidence men and other violators who make crime a way of life, the greatest success in rehabilitation is likely to come from helping them to take on occupational roles not highly dissimilar from their previous criminal roles. The need is for substitute roles that are technically legitimate yet functionally somewhat similar to the previous roles. There has been at least some small tendency for former offenders—men who have been on the fringes of organized crime—to move into the light construction field. They begin with odd-job painting and so on, move on to the installation of restaurant equipment, the renovation of small business establishments, etc. They are free to charge whatever the traffic will bear. Some have made a practice of overcharging by two or three times the normal price. They deal only with those customers who are sufficiently uninformed about current costs that they agree to have the job done for the high price. Certainly the ethics of encouraging former offenders to engage in these practices are altogether open to question. This is a matter that rehabilitative agencies and the society in general must resolve.

As we have said, members of organized crime groups who possess considerable power and prestige are highly unlikely candidates for rehabilitation. The very fact that organized crime exists on a wide scale makes this a foregone conclusion. It means that individuals are able to gain power and prestige that they otherwise would have great difficulty obtaining. One can hardly think it probable that the deputy boss of an organized crime operation in a medium-sized city will throw over his way of life to become the owner of a small painting firm. On the other hand, the society is not prepared to make arrangements to provide him with a legitimate occupation of high standing. The society is not willing because of his previous experience. Illegitimate occupational success precludes legitimate success.

We have no adequate plan for the potentially successful treatment of powerful members of organized crime. In any case they are seldom convicted precisely because they are powerful. With perhaps a very occasional individual exception there will be no solution until we bring into being programs for early prevention, prevention before the fact, of organized crime.

Turning to riotous offenders, again there is not a great deal that can be done to "rehabilitate" them if indeed rehabilitation is needed or relevant. As with organized crime, resources must go largely into prevention before the fact. Assume that a riot has occurred in a black ghetto area. A number of young male residents have been arrested for arson, looting, and a few instances assault. They do not have serious records of previous violations of the law. However, they are convicted and incarcerated. They become trainees in the type of learning center earlier described. What now is to be done? There is really no question of rehabilitation. If conditions for blacks are sufficiently improved, then there will after a period of readjustment be no need to riot, no forces to generate rioting. If conditions for blacks are not significantly improved and they return to the ghetto, then they may very well take part in a riot once again. One way to obviate the future participation of blacks in riots is to co-opt them into the white power structure. This may be unacceptable to some individuals and acceptable to others. In any case it will in good measure result in cutting the more action-oriented blacks off from the rest of their people.

The general problem is in a sense somewhat true of all rehabilitation work. If the forces that generate crime were largely eliminated, then the need for rehabilitation would be minimal. Yet there is a certain significant difference between the riotous offender and, for example, the usual homicidal offender. Regardless of the social forces actually at work to produce both rioting and homicide, the rioter and the homicidal offender tend to see their situations differently and others also see those situations as different. The rioter's behavior tends to be perceived either as an outgrowth of repression of a group, racial or otherwise, or as willful, conspiratorial revolutionary activity. The homicidal act is likely to be seen as more directly a consequence of a constellation of idiosyncratic circumstances; family background, marital strife, personality disorder. How these matters are perceived by offenders and by the general public influence significantly whether rehabilitation can be effective.

In this and the preceding three chapters on corrections, the urgent neeeds for restructuring the roles and organizational forms of the several components of the correctional process have been discussed. The role of the rehabilitationist must be introduced and the role of the "keeper" and the punisher eliminated. Corrections must come to stand for learning the culture rather than learning the criminal subculture. Prisons must be transformed from institutions that negatively label individuals and that further the latent functions of crime. They must become places of positive labeling that provide resocialization into society.

21. A CONCLUDING WORD

1. RECAPITULATION

Implicit in much of the foregoing is the need to reverse the society's approach to crime. The need is to reduce crime by eliminating its sources rather than to increase crime by attacking symptoms, ignoring the fundamental roots of crime and in fact exacerbating the problem. The need is to eliminate rather than to propagate crime. This is a vast demand and it cannot be met overnight. Nor should it. The resultant changes would be so great, so abrupt, that much greater harm would result than that which presently arises from crime.

Through changes in roles and institutional structures, through new organizational forms, through changes in child-rearing and other critical cultural patterns, through public education, substantial progress toward the ends just described can gradually be made.

Meanwhile it is also of the highest priority to treat those who are offenders in such a way that their offenses are not perpetuated and that other offenders are not in the process created. Certainly the police and the courts should be so organized that serious offenders are either incarcerated or supervised outside of institutions and provided with help. At the same time the formal control process should in certain respects be kept to a minimum and punishment avoided. To elaborate: Beginning with apprehension by police, apprehension should be only for what is clearly regarded as socially disruptive crime. The criminal law must be changed so that in the main only murder, manslaughter, assault, kidnapping, arson, forcible rape, and the various forms of theft are crimes. Most victimless crime and other criminal offenses should be construed either as civil offenses or not as offenses at all.

In the courts justice must be rapid, limited and—just. By "limited" we mean that only those cases where the evidence is ample should be tried in criminal courts. By "just" we mean that there should be very few miscarriages of justice. We mean also that the disposition of the case as ordered by the court should be directed toward reducing the likelihood of future offenses, nothing more and nothing less. This means placing offenders on probation whenever feasible rather than in prisons and reformatories where further crime will be learned. True justice also means rehabilitation and not undue frustration when incarceration is necessary. It indicates release on parole as soon as reasonable and continued rehabilitation while paroled.

The ugliness must be removed from the prisons. And there is much of it there: Consciously induced psychological and physical frustration must be replaced by genuine help for the offender. We have for the most part moved away from the practice of killing those who commit serious crimes. This may seem but the first small step on a long journey to reason about crime. And it is. But it is a highly significant step.

Once witches were created by society and held to be responsible for their "witchcraft."[1] Presently the mentally ill, the alcoholic, the drug-addicted are created by society and thought to be in part or in whole responsible for their plight. Those who violate the criminal law are created by the society and are held to be totally responsible for their crimes. Slowly we will come to realize that we engender crime to achieve other ends and that we victimize those made criminal in the process.

2. THE FUTURE

Not only are we an unpreventive people. One of our great drawbacks as a society is a lack of concern for the future. We distrust and abhor planning for the future. Certainly we give lip-service to planning. Even then, our interest is in short-range planning, so short-range that it seems more apropos of the present than of the future. Prevention requires careful planning and it requires long-range planning. Prevention and planning share a common orientation: the future. And despite great technological advances, we are not a future-oriented society.[2]

Those who look to the future, who speculate about life and life problems of the future are sternly disparaged. Those who discuss what life is likely to be like in 2075 or in 2500 A.D. are thought to be less responsible than those who contemplate the here and now. They are looked upon as somewhat akin to the fortune-teller who fleeces his client of a few dollars; they tend to merge with the image of the crackpot. Hence responsible men of science and government avoid public consideration of the future. There may be talk of "a generation of peace," of "a world with freedom from want," but that, the rhetoric, is about as far as the action goes.

The reason for avoidance of concern with the future is clear. We are fearful of it. We feel we are rushing into the future with ever-increasing speed. The rate of change seems to accelerate steadily. We are bombarded by new or newly arranged stimuli hour-in and hour-out. The future appears to be out of control. Best then, it seems to many, is to act as if it were not there—or will not soon be here.

Yet there will be little effective control of pressing human social problems, crime or otherwise, unless there is sound planning which of necessity projects into the future. As said earlier, it does not do to plan simply one or five years ahead. The sweep of social changes predicted over the next decades must be taken into account if we are to carry out effective prevention one or five years from now. By analogy, if you wish to travel to a city some distance away, you first in effect consider the whole route. You do not give attention only to the first few steps. This is what we do, however, in regard to the prevention of crime. We look but one step ahead if we look ahead at all. One might as well not plan; for there is no context for the planned action. *Projections as to the long-range future are a necessary condition for effective planning in regard to the prevention of social problems.*

Hence we need to develop a social science of the future as an accepted, credible discipline or subdiscipline.[3] What will be the shape or shapes of the future? That is to say, what are the most likely outlines of the future shape of events in process? Predicting *alternative* lines of development will be a necessity. If X occurs, then Y is likely to follow. If A occurs instead of X, then B is likely to follow in place of Y and so on. Predictions must be continually reshaped in the light of present conditions. While this is done, renewed efforts at long-range planning must be continuously in progress.

True, it is all very unclear how to do this systematically and coherently. That is simply because we are not used to doing so. There are individuals and organizations, however, which in recent years have made the future their business. To quote Alvin Toffler, a sociologist who has written extensively on the study of the future: "One of the healthiest phenomena of recent years has been the sudden proliferation of organizations devoted to the study of the future. This recent development is, in itself, a homeostatic response of the society to the speed-up of change. Within a few years we have seen the creation of future-oriented think tanks like the Institute for the Future; the formation of academic study groups like the Commission on the Year 2000 and the Harvard Program on Technology and Society; the appearance of futurist journals in England, France, Italy, Germany and the United States; the spread of university courses in forecasting and related subjects; the convocation of international futurist meetings in Oslo, Berlin and Kyoto; the coalescence of groups like Futuribles, Europe 2000, Mankind 2000, the World Future Society."[4]

Some may conclude that a social science of the future cuts the ground from under prevention. For it may be thought that the scientific study of the future implies all is predestined, that nothing we do can make any difference. Why then, some will ask, bother with steps toward prevention if what will be will be? No doubt the broad outlines of what will be will in fact be. Within those outlines, however, there is considerable scope for social action.

To illustrate: Given the trend of events and processes of past decades in the United States, it is reasonable to expect that severe competition in this society will remain; that wide discrepancies in wealth and poverty will continue; that problems of race relations will be with us for years to come; that the gap between youth and adults is unlikely to narrow significantly; that while our involvement in the affairs of other countries (those of Southeast Asia and the Middle East in particular) may well decrease, our presence as one of the two or three decidedly major world powers is likely to continue for many, many years.

Lengthy, highly involved, complex calculations as to the shape of the future are now required. Once this is done, particular approaches to crime prevention can be developed within that context. Those approaches will need to take into account that competition, relative economic deprivation, and racial discrimination and prejudice will be present in the society. While those can in some instances be shifted slightly and circumvented in others, everything considered they are likely to be facts of life for a long time to come.

Therefore we end not with conclusions but with what may lie ahead. Will we tomorrow consider the future more than in the past? Will the shape of the future include increasingly *a concern with* the shape of that future? It would seem so, fortunately. Will our planning, then, for the prevention of crime and other social problems be constructed in the light of the future rather than within the narrow limits of the present and rather than in the terms of the dim reaches of the past? Probably the answer is yes.

APPENDIX

NOTE ON EVALUATION
OF PREVENTIVE PROGRAMS

At various points in the preceding chapters, the necessity for evaluation has been noted. Ideally all preventive programs should be carefully evaluated. While the views of those who design and execute the programs and of those who participate in them are important, it will be unwise to have those individuals conduct evaluations of their own programs. The possibility of bias is obviously great. One or more qualified individuals without a vested interest in the program should be designated, before the program is launched, to oversee its evaluation. Qualified persons will be those with expertise in quantitative analysis of human behavior and with some direct experience in criminal justice. Moreover, sufficient funds should be allocated for an adequate evaluation process. (Presently, this is seldom done.)

Evaluation involves two major components. First, how well does the program achieve its stated goals? Often three stages of analysis are critical here. The first is investigation of relevant characteristics of participants or subjects and of environmental conditions just prior to the onset of the program; frequently measurement of attitudes of participants will be an important part of this investigation. The second stage has to do with the processes that operate during the program. How does it in fact actually work? How do those who take part in the program go about doing what they are expected to do? Or how do they go about doing other than that which is expected? The final stage is a determination of the degrees to which the aims of the program are in varying respects met or unmet. In many instances, the kinds of information gathered in stage one will be repeated in stage three in order that changes in individuals and environment can be measured.

The second major component of evaluation has to do with exploring the ramifications of the given program in other areas of the criminal justice system and of the wider society. This will often involve the discovery and measurement of unintended consequences of the preventive endeavor. If police training programs are highly effective, what consequences does this have for known crime rates in the local area? They may go up because of increased efficiency in recording criminal activity. How does a preventive program in the schools affect other aspects of everyday life in the schools and the community? Does it create or reduce conflict in unintended (or intended) ways? How does a rehabilitation program in a correctional institution affect those inmates who are not a part of it?

What can be learned from the failures and blunders that occur in a program? Not infrequently, more can be learned about how to proceed effectively in the future from failure than from success. Nothing succeeds like success except—sometimes—failure. Relatedly, there will be instances where mistakes, that is, unintended divergences from the planned program, result in extremely constructive consequences. The evaluator should always be on the look-out for these "serendipitous" outcomes. Everyone is aware that some of the most useful discoveries in life have come about by what we choose to call chance.

We have long been aware that evaluation of a new program, preventive or whatever, can be very threatening to those who design and carry out the program and to those who participate in it as well. They are likely to feel that they are being watched, judged, and will be held accountable for any failures. Hence, they may take an uncooperative and in some cases outrightly aggressive stance toward the evaluator and the evaluation process. The best remedy here is to let all involved know ahead of time that evaluation is a normal, useful, and in fact indispensable part of any new preventive program. All individuals having a part in the program—or as many as feasible if there are large numbers—should be helped to understand the following: A new preventive program is an *experiment*. It is designed to find better ways of reducing crime and delinquency. In the true sense, there is no such thing as failure. Whatever happens, much can be learned from it. Except for such possibilities as directors of the program simply "lying-down on the job," there is no necessity and there should be no intent to fix blame. All are engaged in a venture of discovery; none is on trial.

FOOTNOTES

Chapter 1

1. Don C. Gibbons, *Society, Crime, and Criminal Careers*, Englewood Cliffs, N.J.: Prentice-Hall, 1968.
2. Edwin M. Lemert, *Human Deviance, Social Problems, and Social Control*, Englewood Cliffs, N.J.: Prentice-Hall, 1967; Stuart Palmer, *The Violent Society*, New Haven, Conn.: College and University Press, 1972.
3. The same applies to highway deaths and injuries although the rhetoric of highway safety abounds.
4. Thomas Szasz, *The Manufacture of Madness*, New York: Dell, 1971.
5. For various summaries, see Stuart Palmer, *op. cit.*
6. Federal Bureau of Investigation, *Uniform Crime Reports, 1970*, Washington, D.C., U.S. Government Printing Office, 1971, Extrapolation of F.B.I. figures.
7. *Ibid.*, p. 6.
8. *Ibid.*
9. *Ibid.*
10. *Ibid.*
11. Palmer, *op. cit.*
12. *Ibid.*, p. 65.
13. Norval Morris and Gordon Hawkins, *The Honest Politician's Guide to Crime Control*, Chicago: University of Chicago Press, 1969, p. 193.
14. Or a fine or both.

Chapter 2

1. Occasionally the terms first- and second-degree manslaughter are used.
2. Marvin E. Wolfgang and Franco Ferracuti, *The Subculture of Violence,* New York: Barnes and Noble, 1967, pp. 274-275.
3. Personal observation.
4. Wolfgang and Ferracuti, *op. cit.* pp. 275-279, 325-327.
5. Stuart Palmer, "Murder and Suicide in 40 Non-Literate Societies," *Journal of Criminal Law, Criminology and Police Science,* Sept.-Oct. 1965, pp. 320-324.
6. For example Paul Bohannan, ed., *African Homicide and Suicide,* Princeton, N.J.: Princeton University Press, 1960.

7. Human Relations Area Files.

8. *Ibid.*

9. This of course is in large measure also the case in the northern black urban ghettoes.

10. Marvin E. Wolfgang, *Patterns in Criminal Homicide,* Philadelphia, Pa.: Princeton University Press, 1958.

11. Alex D. Pokorny, "Human Violence: A Comparison of Homicide, Aggravated Assault, Suicide and Attempted Suicide," *Journal of Criminal Law, Criminology and Police Science,* Vol. 56, Dec. 1965, pp. 488-497.

12. Stuart Palmer, *The Violent Society, op. cit.*

13. For general discussion, see George D. Newton and Franklin E. Zimring, *Firearms and Violence in American Life,* A Staff Report to the National Commission on the Causes and Prevention of Violence, Washington, D.C.: U.S. Government Printing Office, 1970.

14. Wolfgang, *op. cit.*

15. Palmer, *op. cit.;* Pokorny, *op. cit.*

16. *Ibid.;* Palmer *op. cit.,* Wolfgang, *op. cit.*

17. *Ibid.*

18. Federal Bureau of Investigation, *op. cit.,* 1967.

19. Stuart Palmer, *A Study of Murder,* New York: Crowell, 1960.

20. Stuart Palmer, *The Violent Society, op. cit.*

21. *The American Almanac, 1972,* (revised version of *The Statistical Abstract of the United States),* New York: Grosset and Dunlap, 1972, p. 128.

22. *Report of the National Advisory Commission on Civil Disorders,* New York: Bantam Books, 1968, p. 254.

23. *The New York Times,* July 18, 1972, p. 1.

24. Stuart Palmer, *op. cit.*

25. Federal Bureau of Investigation, *op. cit.,* 1971.

26. Stuart Palmer, *op. cit.*

27. *Ibid.*

28. *Ibid.*

29. Stuart Palmer, *A Study of Murder, op. cit.*

30. *Ibid.,* Ch. 3.

31. *Ibid.*

32. *Ibid.*

33. Stuart Palmer, *Deviance and Conformity,* New Haven, Conn.: College and University Press, 1970.

34. Wolfgang and Ferracuti, *op. cit.*

35. Wolfgang, *op. cit.,* Ch. 8.

Chapter 3

1. Federal Bureau of Investigation, *Uniform Crime Reports,* 1970, Washington, D.C.: U.S. Government Printing Office, 1971, p. 6.

2. *Ibid.,* p. 12.

3. *Ibid.*

4. *Ibid.*

5. *Ibid.*

6. *Ibid.*

7. *Ibid.*
8. See Alex D. Pokorny, "Human Violence: A Comparison of Homicide, Aggravated Assault, Suicide and Attempted Suicide," *Journal of Criminal Law, Criminology and Police Science,* Vol. 56, Dec. 1965, pp. 488-497.
9. David J. Pittman and William Handy, "Patterns in Criminal Aggravated Assault," *Journal of Criminal Law, Criminology and Police Science,* Vol. 55, No. 4, Dec. 1964, pp. 462-470.
10. *Ibid.*
11. Federal Bureau of Investigation, *op. cit.*
12. *Ibid.,* p. 6.
13. *Ibid.,* p. 14.
14. Paul H. Gebhard, *et. al., Sex Offenders,* New York: Harper and Row, 1965.
15. A. R. Pacht *et. al.,* "Diagnosis and Treatment of the Sexual Offender: A Nine-Year Study," *American Journal of Psychiatry,* CXVIII, Mar. 1962, pp. 802-808.
16. Don C. Gibbons, *Society, Crime, and Criminal Careers,* Englewood Cliffs, N.J.: Prentice-Hall, 1968, p. 385.
17. Mennachim Amir, "Forcible Rape," *Federal Probation,* XXXI, Mar. 1967, pp. 51-58.
18. *Ibid.* See in this connection the yearly *Uniform Crime Reports.*
19. *Ibid.*
20. Federal Bureau of Investigation, *op. cit.,* p. 15.
21. *Ibid.,* p. 6.
22. *Ibid.,* p. 15.
23. *Uniform Crime Report,* 1967, p. 15.
24. Federal Bureau of Investigation, 1971, *op. cit.,* p. 18.
25. *Ibid.*
26. National Commission on the Causes and Prevention of Violence, *To Establish Justice, to Insure Domestic Tranquility,* New York: Award Books, 1969, p. 24.
27. Julian R. Roebuck and Mervyn L. Cadwallader, "The Negro Armed Robber As A Criminal Type: The Construction and Application of a Typology," *Pacific Sociological Review,* 4, Spring, 1961, pp. 21-26.
28. *op. cit.*

Chapter 4

1. Federal Bureau of Investigation, *Uniform Crime Reports,* 1970, Washington, D.C.: U.S. Government Printing Office, 1971, p. 6.
2. *Ibid.,* pp. 21, 25, 30 respectively.
3. *Ibid.,* p. 21.
4. *Ibid.,* pp. 21, 25, 30 respectively.
5. So are robbers. Regarding this, see: Don C. Gibbons, *Society, Crime, and Criminal Careers,* Englewood Cliffs, N.J.: Prentice-Hall, 1968, pp. 252-258.
6. *Ibid.*
7. Federal Bureau of Investigation, *op. cit.,* p. 25.
8. *Ibid.*
9. Mary O. Cameron, *The Booster and the Snitch,* New York: The Free Press, 1964.

10. *Ibid.,* p. 118.
11. Gibbons, *op. cit.,* pp. 287-292.
12. Federal Bureau of Investigation, *op. cit.,* p. 28.
13. *Ibid.,* p. 30.

Chapter 5

1. Don C. Gibbons, *Society, Crime, and Criminal Careers,* Englewood Cliffs, N.J.: Prentice-Hall, 1968, pp. 250-251.
2. *Ibid.*
3. *Ibid.*
4. Edwin M. Schur, *Our Criminal Society,* Englewood Cliffs, N.J.: Prentice-Hall, 1969, p. 179.
5. *Ibid.*
6. Edwin M. Lemert, *Human Deviance, Social Problems, and Social Control,* Englewood Cliffs, N.J.: Prentice-Hall, 1967, Chs. 7-9.
7. *Ibid.*
8. *Ibid.*
9. *Ibid.*
10. Some sociologists consider only the second form to constitute white-collar crime. See Gibbons, *op. cit.,* p. 214.
11. Norman Jaspar and Hillel Black, *The Thief in the White Collar,* Philadelphia, Pa.: Lippincott, 1960.
12. Federal Bureau of Investigation, 1961, *op. cit.*
13. Donald R. Cressey, *Other People's Money,* New York: Free Press, 1953.
14. Edwin H. Sutherland, *White Collar Crime,* New York: Dryden, 1949.
15. Richard H. Smith, "The Incredible Electrical Conspiracy," *Fortune,* April 1961, pp. 132-18 and May 1961, pp. 161-224.
16. *Ibid.*
17. For general discussion, see Schur, *op. cit.*

Chapter 6

1. Edwin M. Schur, *Crimes Without Victims,* Englewood Cliffs, N.J.: Prentice-Hall, 1965.
2. *Ibid.*
3. Edwin M. Schur, *Narcotic Addiction in Britain and America,* Bloomington, Ind.: Indiana University Press, 1962.
4. *Ibid.*
5. *Ibid.*
6. Stuart Palmer, *The Violent Society,* New Haven Conn.: College and University Press, 1972, Ch. 8.
7. For summary, see *Ibid.*
8. *Ibid.*
9. *Ibid.*
10. Jerome Skolnick, *The Politics of Protest,* A Staff Report to the National Commission on the Causes and Prevention of Violence, Washington, D.C.: U.S. Government Printing Office, no date.

11. *Ibid.*

12. Lemberg Center for the Study of Violence, *Riot Data Review*, Waltham, Mass.: Brandeis University, May 1968 and Aug. 1968.

13. *Ibid.*

14. *Report of the National Advisory Commission on Civil Disorders*, New York: Bantam Books, 1968, p. 116.

15. Hugh D. Graham and Ted R. Gurr, *Violence In America*, New York: New American Library, 1969.

16. Skolnick, *op. cit.*, p. 111.

17. *Report of the National Advisory Commission on Civil Disorders*, *op. cit.*

18. *Ibid.*; see also Palmer, *op. cit.*; and Skolnick, *op. cit.*

19. *Ibid.*

20. *Report of the National Advisory Commission on Civil Disorders*, *op. cit.*

Chapter 7

1. I have discussed this in many previous works. See, for example, Stuart Palmer, *The Violent Society*, New Haven, Conn.: College and University Press, 1972.

2. John Dollard *et al.*, *Frustration and Aggression*, New Haven, Conn.: Yale University Press, 1961.

3. For general discussion, see: Leonard Berkewitz, *Aggression: A Social Psychological Analysis*, New York: McGraw-Hill, 1962; Arnold H. Buss, *The Psychology of Aggression*, New York: Wiley, 1961.

4. Robert K. Merton, "Social Structure and Anomie," *American Sociological Review*, Oct. 1938, vol. 3, pp. 672-682.

5. For one extension of this, see Stuart Palmer, *Deviance and Conformity*, New Haven, Conn.: College and University Press, 1970.

6. Andrew F. Henry and James F. Short, Jr., *Suicide and Homicide*, Glencoe, Ill.: Free Press, 1954.

7. Alvin Gouldner, "The Norm of Reciprocity," *American Sociological Review*, 25, 1960, pp. 161-177; George C. Homans, *Social Behavior: Its Elementary Forms*, New York: Harcourt, Brace and World, 1961; Marcel Mauss, *The Gift*, trans. by I. Cunnison, Glencoe, Ill.: Free Press, 1954.

8. Palmer, *op. cit.*

9. Jacqueline Straus and Murray Straus, "Suicide, Homicide, and Social Structure in Ceylon," *American Journal of Sociology*, vol. 58, Mar. 1953, pp. 461-469.

10. Regarding blame, see Henry and Short, *op. cit.*

11. Austin Porterfield *et. al.*, *Crime, Suicide and Social Well-Being in Your State and City*, Fort Worth, Texas: Leo Potisham Foundation, 1948.

12. For further discussion, see Palmer, *op. cit.*

13. Arthur Lewis Wood, "A Socio-Structural Analysis of Murder, Suicide and Social Structure in Ceylon," *American Sociological Review*, 26, 1961, p. 752.

14. Edwin Sutherland and Donald Cressey, *Principles of Criminology*, Chicago: Lippincott, 1960 for fundamental statement regarding

criminal subcultures; see also Richard Cloward and Lloyd Ohlin, *Delinquency and Opportunity,* Glencoe, Ill.: Free Press, 1960; Albert K. Cohen, *Delinquent Boys,* Glencoe, Ill.: Free Press, 1954.

15. Sutherland, *op. cit.*
16. *Ibid.*
17. Cohen, *op. cit.*
18. Cloward and Ohlin, *op. cit.*
19. Walter B. Miller, "Lower Class Culture As a Generating Milieu of Gang Delinquency," *Journal of Social Issues,* 14, 1958, pp. 5-19.
20. Martin Gold, "Suicide, Homicide and the Socialization of Aggression," *American Journal of Sociology,* LXIII, 1958, pp. 651-661.
21. *Ibid.*
22. Marvin E. Wolfgang and Franco Ferracuti, *The Subculture of Violence,* New York: Barnes and Noble, 1967.

Chapter 8

1. Robert K. Merton, *Social Theory and Social Structure,* Glencoe, Illinois: Free Press, 1957.
2. Emile Durkheim, *Rules of Sociological Method,* 8th ed., trans. by S. Solvay and J. Mueller and edited by G. Cattin, Glencoe, Ill.: Free Press, 1950, pp. 65-73.
3. Georg Simmel, *Conflict,* trans. by Kurt Wolff, Glencoe, Ill.: Free Press, 1955.
4. Kai Erikson, *Wayward Puritans,* New York: Wiley, 1966.
5. Stuart Palmer, *The Violent Society,* New Haven, Conn.: College and University Press, 1972; also Erikson, *op. cit.*
6. Thomas Szasz, *The Manufacture of Madness,* New York: Dell, 1971.
7. Lewis A. Coser, *Continuities in the Study of Social Conflict,* New York: Free Press, 1967, Ch. 4.
8. *Ibid.*
9. Elmer H. Johnson, *Crime, Correction and Society,* Homewood, Ill.: Dorsey Press, 1964, p. 455. Updated from Johnson's figures.
10. *Ibid.,* pp. 495-496.
11. Edwin Sutherland and Donald Cressey, *Principles of Criminology,* 7th ed., Philadelphia, Pa.: Lippincott, 1966, p. 36.
12. Edwin M. Lemert, *Human Deviance, Social Problems and Social Control,* Englewood Cliffs, N.J.: Prentice-Hall, 1967, p. v.
13. For a discussion, see Edwin M. Schur, *Crimes Without Victims,* Englewood Cliffs, N.J.: Prentice-Hall, 1965, especially p. 142.
14. Again, for discussion see *Ibid.,* especially pp. 126-127.
15. On the same point, see Howard S. Becker, *Outsiders,* New York: Free Press, 1963.
16. Schur, *op. cit.*
17. *Ibid.,* Schur summarizes the literature well.
18. *Ibid.,* p. 141.
19. Jerome Skolnick, *The Politics of Protest,* A Task Force Report to the National Commission on the Causes and Prevention of Violence, Washington, D.C: U.S. Government Printing Office, no date, Ch. 9.

20. Roger Brown, *Social Psychology,* New York: Free Press, 1965, p. 709.

21. *The First Two Years: Annual Report to the Board of Governors, 1968,* Lemberg Center for the Study of Violence, Brandeis University, Waltham, Mass.

22. Neil J. Smelser, *Theory of Collective Behavior,* New York: Free Press, 1963, p. 385 especially.

Chapter 9

1. Even when allowing for improved reporting and recording procedures.

2. The controversy over this rages on.

3. Personal observation in a New York Criminal Court.

4. Granting wide variations, especially among newspapers.

5. Gresham Sykes, *Society of Captives,* Princeton, N.J.: Princeton University Press, 1958.

6. Stuart Palmer, *The Violent Society,* New Haven, Conn.: College and University Press, 1972, Chs. 4 and 9.

7. *Ibid.,* See also Jerome Skolnick, *The Politics of Protest,* Washington, D.C.: U.S. Government Printing Office, no date.

8. *Ibid.;* Palmer, *op. cit.*

9. See reports of various state commissions on crime.

10. See various yearly issues of *Uniform Crime Reports.*

11. Federal Bureau of Investigation, *Uniform Crime Reports, 1970,* Washington, D.C.: U.S. Government Printing Office, 1971, p. 30.

12. *Ibid.,* p. 32.

13. *Ibid.*

14. Various issues of *Uniform Crime Reports.*

15. Skolnick, *op. cit.,* for discussion.

16. Again, especially *Ibid.*

17. *Ibid.*

18. 1961.

19. *New York Times,* various dates on and surrounding April 27, 1970.

20. Stuart Palmer, "On the Unintended Consequences of Social Control," presented at annual meeting of American Sociological Association, San Francisco, Sept. 1969.

21. Skolnick, *op. cit.*

22. Federal Bureau of Investigation, *op. cit.,* p. 44.

23. *Ibid.,* p. 52.

24. Skolnick, *op. cit.,* p. 203.

25. *Ibid.,* pp. 206-208.

26. *Ibid.,* Ch. 7. The problem has escalated since the Skolnick report in the late 1960's.

27. *Ibid.,* p. 210.

28. Edwin Sutherland and Donald Cressey, *Principles of Criminology,* 8th ed., Philadelphia, Pa.: 1970, pp. 50-51.

29. Personal perusal of court records.

30. Especially important is an understanding of crime as an integral part of the social system.

31. For example, "treason" against the state, even small-scale robbery.

32. United States Department of Justice, *National Prisoner Statistics, Capital Punishment, 1930-1970,* Washington, D.C.: Bureau of Prisons, No. 46, Aug. 1971.

33. *Ibid.*

34. See action of U.S. Supreme Court (at time of this writing) as noted below.

35. See earlier discussion of the "electrical conspiracy."

36. Marvin E. Wolfgang, *Patterns in Criminal Homicide,* Philadelphia, Pa.: University of Pennsylvania Press, 1958.

37. *Ibid.,* p. 300.

38. Marvin E. Wolfgang, *et. al.,* "Comparison of Executed and Commuted on Death Row," *Journal of Criminal Law, Criminology and Police Science,* 53, Sept. 1962, pp. 301-311.

39. Harold Garfinkel, "Research Note on Inter- and Intra-Racial Homicides," *Social Forces,* 27, 1949, pp. 369-381.

40. Frank Hartung, *On Capital Punishment,* Detroit, Mich.: Wayne State Department of Sociology and Anthropology, 1951; Lewis E. Lawes, *Twenty Thousand Years in Sing Sing,* New York: Long and Smith, 1932.

Chapter 10

1. David Dressler, *Practice and Theory of Probation and Parole,* New York: Columbia University Press, 1959.

2. Gresham Sykes, *The Society of Captives,* Princeton, N.J.: Princeton University Press, 1958.

3. See Chs. 19 and 20 below.

4. *Ibid.*

5. *Ibid.* See also Donald Clemmer, *The Prison Community,* New York: Rinehart, 1958.

6. *Ibid.*; Dressler, *op. cit.*; Sykes, *op. cit.*

7. Edwin M. Schur, *Narcotic Addiction in Britain and America,* Bloomington, Ind.: Indiana University Press, 1962.

8. Edwin M. Schur, *Our Criminal Society,* Englewood Cliffs, N.J.: Prentice-Hall, 1969, Ch. 6.

9. *Ibid.*

10. Edwin M. Schur, *Crimes Without Victims,* Englewood Cliffs, N.J.: Prentice-Hall, 1965, p. 142.

11. See the various discussions by Schur referred to above for general context.

12. Schur, *Crimes Without Victims, op. cit.,* pp. 152-156.

13. *Ibid.,* p. 154.

14. The President's Commission on Law Enforcement and Administration of Justice, *The Challenge of Crime in a Free Society,* Washington, D.C.: U.S. Government Printing Office, 1967, pp. 225-226.

15. *Ibid.,* p. 227.

16. For general discussion of social class gulf between therapist and patient, see August B. Hollingshead and Frederick Redlich, *Social Class and Mental Illness,* New York: Wiley, 1958.

17. Lewis Yablonsky, *Synanon: The Tunnel Back,* New York: Macmillan, 1964.

18. *Ibid.*; Schur, *Our Criminal Society, op. cit.,* p. 214.

19. *Ibid.*

20. Personal observation.

21. Again, personal observation, and discussion with Odyssey House personnel.

22. Stuart Palmer, "On the Unintended Consequences of Social Control," Annual Meeting of *American Sociological Association,* San Francisco, Sept. 1969.

23. Daniel Walker, *Rights in Conflict,* New York: Bantam Books, 1968.

24. Jerome Skolnick, *The Politics of Protest,* Washington, D.C.: U.S. Government Printing Office, no date.

25. *Ibid.*; Palmer, *op. cit.*

26. Skolnick, *op.cit.*

27. *Ibid.*

28. *The New York Times,* Oct. 11, 1970, p. 7.

29. *Newsweek,* Oct. 19, 1970, p. 102.

Chapter 11

1. George Homans, *The Human Group,* New York: Harcourt, Brace and World, 1950.

2. This is common fare in the mass media and in much political rhetoric. It has become embedded in the current conventional wisdom. Little if any empirical data support the belief.

3. Richard A. Cloward, "The Prevention of Delinquent Subcultures: Issues and Problems," in William R. Carriker, ed., *Role of the School in the Prevention of Juvenile Delinquency,* Washington, D.C.: U.S. Dept. of Health, Education and Welfare, 1963, pp. 69-84.

Chapter 12

1. President's Commission on Law Enforcement and Administration of Justice, *The Challenge of Crime in a Free Society,* Washington, D.C.: U.S. Government Printing Office, 1967.

2. Other federal agencies, such as the Department of Health, Education and Welfare, provide funds for specific programs on a highly selective basis.

3. While some large states require regional councils, it is becoming more and more apparent that, generally speaking, advisory groups to the commissions for specific problem areas, e.g., delinquency, court reform, rehabilitation, and so on, are more effective.

4. For some time, Massachusetts provided informal group therapy for prison guards. Maryland, among other states, has carried on programs involving judge-inmate discussion groups.

5. *Op. cit.*

6. *Ibid.*

7. *Ibid.*
8. *Ibid.*
9. *Ibid.*
10. *Ibid.*
11. Ralph W. England, Jr., "A Study of Post-Probation Recidivism Among 500 Federal Offenders," *Federal Probation,* 19 (September, 1955), pp. 10-16.

Chapter 13

1. President's Commission on Law Enforcement and Administration of Justice, *The Challenge of Crime in a Free Society,* Washington, D.C.: U.S. Government Printing Office, 1967.
2. *Ibid.*
3. See for example various recent works of Frank Riessman and of James Coleman.
4. Stuart Palmer, *A Study of Murder,* New York: Crowell, 1960.
5. Certain public, and especially private, schools excepted.
6. *Op. cit.*
7. *Report of the National Advisory Commission on Civil Disorders,* Washington, D.C.: U.S. Government Printing Office, 1968.
8. *The American Almanac* (Revised Version of *The Statistical Abstract of the United States),* New York: Grosset and Dunlap, 1972, Section 4.
9. *Report of National Commission on Marihuana and Drug Abuse,* New York: New American Library, 1972.
10. For example, Edwin M. Schur, *Our Criminal Society,* Englewood Cliffs, N.J.: Prentice-Hall, 1969.

Chapter 14

1. Stuart Palmer, *The Violent Society,* New Haven, Conn.: College and University Press, 1972, Part I.
2. See, for example, recent works of Frank Riessman and William Kvaraceus.
3. Richard A. Cloward, "The Prevention of Delinquent Subcultures: Issues and Problems," in William R. Carriker, ed., *Role of the School in the Prevention of Juvenile Delinquency,* Washington, D.C.: U.S. Dept. of Health, Education and Welfare, 1963, pp. 69-84; Irving Spergel, "Gang Warfare and Agency Response," in Dale B. Harris and John A. Sample, eds., *Violence in Contemporary American Society,* University Park, Pa.: The Pennsylvania State University Press, 1969.

Chapter 15

1. William A. Westley, *The Police: A Sociological Study of Law, Custom and Morality,* (unpublished doctoral dissertation, Department of Sociology, University of Chicago, 1951).
2. President's Commission on Law Enforcement and Admistration

of Justice, *The Challenge of Crime in a Free Society,* Washington, D.C.: U.S. Government Printing Office, 1967.

3. *Ibid.*

4. *Ibid.,* p. 99.

5. *Ibid.*

6. *Ibid.*

7. Jerome Skolnick, *The Politics of Protest,* A Staff Report to the National Commission on the Causes and Prevention of Violence, Washington, D.C.: U.S. Government Printing Office, Ch. 7.

8. *The Challenge of Crime in a Free Society, op. cit.*

9. *Ibid.* Ch. 4.

10. Skolnick. *op. cit.,* Ch. 7.

11. Marvin E. Wolfgang and Franco Ferracuti, *The Subculture of Violence,* New York: Barnes and Noble, 1967.

12. *Ibid.*

13. *Ibid.*

14. *Ibid.*

15. Donald R. Cressey, *Theft of the Nation,* New York: Harper, 1969.

16. Skolnick, *op. cit.*

17. Author's shorthand definition of leadership.

18. Stuart Palmer, "On the Unintended Consequences of Social Control," Annual Meeting of the American Sociological Association, San Francisco, 1969.

19. Currently being put into practice on an experimental basis in New York, Albany, and several other cities.

Chapter 16

1. This unfortunate trend is now to some degree reversing itself.

2. In some states, such as New York, there is now movement toward that end.

3. New Hampshire is a partial case in point.

4. Elmer H. Johnson, *Crime, Correction and Society,* Homewood, Ill.: The Dorsey Press, 1964.

5. *New York Times,* Dec. 8, 1970.

6. George D. Newton and Franklin E. Zimring, *Firearms and Violence in American Life,* A Staff Report to the National Commission on the Causes and Prevention of Violence, Washington, D.C.: U.S. Government Printing Office, no date, *circa* 1970.

7. *Ibid.*

8. Federal Bureau of Investigation, *Uniform Crime Reports for the United States, 1970,* Washington, D.C.: U.S. Government Printing Office, 1971, pp. 9, 12, 15.

9. *Ibid.,* p. xiv.

10. *Ibid.* p. xv.

Chapter 17

1. President's Commission on Law Enforcement and Administration of Justice, *The Challenge of Crime in a Free Society,* Washington, D.C.:

U.S. Government Printing Office, 1967.
2. *Ibid.*
3. Currently being conducted in New Hampshire and several other states.
4. President's Commission on Law Enforcement and Administration of Justice, *op. cit.*
5. Used twice by the author with useful consequences.

Chapter 18

1. President's Commission on Law Enforcement and Administration of Justice, *The Challenge of Crime in a Free Society,* Washington, D.C.: U.S. Government Printing Office, 1967.
2. Stuart Palmer, *Deviance and Conformity,* New Haven, Conn.: College and University Press, 1970.
3. Stuart Palmer, *The Violent Society,* New Haven, Conn.: College and University Press, 1972, Part I.
4. *Ibid.*
5. *Ibid.*
6. Palmer, *Deviance and Conformity, op. cit.*
7. Palmer, *The Violent Society, op. cit.*

Chapter 19

1. President's Commission on Law Enforcement and Administration of Justice, *The Challenge of Crime in a Free Society,* Washington, D.C.: U.S. Government Printing Office, 1967.
2. *Ibid.* for relevant material.
3. Edwin M. Lemert, *Human Deviance, Social Problems and Social Control,* Englewood Cliffs, N.J.: Prentice-Hall, 1967.
4. Gresham Sykes, *The Society of Captives,* Princeton, N.J.: Princeton University Press, 1958.

Chapter 20

1. Increasing emphasis attaches to the victim of crime. The First International Symposium on Victimology meets in Israel in 1973.
2. President's Commission on Law Enforcement and Administration of Justice, *The Challenge of Crime in a Free Society,* Washington, D.C.: U.S. Government Printing Office, 1967.
3. Edwin M. Schur, *Our Criminal Society,* Englewood Cliffs, N.J.: Prentice-Hall, 1968.

Chapter 21

1. Kai Erikson, *Wayward Puritans,* New York: Wiley, 1966.
2. Alvin Toffler, *Future Shock,* New York: Random House, 1970.
3. *Ibid.*
4. *Ibid.*

INDEX

Abortion, 10
Action commissions, 121-123
Action programs, 121-122,
    124-134
  catalysts, 127-130
  citizen involvement in,
    124-127
  research in relations to,
    130-134
Addiction to drugs, *see* Drug
  abuse
Age of offenders
  aggravated assault, 25-27
  auto theft, 41
  burglary, 37
  embezzlement, 47
  forcible rape, 28-30
  homicide, 19-20
  rioting, 56
  robbery, 32-33
  theory of subcultural
    learning and, 65-66
Aggravated assault, 25-27
  statistics, 7, 14, 16, 25
Alcohol
  forcible rape and, 29
  forgery and, 44
  homicide and, 23
Altruism, 117, 118
American Indians, 13-14, 55

Amphetamines, 52, 54
Anomie, 61
Armed robbery, *see* Robbery
Arrests, percentage of, 85
Arson, 167
Assault, 3, 10, 167-168
  with intent to kill, 9
  See also Aggravated
    assault
Auto theft, 39-42
  statistics, 6, 8, 36, 37
Bail bondsmen, 182
  role of, 112
Bail system, 182
Bank robberies, 32
Barbiturates, 52, 54
Bargain justice, 89-90, 177,
  182-183
Battery, 25
Behavioral science, in public
  schools, 140-145
Black Panthers, 88
Black-collar crimes, 10,
  43-46, 49, 167
Blacks
  aggravated assault, 26, 27
  burglary, 38
  convictions, 91-92
  forcible rape, 28-30
  homicide, 15, 18, 20

labeling process, 73
riots, 55-58, 239
robbery, 32-34
role of, 112
southern police and, 72
Boosters, 39
Bureau of Narcotics, 96
Burglary, 3, 9, 10, 35-39, 167
sentences for, 91
statistics, 6, 8, 35-38

Catalytic agents for social
change, 127-130, 153
Cat-burglars, 38
Check forgers, 44-46, 169
Chicago riot of 1919, 55
Chicago riot of 1968, 101
Children
attitude towards schools,
137-139
behavioral science courses
and, 140-145
correctional treatment for,
213-216
frustration in, and homi-
cide, 21-22
neighborhood service cen-
ters and, 156-160
public education of, 135-
137
See also Youth
Churchill, Winston, 91
Cities
aggravated assault, 25
burglaries, 36-37
forcible rape, 27-29
homicides, 15-16, 20
larceny, 39
robbery, 32-33

Citizen involvement, 124-
127, 168
Codeine, 52
Colombia, homicide rate in,
12-13
Commission directors, 113
Commission on the Year
2000, 245
Communication of certain-
ty, 173
Community service officers,
164-165
Confidence games, 43-44,
169
Control process, 4-5, 81-104,
241
drug abuse, 95-100
labeling process, 81-83,
103
prison, 93-95, 102-103, 242
riots, 100-103, 171-174
self-fulfilling prophecy, 81-
83, 107
unconvicted persons, pun-
ishment of, 102-103
See also Courts; Police
Convictions, 91-93
Correctional learning centers, 217-240
general characteristics,
217- 221
integration into commu-
nity, 230-233
operation of, 225-230
professional staff, 221-224
special types of offenders,
233-240
Correctional training programs, 191-206

one-year professional de-
    gree, 202-206
    personnel, 191-196
    types of, 196-202
Correctional treatment pro-
    grams, 207-216
    children, 213-216
    rehabilitation, 207-209
    violent adults, 209-213
Courts, 89-92, 177
    cooperation of, 116-118
    reorganization of, 179-185,
        241
    riots and, 101
Crime commissions, 122-123
Crime control, see Control
    process
Criminal society, 3-10
    crime, defined, 8-10
    lack of prevention, 5
    statistics, 6-8

Defense attorneys, 180-181
    bargain justice and, 89-90,
        182-183
    riots and, 101
    training of, 186-187
Delinquency, 4, 156-160
    subcultures of crime and,
        65- 66, 78
    See also Children; Youth
Democratic national con-
    vention (1968), 101
Denmark, homicide rate in,
    12
Denver police theft ring, 86-
    87
Deprivation of liberty, 94
Detroit riot of 1943, 55

Drug abuse, 10, 51-54, 167
    control of, 95-100
    police and, 169-170
    public education and, 144-
        145
    theories of, 75-76
    treatment for, 234, 236-237
Drunkenness, public, 9
Dunne, John, 103

Education, see Public educa-
    tion
Eisenhower Commission
    (National Commission
    on the Causes and Pre-
    vention of Violence), 33
Embezzlement, 3, 10, 43, 46-
    49
Europe 2000, 245
Evaluation, of preventive
    programs, 249-251
Execution, 90-91

Family service centers, see
    Neighborhood service
    centers
Federal Bureau of Investiga-
    tion, 6, 19, 26, 31-32, 35,
    39, 171
Federal Communications
    Commission, 146
Federal government fund-
    ing, 121-123, 130-131,
    141, 152-153, 191-192
Felonies, 6, 9-10, 85
    See also names of felonies
Firearms
    control of, 187-189
    homicides, 16

robbery, 31
Forcible rape, 3, 9, 10, 27-31, 167-168
statistics, 7, 14, 16, 27-30
Forgery, 43-46, 169
Fraud
black-collar, 10, 43-46, 49, 167
white-collar, 10, 46-49, 91, 169, 178
Frustration, 103, 107
childhood and homicide, 21-22
police, 161
reduction of, 114-116
theory of, 59-64
Futuribles, 245

Gambling, 10
General Electric Company, 48
"Goof balls," 52
Grand larceny, 6, 8, 9, 36, 37, 39
Grants, 122-123, 183
Great Britain, treatment of drug addicts in, 97-98
Group rapes, 31
Gun control, 187-189
Gun Control Act of 1968, 188-189

Hallucinogens, 52-54
Handguns, control of, 188-189
Harvard Program on Technology and Society, 245
Heroin, 52, 53
Homicide, 3, 11-23, 167-168
characteristics of offenders, 17-23
convictions, 91
geographical variations, 12-15
homicidal situation, 15-17
justifiable, 11
meaning of, 11-12
needs and, 111
police as victim of, 87
social conditions and, 63-64
theory of subcultural learning and, 66-67
Homosexuality, 10, 169-170
treatment for, 234-236
Hopi Indians, homicide rate of, 13
Iceland, homicide rate in, 12
"Illegal laws," 178
Institute for the Future, 244-245

Judges, 90, 178-181
bail system, 182
bargain justice, 89-90, 183
labeling process, 82
probation, 93
riots, 101-102
role of, 113, 187
sentencing, 183-184
training of, 185-187
Judicial system, 177-189
gun control, 187-189
law, reform of, 177-179, 241-242
See also Courts; Judges
Jurors, 184
Jury system, 113-114

Justifiable homicide, 11

Kerner Commission, 56, 140
Kidnapping, 167
Kleptomania, 40-41
Knives
    aggravated assault, 26, 27
    homicides, 16
    robbery, 31

Labeling process, 73-75, 81-
    83, 103, 107, 127, 156-157
Larceny, 3, 39-42, 91, 167,
    169
    grand, 6, 8, 9, 36, 37, 39
    petty, 9, 91
    statistics, 6, 8, 36, 37, 39
Latent functions, theory of,
    69-73 107, 163
    needs and, 110-114
Latin America, homicide
    rate in, 12
Lemberg Center for the
    Study of Violence, 65
Liberty, deprivation of, 94
Life imprisonment, 90
Local government funding,
    121, 131, 141, 153, 192
Looting, 178
LSD, 53

Manifest functions, 69
Mankind 2000, 245
Manslaughter, 9, 10
    degrees of, 11-12
    statistics, 6
Maori Indians, homicide
    rate of, 13-14
Marihuana, 52, 53

Mass disorder, see Riots
Mass media, 179
    education through, 145-
    147
    labeling process and, 82
Methadone, 98
Mexico, homicide rate in, 12
Middle-class morality, 150-
    151
Minority groups, and police,
    162-163
    See also Blacks
Misdemeanors, 9-10
Money, and altruism, 117,
    118
Morphine, 52
Murder, 9, 10
    convictions, 92
    degrees of, 11, 12
    penalties for, 90
    statistics, 6-8
Murphy, Patrick, 187
National Advisory Commis-
    sion on Civil Disorders,
    140
National Commission on the
    Causes and Prevention
    of Violence, 166
    Task Force on Firearms,
    188
National Institute of Law
    Enforcement and Crimi-
    nal Justice, 131
National Rifle Association,
    187
National Service Academy,
    166
Needs, and latent functions,
    110-114

Negligent manslaughter, 11-12
Neighborhood police teams, 174-176
Neighborhood service centers, 149-160
children and, 156-160
need for, 149-152
organization of, 152-156
Netherlands, homicide rate in, 12
New England
aggravated assault, 25
forcible rape, 27
homicide, 14-15
robbery, 32
New York City
jail riots, 102-103
police force, investigation of, 87
New York State Senate, Committee on Crime and Corrections, 103
New York Times, 87
Newark riot of 1967, 55
Nonliterate societies, homicide rates in, 13
Nonnegligent manslaughter, 11
Norway, homicide rate in, 12

Odyssey House, 99-100
Opiates, 52, 53
Opium, 52
Order of Police, 88
Organization mechanisms for change, 121-124
Organized crime, 171, 234, 237-239

Pair rapes, 31
Parole, 191, 125-127, 191
Parole officers, 95
training of, see Correctional training programs
Permissiveness, 114-115
Petty larceny, 9, 91
Peyote, 53
Philadelphia, Pennsylvania, 15, 20, 29
Pilferers, 39-40
Pocket-picking, 39
sentences for, 91
Police, 83-89, 161-176, 241
community and, 161-164
cooperation of, 116-118
crime by, 86-87
frustration, 161
as homicide victims, 87
neighborhood teams, 174-176
professionalization of, 161-167
riot control, 100-101, 171-174
specific offenses and, 167-171
Police agents, 164-165
Politics of Protest, The (Skolnick), 166
President's Commission on Law Enforcement and Administration of Justice, 130, 131, 136-137, 140, 162, 164-165, 217
Prestige
altruism and, 117
auto theft and, 41-42
burglary and, 37

forcible rape and, 29
frustration and, 62
homicide and, 17-20
robbery and, 32
Preventive detention, 81-82
Preventive detention laws,
    178
Price-rigging, 3, 10, 43
Prison, 93-95, 102-103, 242
Prison guards, 102-103
    role of, 112
    training of, see Correc-
        tional training pro-
        grams
Probation, 93-95
Probation officers
    role of, 132-134
    training of, see Correc-
        tional training programs
Probationers, research on
    roles of, 132-134
Professional heavies, 38
Professionalization of po-
    lice, 161, 162, 164-167
Property crimes, 10
    statistics, 6-8
    See also Auto theft; Bur-
        glary; Larceny; Rob-
        bery
Prosecutors, 180-181
    bargain justice and, 89-90,
        182-183
    labeling process and, 82
    riots and, 101
    training of, 185-187
Prostitution, 169-170
    treatment for, 234-236
Public drunkenness, 9
Public education, 135-147

behavioral science,
    teaching of, 140-145
changing school curricula,
    137-139
mass media and, 145-147
Purse-snatching, 39

Race
    aggravated assault and,
        25-27
    burglary and, 38
    convictions and, 91-92
    forcible rape and, 28-30
    forgery and, 44
    homicide and, 13-15, 17-20
    labeling process and, 55-58
    rioting and, 55-58, 239
    robbery and, 32-34
Rape, forcible, 3, 9, 10, 27-31,
    167-168
    statistics, 7, 14, 16, 27-30
Reciprocity, 62-65, 72, 187,
    236
Rehabilitation, 4-5, 94-95,
    118-120
    See also Correctional
        learning centers; Cor-
        rectional treatment
    programs
Research, in relation to ac-
    tion, 130-134
Riots, 10, 54-58, 76-78
    control, 100-103, 171-174
Robbery, 3, 9, 10, 31-34, 167-
    168
    sentences for, 91
    statistics, 7, 14, 16, 31-33
Roles, 111-113, 116-118, 127,
    241

blacks, 112
bail bondsmen, 112
conflict theory, 77-78
judges, 113, 187
police, 161-164
prison guard, 112
rehabilitationist, 240
research on, 132-134
student and faculty, 139
therapy, 195-212, 215
Rural places
burglaries, 37
forcible rape, 28
homicide, 15, 16
robbery, 32

School curricula, changing
of, 137-139
Second-degree murder, 11
Self-fulfilling prophecy, 81-
83, 107
Sentencing, 90-93, 183-184
Service centers, see Neighborhood service centers
Sex of offenders
aggravated assault, 25-27
auto theft, 41
burglary, 37-38
convictions, 91
forgery, 44
homicide, 17-20
larceny, 39-40
rioting, 56
Sherman Antitrust Act, 48
Shoplifting, 39-41, 169
Skyjacking, 167
Snitches, 39-40
South Atlantic states
aggravated assault, 25

homicide, 14-15
Southern states
forcible rape, 14, 27
homicide, 14-15
robbery, 14, 16, 32
Social class, 3
aggravated assault, 25-27
assault, 67
auto theft, 67
burglary, 67
embezzlement, 47
forcible rape, 29, 67
homicide, 15, 17-20, 67
larceny, 67
rioting, 56-57
robbery, 32, 67
theory of subcultural
learning and, 65-67
State government funding,
121, 131, 141, 152-153,
192
Study commissions, 121-122
Subcultural learning, theory
of, 64-68, 107
Suburban areas
aggravated assault, 25
burglaries, 37
forcible rape, 28
homicide, 16
Suicide, 61, 63
Synanon, 99, 236
Task Force Report on Mass
Disorder, 76
Theory, see Frustration,
theory of; Labeling pro-
cess; Latent functions,
theory of; Subcultural
learning, theory of
Torts, 8-9

Training programs, *see* Correctional training programs

Treatment programs, *see* Correctional treatment programs

Uniform Crime Reports, The 27, 32

U.S. Department of Health, Education and Welfare, 131

U.S. Department of Justice, Law Enforcement Assistance Administration, 122

U.S. Public Health Service, 98

United States Supreme Court, 91

University of New Hampshire, 125

Unreciprocity, 62-64, 78, 107, 173, 187

Vagrancy, 9

Victimless crime, 51-54, 75-76, 169-170, ,177, 242

classification of, 10

Violent crimes

classification of,9-10

statistics, 6-8

Vocational schools, 138

Western states

burglaries, 35, 36

forcible rape, 27

Westinghouse Company, 48

White-collar crimes, 10, 46-49, 91, 169, 178

Whites

burglaries, 38

convictions, 91-92

forcible rape, 28-29

homicide, 15, 18, 20

police and, 162

Witnesses, 184

World Future Society, 245

Youth

auto theft, 41

burglary, 37

forcible rape, 28-29

homicide, 19-20

recruitment to police force, 163

rioting, 56

robbery, 32-33

service centers, *see* Neighborhood service centers

See also Children

Youth Service Bureaus, 136